Also from Westphalia Press
westphaliapress.org

Dry-Fly Fishing

A Guide with a Scottish Perspective

by R. C. Bridgett

WESTPHALIA PRESS
An imprint of Policy Studies Organization

Westphalia Press
An imprint of Policy Studies Organization
1527 New Hampshire Ave., NW
Washington, D.C. 20036
info@ipsonet.org

ISBN-13: 978-1-63391-148-2
ISBN-10: 1633911489

Cover design by Taillefer Long at Illuminated Stories:
www.illuminatedstories.com

Daniel Gutierrez-Sandoval, Executive Director
PSO and Westphalia Press

Updated material and comments on this edition
can be found at the Westphalia Press website:
www.westphaliapress.org

DRY-FLY FISHING

BY

R. C. BRIDGETT, M.A., B.Sc.

PREFACE

ANOTHER book on the dry-fly should perhaps be accompanied by an apology, so many anglers having already written in praise of the most seductive lure that can be offered to a trout ; but I have been so frequently asked to produce an elementary work on the fascinating subject that I have at last consented.

Those who have been fishing the floating fly for many years may be surprised to learn how much misconception exists regarding their favourite method. It is still looked upon in many quarters as something mysterious, something demanding superlative skill and even erudition, something applicable only to certain waters ; whereas the fact is that it is as simple as it is deadly, and more generally useful than any other.

My chief purpose is to make known the virtues of the dry-fly to Scottish anglers and others, whose great privilege it is to fish streams of cheerful flow ; to show them how they may take trout with the fly both from the sparkling currents and the placid pools, not only in spring, but also in the height of summer, not under cover of darkness, but in the happier sunlight. In June, July and August, during which period most fishing is done and fewest fish are captured, it is impossible to obtain sport by day with the ordinary patterns of wet-fly in any but the most inaccessible waters; consequently the fisher seeks the river by night. He would, I am sure, much rather fish during the day, but his first desire is to catch trout, and he solves the difficulty by going out only after sunset, whereas a much better solution from every point of view awaits him, viz. a floating fly.

I do not ask him to discontinue the use of any lure, but wish only to introduce to him another, and I assure him that, if he can place correctly at the first cast the correct pattern of dry-fly to a rising trout, he will succeed in raising the fish.

As I address those who have experience of fly-fishing, and as I am of opinion that even the most elaborate printed instructions on the science and art of casting are of negligible value, I have given little or no attention to this branch of the subject. The wet-fly fisher can already perform some tricks with the rod and, when he adopts the floating fly, he will soon develop his skill sufficiently to enable him to circumvent the usually fatal " drag."

I have to thank Mr. Edward Curwen for the beautiful drawings he has provided, and other friends who have been kind enough to give assistance with the remaining illustrations.

My thanks are due also to the Editor of the *Glasgow Herald* for permitting me to use such parts of the book as have already appeared in that journal.

R. C. B.

CONTENTS

ILLUSTRATIONS

COLOURED PLATES

LINE ILLUSTRATIONS AND DIAGRAMS

DRY-FLY FISHING

CHAPTER I

THE OBJECT OF FISHING

THE primary object of trout-fishing is to catch trout. If, however, the angler had no desires above and beyond the mere slaying of fish, his favourite appliances would be the net, the explosive, the lime-shell, and the otter. These are so extremely effective that it is well they are viewed with disfavour, for, otherwise, both trout and anglers would have ceased to exist long ago, and much happiness would have been lost to the world.

The angler imposes upon himself certain restrictions. His overwhelming desire, amounting to a passion, occupying his waking thoughts, and even obtruding itself upon his dreams, is to capture trout ; but at the same time he stipulates that the pursuit will give him pleasure and sport. The quest must also be attended with some, but not too much, difficulty. If there is either too much or too little, then no sport can ensue. For example, if he fishes the wet-fly in July on a much-frequented stream, he finds it so difficult to catch a single trout that sport vanishes ; if he works the otter on some remote mountain tarn, he may find it so easy to fill his basket that again sport is altogether awanting. Above all things, he desires trout, but he must be called upon to display skill in deceiving them, and exercise supreme care in dealing with them.

It is rather curious that, while every angler is anxious to catch fish and still more anxious to bring them home, very few thereafter want them for themselves. It is not a desire to eat that drives men to the river. If that were the case, none would be particular as to method, none would shudder at illegalities. Why is it that an empty creel is considered a great calamity?

The trout are necessary to justify to others the undertaking of an expedition, and to provide clearly visible proof of its success. The angler must have them to give to his friends, who will be convinced of his piscatorial prowess. If these friends are stupid enough to congratulate him on his luck, he is annoyed, because, of course, fish are caught by skill; should they meet him at the end of a blank day and commiserate him on his bad luck, he is comforted, because certainly it is misfortune that prevents trout being caught. He would much rather have commendation than condolence; hence trout are a necessity. They represent the realisation of an ambition; they demonstrate the successful accomplishment of an enterprise.

In addition the angler demands that the trout he catches will provide him with sport. Individuals differ as to their conception of what constitutes sport. One will fish in a dirty, yellow, flooded water with coarse tackle and coarser worms, and find cause for congratulation in several dozens of trout caught under such conditions. There is a little skill required even in this, probably the lowest branch of angling ; it consists in a knowledge of the parts favoured by trout at the various stages of the flood, and in an ability to detect and answer at the right moment an offering fish.

Another refuses to regard it sportsmanlike to take trout when their vision is blinded by the murkiness of the water, considers it unfair, finds no pleasure whatever in heaving them on the bank, and is quite prepared to affirm that the former would take trout with a net or by other illegal means whenever there was no serious risk of being discovered.

Some find infinite pleasure and sport in fishing by night ; others regard it as but little removed from poaching. Some restrict themselves to natural baits, some to artificials of various kinds, while others use all legal lures in their respective seasons. In all probability everyone has a lure which he prefers above all others ; for one reason or another it appeals specially to him. It may bring him consistently good results ; he may imagine or know that it produces the finest class of trout ; it may be the most suitable for his favourite water ; it may give little trouble to acquire and manipulate ; he may merely have enjoyed one great and glorious day with it.

No one should dare to dictate to the angler what he should use and what he should not, when he should fish and when he should refrain from fishing. Some do not find any pleasure in fishing in floods, but others may then find their greatest happiness.

Night-fishing has its delights : great baskets can
be killed with the fly, the fly and maggot, the dock-
grub, and the minnow.   Nevertheless, it is entirely
unnecessary to be on the river at night.   Many
anglers have discovered that it is possible to capture
more trout and better trout in the full light of day,
and moreover obtain more enjoyment in their
capture, than ever they used to do in the darkness.

The purpose of this book is to describe the lure
which makes such a remarkable thing possible,
which removes all necessity for fishing under the
stars or in flooded water.   That lure is the dry-fly.
If the angler finds that his pleasure varies directly
with the number of fish hooked and landed, if he
measures it by the average weight of his catch, if he
judges it by the number of large trout caught during
a season, if he estimates it by the quality of the
sport obtained under difficult conditions, or in any
praiseworthy way whatever, he will at once acknowledge it largely increased when he adds to his list
of lures the floating fly.

He is not advised to discontinue the use of any
lure, because after all a basket of trout is what
everyone desires, and that cannot always be obtained even with a dry-fly.   That lure is not absolutely infallible ; at certain times and under certain
conditions, not few in number, but occurring with
great frequency all through the season, no other is
comparable with it.

Nor is he asked to abstain from fishing in the
circumstances above described.   That would be
quite superfluous, as such practices will automatic-
ally cease, when the necessity for them disappears,
and that will be when the floating fly becomes

known to all. There is, however, so much fascination in this lure that, when he learns its powers and appreciates its capabilities, he will in all likelihood, as many others before him have done, discard most of his present possessions, and devote all his attention to his new acquisition.

If that should happen, it is to be hoped that he will not scorn, or pretend to scorn, other methods of filling the basket, as well as those who continue to use them, for without their years of research and without the knowledge of trout and their ways that the advocates of other lures have been the means of furnishing, the art of dry-fly fishing would not have been evolved. On one point all, who are qualified by experience to pass an opinion, are in agreement, viz. that the floating fly is the most reliable and most sporting lure that has been perfected.

It has been wisely said of fishing in general that its practice is calculated to induce forgetfulness of all worries that can render miserable the life of man. The dry-fly fisher can claim, and, moreover, easily substantiate his claim, that his branch of the art of angling can never fail to produce complete oblivion to all but the object in immediate view. He must, of necessity, watch with engrossed attention for the rising trout, or determine from his experience the exact position of an expectant one, study and discuss with himself the difficulties of its situation produced by contending currents formed by stones or banks of weed seen and unseen, discover the species of fly that is being pronounced acceptable or is expected, and select its counterpart.

His prospective victim may be an old and wary

trout, far advanced in knowledge of artificial flies,
ready to take alarm at flash of rod or glimpse of
the most fragile gut. Possibly it has been hooked
a score of times, and the memory of the piercing
barb or the suffocating strain may be strong and
clear. It may be that, to ensure success, the cast
must be delivered to fall in such a way that the
fly reaches the trout before the betraying gut
arrives, a trick which will reap great rewards, but
which requires assiduous practice and the acquisition
of a knack that is difficult.

When the fly is sent out on its mission, it may
hover hesitatingly, as if uncertain yet of making
the attempt, but gradually it settles slowly down,
until it sits riding the rippling wave forward to the
fateful spot. Its progress must be closely watched,
for it may disappear, and the moment of its going
be unmarked, and a golden opportunity be gone
for ever. With so much to do, all else is forgotten,
and the dry-fly angler obtains the happiness that
alone can come by the moorland pool or the sparkling
stream. After the trout is securely hooked, all
is commonplace though exciting enough ; but it
is the prelude to the fight that requires the thought,
demands the preparation, and claims the undivided
attention.

Some who have spoken regarding the dry-fly
have unfortunately done the sport great harm,
and retarded very seriously the advance of the
angler's education. To very many they seem to be
striving to put themselves into a position of splendid
isolation, and to claim for their methods, and also
for themselves, a vast superiority. They appear to
disparage o⸺ ⸺ ⸺   ¹ ⸺⸺ ⸺⸺⸺⸺ proclaiming

that they alone are sportsmen, that the floating fly is the only honourable, the most scientific means of capturing trout, and suggesting that it is to be used only by a few mortals, who have been endowed by Nature with extraordinary intelligence.

It is not surprising that only a comparatively small number of anglers have had the courage or the vanity to adopt a lure which demands so much. Any legal lure is honourable, if used in waters where it is not forbidden by general agreement. The dry-fly is not the most scientific lure, that is to say, it does not call for the most expert knowledge; the place of honour is occupied by the artificial nymph.

It has been laid down that a dry-fly must be presented only to a rising trout. Now every angler knows that there are days, many of them in the course of a season, when he will not see a single fish rising. Is he, after journeying fifty miles or more to the river, to weary his soul out waiting for the rise that never comes? Does he cease to be a sportsman if he enjoys himself casting the wet-fly, worm, dry-fly, or any other lure? The art of dry-fly fishing consists of fishing with a floating fly. Every sensible angler will place it over a rise when that is possible, and into likely places when no fish are rising. He will act in precisely the same way as the wet-fly man acts; the only difference between the methods is, that in the one case the fly floats and in the other it sinks.

The man who praises the clear-water worm does not declare that we must on no account offer a worm to a trout until we first discover that the trout is feeding on worms. If he did, he would be no more ridiculous than the dry-fly purist. The latter seeks to lure a " tailing " trout, that is to say, one grubbing about in the weeds, searching not for fully-fledged flies but for nymphs and shrimps, and betraying its presence and occupation from time to time by throwing its tail above the surface. It would be more logical to offer it a wet-fly or a worm, and more in accordance with his own principles.

The dry-fly, used as indicated in the following chapters, assists the angler to accomplish every object he has in view when out on a fishing expedition. He catches trout in a fascinating, sporting manner, indulges in a pleasant recreation, enjoys in the sunlight the beauties of the country, exercises and increases his skill in manipulating the rod, reading the stream, and overcoming his captives, all of which he might also do sometimes, whatever his lure ; but the floating fly will ensure their continuance during that period of the year which is at present least kind to him, and at other times it will certainly not fail him.

There are a few who say that the practice of dry-fly fishing has one great effect, viz. that it destroys the most reprehensible desire for big kills, and yet they give instructions in the art, so that anglers may be enabled to catch more trout than ever they did before. They record instances where the superiority of the dry-fly over other lures was clearly demonstrated, and relate how certain pools, considered to contain impossible fish, were made to yield freely of their magnificent specimens.

The expert with the dry-fly does not lose his desire for a big basket—no angler ever does. On the contrary, he accomplishes his ambition. He, however, raises his standard, either intentionally or unconsciously ; he ceases to be responsible for the death of small trout, but tries his hardest to overcome, and succeeds in overcoming, the biggest fish the river contains.

CHAPTER II

THE NECESSITY FOR THE DRY-FLY

THE dry-fly is already a necessity on many rivers, and as fishers increase in number and wander ever farther afield in pursuit of the trout, so will the list of waters which will yield results to a submerged imitation of a fully developed fly become reduced.

Consider a day of early April, when beside the river the angler rests expectant. Across the broad expanse of brilliant blue great clouds sail before the fresh west wind; now the sun blazes through a cleft in brilliant rays, lighting up the pool, revealing every rock set amid the gleaming gravel; now it is obscured, and the air feels chill; the water is dark and dismal.

The river is flowing full and free, merry and lively; the brightness is not dimmed by summer weeds; the wave-crests sparkle when the cloud passes; but of life beneath the waters there is no sign. Every trout seems to have been swept along the floods of winter. The angler begins to stir with impatience, but let him wait a little longer.

On the wings of the breeze is borne a shower of March Browns, a most welcome sight, welcome because they mark the passing of weary idleness and herald the coming of activity. Winter has passed away, and the season of plenty is at hand. The flies alight upon the pool ; the wind buffets them about, blowing them across to the farther shore towards the saughs, that also have answered the call of spring. The brown insects dance from wave to wave of the rushing throat, but there is no time to observe them all, for, from the first moment of their advent, the trout are leaping joyously, leaping to welcome the gift of April, leaping until not one fly remains.

The angler's rest ceased with the first grand leap, his rod has awhile been active ; but, though he finds its labours not quite without reward, he is perplexed with doubts and vexed with questionings.

Why should his fly disappear beneath the surface, when the beautiful insect it copies sails the wave ? Though it be an exact imitation in form, size, and colouring, can it give him faithful service when it errs in such a conspicuous and important particular ? Why does it not remain in full view, bobbing to every wavelet, sitting naturally on the water, answering the wind and the current ?

Will the wise and wary trout not look with suspicion upon his lure, made with infinite pains and skill though it be, and treat it with the contempt it merits ? The younger fry, not yet versed in the wiles of man, and still unaware of the dangers that surround them, may accept the unnatural object without hesitation ; but the older, experienced trout will flee from its vicinity.

With so much to persuade him the angler will retrieve his unsuccessful fly, which miserably fails to yield the sport that the pool can give, and the conditions allow ; he will dry it carefully, anoint it with some preparation which will enable it to resist the water, and send it forth endowed with greatly increased capacity to compete with the living insects for the attention and acceptance of the eager trout. No longer will it be ignored, but at every subsequent shower of March Browns it will deceive a fish or two, and the basket will begin to grow agreeably heavy.

The only really wonderful fact about the dry-fly is that it was not invented first. Instead of being a development of the wet-fly, it should have been its precursor. Why did these old anglers, who have assisted so much by their study of the food of trout and by their laborious search for materials wherewith to copy the various species of flies, attend only to certain details, highly essential no doubt, and ignore the most important characteristic? Of course, in these far-off days trout were numerous and unsophisticated, and anglers were few, so that little thought was demanded; but even that fact does not excuse or explain the omission.

Some may respond that it is easy to be wise after the event. They should, however, note that the use of a floating fly was advocated at least seventy years ago, and that the idea has occurred to many anglers who had previously never read a single word about it or seen anyone using it. It is certainly surprising that the art of dry-fly fishing has taken so long to become well-known.

As long as trout are accustomed to see flies, living or dead, sailing on the surface of the water, and are willing to take them, so long must the angler take heed that his artificials behave in exactly the same way. Wherever trout have reached a degree of wariness sufficient to make them suspicious of a winged lure borne down beneath the surface in answer to a current or other force, then he must make sure that his fly will not be unnatural in action.

In some streams, thrashed every day by many anglers, it is a well-known fact that sport is generally poor during the summer months. It is commonly stated that the reason for this is that the trout are well-fed, and neither require nor desire food. With that some disagree, maintaining that the fish have had such abundance of insect-food that they are completely sated with it, and wish a change of diet. Acting on this assumption, they fish the worm in clear water and prove conclusively that the trout are very keen on food ; but it does not follow that flies are temporarily out of favour.

On a cold day in July or on a warm summer evening, flies are plentiful, and trout will take them quite as greedily as at any other time. The fact is that flies never are unwelcome, but on certain days, particularly in summer, they are very scarce, conditions being not such as they prefer. It is very seldom indeed that on a river a hatch is not accompanied by a rise ; but the trout have learned a lot during the spring, re-learned all that they forgot during the winter, and the result is that they are less easy to deceive.

The ordinary wet-fly is now practically worthless ; but a dry-fly, if floated carefully over a feeding fish, is almost certain to produce a rise. Those anglers who object to natural baits of all kinds will find that a floating fly will bring to an end much of the disappointment they experience in the difficult days of July and August.

It would be perfectly fair to ask why it is that the

wet-fly meets with any success at all, when it acts in such an unnatural manner. That success should attend the use of spiders or wingless flies is not surprising, because some of the best patterns suggest tolerably well nymphs and other subaqueous creatures. The majority of wet-flies, however, are dressed in imitation of fully developed flies, and yet are fished beneath the surface, that is to say, they are put into a position which the natural fly can seldom occupy.

When thus submerged, the wings in many flies fold over the hook, and covering slightly the body and modifying its colour, presumably give the lure the shape and shade of a nymph. Being under water and subjected to movement by the current and perhaps also by the rod, the so-called fly resembles the nymph in another particular, viz. action, and therefore it is accepted. In short, though designed to represent a fly, it accidentally suggests something else well enough to delude a hungry fish.

Again, it seems reasonable to assume that a trout has no clear view of the surface ; in certain circumstances at least, for example, when the water is ruffled by a breeze or current, it is possible that it cannot see exactly whether a fly is on the surface or slightly above or below it. Consequently it may rise for a fly which has not yet reached the water, just as it may take one that has sunk an inch or two.

It is now understood that a trout is able to see objects coming through the air towards the water. Those who dap with the natural fly must have had the experience of exciting the curiosity of several trout in a pool and leading them about by dangling the fly in the air ; it is possible at this game to select the best trout out of the following company. Most wet-fly fishers will agree that on the river a great many rises occur at the moment the flies alight on the surface. Everyone must have observed a trout break water as soon as, or even before, the fly arrives, as if it had been awaiting and expecting the event. The trout is there on the surface actually before the fly.

Intent on feeding, the fish eagerly watches for the appearance of food, and takes the artificial the instant it arrives, not knowing whether it is going to act in unnatural fashion by sinking in the water. The trout accepts the fly without suspicion, because the fly is acting precisely like a natural insect. It cannot tell whether the fly is similar to those already accepted, and it has no reason to suspect its genuineness. Hence it is that the wet-fly sometimes meets with a fair response.

At every part of the season and in all streams inhabited by worthy and wary trout, the dry-fly is essential when the fish are feeding on flies in their winged state. Other lures may then produce a trout or two ; but if the maximum of sport is to be forthcoming, then the fly used must be a good imitation of the insect on the water, and it must likewise float.

The dry-fly is not a satisfactory lure when trout are feeding exclusively on subaqueous forms of flies or on any of the many and varied creatures which pass all their days beneath the surface ; but it is often a means of securing a fair basket, though not a rise is seen.

A rise is an effect of which a fly is the cause, and if the fly is absent the rise cannot take place—an axiomatic truth which is sometimes overlooked. If, however, the fly is supplied, even though it be an artificial fly, a trout will accept it, provided always that the fish is in a humour to feed, and is satisfied in all respects with the object placed before it.

In summer the trout are certainly not always on the look-out for food ; they can afford to do without for a short time, if necessary ; they do not meet the flies half-way, unless a hatch is on ; they examine and either reject or accept according to their conclusions from the inspection. Under these conditions, and whenever surface food is being taken, not only in summer but at all times, not only in the most severely fished rivers but now in almost all waters, the angler's fly must behave in all respects like the natural fly it is intended to represent.

CHAPTER III

OBJECTIONS ANSWERED

THOUGH the advantages of the dry-fly have been known to many for a considerable number of years, the science and the art of dry-fly fishing make progress at a pace which seems amazingly slow to those who have discovered how infinitely superior at certain times the lure is to all others.

Its merits have not been jealously kept secret. Anglers do not conceal their discoveries from their fellows, or refrain from discussing with them their experiences and theories. On the contrary, the glories of the sport have been frequently extolled and gracefully described. The reason for the slow advance lies elsewhere. The general conservatism of anglers will undoubtedly have had some retarding effect ; but it is certainly not alone responsible.

The fact is that some of those, who have done their best to make the virtues of the floating fly widely known, have not succeeded, because they have contrived to surround the whole subject with an atmosphere of mystery, and have appeared to look down upon the unconverted. Moreover, they give the impression that the lure is of limited application, instead of which there is none which enjoys a longer effective season, or can be profitably employed on a greater variety of waters. Many misconceptions still exist, and these we endeavour to remove.

Frequently it is objected against the dry-fly that its use is confined to a few streams smooth flowing and of crystal clearness in the South of England. There can be no greater fallacy; but it persists, in spite of numerous attempts to eradicate it. What has been declared is to the effect that on such streams the dry-fly is the only lure worth using, from which the only logical inference is that it will be extremely good on less difficult waters. If it is deadly on the chalk-stream inhabited by heavy, wary, well-fed trout, it should be effective everywhere, and it is. Wherever a natural fly will float, wherever a trout can lie, there also will a dry-fly sail, and entice fish to their doom.

By means of the floating fly we have killed trout, not one or two specimens, stupid or tired of life, but fine creels of wary fish, not diminutive, ignorant fingerlings, but grandest trout of highly desirable dimensions on all sorts of waters throughout Scotland; e.g. on the Clyde from Carstairs to the headwaters of Daer and Potrail, on Tweed from St. Boswells to Talla, on the lochs of Islay and Bute, on reservoirs and ornamental ponds, on the brawling Stanhope Water, on the sluggish Balvaig, on Loch Dochart, Loch Voil, and Loch Lubnaig, on the smallest of burns, on the rivers of Fifeshire, in wild, rocky Glen Shee and Strathardle, on Loch Leven itself, in fact, everywhere that we have gone in pursuit of the trout.

Another objection sometimes raised is that the practice is attended with enormous expense, that it involves the purchase of a special rod, reel and line, gut and flies. It is certainly true that the dry-fly angler becomes so much enamoured of his art, that he cannot know contentment until he has everything in keeping with it and worthy of it. Dry-fly fishing does not require these things; it deserves them.

Any rod will serve for a beginning, but if it chance to be a light single-handed weapon, the initial attempts will be more enjoyable, and proficiency will not be long delayed. Special flies are not even necessary. Almost any wet-fly river pattern will kill a trout, if it is made to float by being oiled or touched with vaseline. The fly-fisher's present possessions can be made to serve, and will be sufficient to convince him that a dry-fly is a more fascinating lure than any he has previously used. The acquisition of more suitable appliances will follow inevitably, and all expenditure will be cheerfully incurred.

Again, the objector says that the art is difficult to acquire and necessitates years of practice. He dismisses the suggestion that he should try dry-fly fishing with, " It is far too scientific for me." We do not advise anyone on his first expedition to the river to attempt the capture of a trout by means of a floating fly ; such a thing would strike us as somewhat ridiculous. The angler must go through an apprenticeship, a long course of clear-water worm-fishing, so that he may learn something of the haunts of trout, their favourite lies in burns and rivers, practise the art of self-concealment, and acquire experience in bringing a captive to the net or bank ; following this would come some wet-fly fishing in

spring time, when he would learn to cast a fly lightly
on the water, answer a rising trout, and at the
same time obtain some knowledge of the various
species of flies and their seasons.

In time he will be in a position to advance to the
higher branches of angling, and only after he has
arrived at this state should he think of dry-fly
fishing. He will have much expert knowledge of
trout and their ways ; all he now requires consists
of further information regarding flies and a little
instruction in the art of manipulating a floating
artificial.

Many another has said, "I am too old to learn
it." If he is old in fishing experience, he would learn
in the minimum of time. If he is young in experience and old in years, the answer would not have been
given, for the question would not have been asked.

Those who already fish the wet-fly upstream have
almost nothing to learn ; if they will simply oil
their flies, they are dry-fly fishers. Those who still
believe in fishing downstream with the fly, have only
to turn their eyes to the hills and arrange that the
trout, they desire to catch, sees a fly before it sees
an angler. There is nothing mysterious or difficult
in dry-fly fishing to those who have practised the
more elementary methods of angling.

Perhaps the chief objection to the dry-fly is one
seldom expressed or admitted. It is difficult to
break away from long-established custom, and the
wet-fly angler, before he can adopt the dry-fly, is
called upon to relinquish two habits deeply rooted
within him by the practice of many years. He is
required to float his flies and to reduce the number on
his cast.

The former change is probably viewed with comparative equanimity; but the latter entails a departure which seems to presage disaster. He fishes the loch with a cast of four flies, while on the river he may be accustomed to use even more, and to reduce their number appears to him as equivalent to a sacrifice of chances. This is a difficulty we quite appreciate. Many a day on the loch every fly of the quartette will score its share of points; in fact, sometimes the honours may be equally divided. One may be excused for concluding that, had one of the flies been absent, the total catch on such a day would have been only 75 per cent. of what it was, and it is impossible to determine whether the deduction is correct or not.

The greater the number of flies on a cast, the larger may be the area of water searched, and consequently more trout will have an opportunity of seeing them. This is obviously the case when the cast is delivered across the stream; but it is equally apparent that, for the majority of casts on a loch, and for one directly upstream on a river, ten flies will search no greater area than one.

The angler, however, argues that one pattern may be refused and another prove acceptable, or one may awake sufficient interest in a trout to make it take the next. He, therefore, provides a fair variety, ties to his cast as many flies as he can conveniently manipulate, and works hard believing that he has ensured for himself the maximum of sport. His reasoning is sound and sensible, and, if he applies these principles to the loch, his basket will be as good as the conditions, his luck, and his skill permit; but if he extends them to the river he is guilty of ignoring the introduction of a factor which will upset his calculations.

Let him consider for a moment whether it is not possible that one fly may interfere with another, and so completely deprive it of all attractiveness, for that is what may very readily happen in a river. One member of a team may be caught up in an eddy and, if that happens, it will either retard or hasten unnaturally the progress of the rest; the result is that a willing trout rushing open-mouthed upon its doom swerves aside in alarm. Such things may, if unseen, remain unsuspected; but they are nevertheless the means of snatching away many a triumph. There is not the slightest doubt that the wet-fly fisher on the river would vastly benefit by limiting himself to one or two flies; on the loch, in the absence of currents and eddies, the need for reduction does not exist.

The great authorities on dry-fly fishing recommend the use of only one fly, or perhaps it were more correct to say that, not realising this very serious matter, viz. the reduction in the number of flies, they take it for granted that not more than one will be used. Only in some parts of small waters and exceptional places in the larger rivers is it really essential so to restrict oneself. In the great majority of the pools and streams, there is no objection to the use of two flies, unless it be when the downfall of some individual trout of large size and wide reputation is being attempted. Then, of course, it is advisable to have all attention concentrated on one particular spot. In due course we shall endeavour to adduce reasons for thus advising contrary to recognised authority; but not the least of these is that the use of two flies on the cast helps the angler to pass safely over the transition period between the wet-fly and the dry.

We should not have any compunctions about using three dry-flies at once. We have done so, but we find it impossible to keep more than two under observation at the same time, and carefully watched they must be, if a rise is to have its desired end. None can say how or when the fly will disappear, and, unless the eye sees and marks its going, the wrist cannot be prepared to respond.

None can prove to the beginner in the art of dry-fly fishing, but he will prove for himself at his initial attempt, that, instead of subtracting from his chances of sport, the use of one or at most two flies will greatly increase them. On this point one cannot hope to convince another ; but it is easy to convince oneself.

It has been said, and truly said, that the dry-fly is a splendid lure on calm bright days, when the loch and pool are smooth as glass. A great many anglers, who should have had more sense, have misinterpreted that statement, and taken it to mean that only under such conditions is the dry-fly profitable. We are continually meeting anglers who are under this impression ; the floating fly, immediately it is mentioned, calls up visions of conditions which do not generally inspire hope ; it is associated in the minds of very many with cloudless, windless skies, unruffled pools, and quivering atmosphere. The misconception is unfortunate, inexcusable perhaps, but certainly very common. It is not our desire to claim more for the dry-fly than it deserves ; but without doubt it is a killing lure on all waters

and at all times when trout are taking flies from the
surface or would be willing to take them if they
were there.

The fact that the weather is breezy or calm, bright
or dull, wet or dry, in no way affects the deadliness
of the dry-fly. We prefer a good breeze to a calm
and, unless it is very strong, care not whether it is
up or down stream ; we imagine that then the trout
are in better humour. On the loch we are happy,
when the fish are rising well in a dead calm ; but the
advent of a ripple or a wave does not by any means
signify that the cast must be replaced by one bearing
the customary four wet-flies. If the flies hatch and
the trout rise, the dry-fly will continue to satisfy.
Nothing can be more dreary than the loch when it
is absolutely unruffled by wind and undimpled by
rising fish. Angling with any lure is then supreme
weariness ; but we would rather in such circumstances
fish the wet-fly than the dry, because it gives us
more work to do, and also because we find that a
deeply-sunk lure drawn jerkily towards the surface
has great attractions.

Some rivers are declared to be dry-fly waters,
while others are designated wet-fly waters. That is
another example of the mass of amazing nonsense
connected with fishing, for it simply means that
those, who so speak, say that on some streams fully
matured flies are produced from nothing, a remarkable example of spontaneous generation, and that
on others they are developed gradually through
several stages from the ovum, a process sometimes
occupying two and three years. Wherever there are
aquatic flies, there must have been larvæ and
nymphs and, wherever the latter occur, there will in

time the former arrive, provided that no accident supervenes. As trout feed on flies in all their stages in all streams, therefore lures representing immature forms and lures resembling perfect insects can be used with great hope of success everywhere that flies and trout are found. Any river is a dry-fly water when the trout are rising to take flies from the surface, and the same river is a wet-fly water when the trout are feeding on nymphs.

In brawling Highland streams, where for long stretches the water is foaming white, tortured by rocks into innumerable cascades, we have used the floating fly, and with it have taken many dozens of trout from the tiny pockets. To fish completely fifty yards of such a reach takes up fully an hour zigzagging backwards and forwards across the stream, searching every little corner of smooth surface, for every step has to be carefully chosen. Of course the dry-fly is entirely unnecessary in such water. The wet-fly proved quite as effective a lure, or at any rate it answered perfectly well ; but we used the dry-fly at times merely to prove to our own satisfaction that it is not confined to any particular type of water.

The Balvaig is in certain parts so slow that it is well-nigh impossible to detect any current in it, and we have had good sport on it with both wet and dry flies. On the Clyde immediately below Elvanfoot there is a long diversified stretch which the angler would at once declare to be absolutely ideal water for the use of the worm and creeper, and so it is ; but it likewise has afforded us some of the best and most interesting dry-fly fishing that we have experienced.

We have attempted to persuade the angler that there are no objections to the dry-fly as a lure ; but there is one—it is not our intention to deal with it—viz., that, if its use becomes general, the few trout remaining in our rivers will abstain from flies altogether.

CHAPTER IV

ADVANTAGES OF THE DRY-FLY

MANY anglers welcome and thoroughly enjoy the stone-fly season, because they are then accustomed to obtain sport of a very high order, probably the best of the whole year. Baskets are then as a rule well filled, and the trout captured are of grand average size, comparable with those that fall to the attractions of the minnow in a full black water.

The reason for this is that the bait used is a living fly, which, if not subjected to any unnatural motion, is viewed without any semblance of suspicion and accepted without hesitation by the trout, provided always that they do not catch a glimpse of the angler.

The extremely deadly nature of the worm in clear water is similarly explained; but that bait, the use of which teaches the angler so much concerning trout, does not reach the summit of acceptability until the stone-fly has passed away, and the reason simply is that after that period surface-food is liable to be somewhat scarce. Whenever the conditions are favourable to the hatching of flies, the trout become as keen on flies as ever; they are not sated with them, as is sometimes declared, but abstain only because aquatic winged insects are frequently not available. They look for food below and take the worm, not because they are accustomed to it, for that they cannot be when waters are low, but because it is alive and happens to arrive where they are. The artificial fly is not readily taken when surface-food is absent, because trout are searching the depths and not scanning the surface.

If at all periods of the year flies like unto the stone-fly in size and number were obtainable, there would be no necessity for a dry-fly, except for such anglers as prefer on all occasions an artificial lure. Since natural flies do not exist so accommodating in every respect as the stone-fly, the fly-fisher desirous of prolonging the period of good sport, must have the nearest approach to the natural insect that has been made, in other words, the floating fly. As that lure so very closely resembles a living creature in shape, size, shade, and behaviour, the last particular being probably the most important, it deceives very nearly as many and as good trout as any natural bait entices. The great advantage of the floating fly is that it takes trout of fine average size, the best the river contains. In short, it allows the glories of the stone-fly season to continue throughout the year.

It is curious that the great majority of stone-fly anglers fish it on the surface and yet, when they are forced to use an artificial, which they do simply because a natural fly suitable for impaling upon a hook is not available, they allow it to sink beneath. If an artificial represents a living fly, surely it should behave as one, and float.

Another great advantage of the dry-fly is that

every capture effected with it brings delights unknown to those who confine themselves to other
lures. The fly is in full view of the angler, who
can plainly watch its progress on the water, follow
its fortunes, and all the time he is in a state of
expectancy and tension. Probably he has marked
down a rising fish and offered it the counterpart
of what it has just taken. If his fly vanishes
from sight, he is pleased, because what he expected
to happen, what he has striven to achieve, has
occurred ; if it passes on unheeded, he is surprised,
perhaps a little disappointed, because he has failed
for one reason or another to satisfy the trout.

If a wet-fly angler casting over fish feeding on
the surface draws a pool blank, he may be disappointed ; but he has no right to be, because
he is endeavouring to persuade the trout to accept
something that they obviously do not at the moment
wish ; they cannot be expected to carry out his
desires ; he ought to satisfy theirs, seeing that
they are the object of his pursuit.

Certainly there is something very fine in the
boil of a trout to a sunk fly. The suddenness
of it is very thrilling ; so unexpected is the break
on the surface that it is easy to omit administering
the required strike. Such an event strongly appeals
to us, and under certain conditions we use the
wet-fly in the hope that it will often occur, but
we enjoy also laying and watching the fly that
floats. In salmon-fishing the sudden apparition
of the great fish, the terrific snatch at the fly that
sets the angler trembling with excitement, form
a large part of the attractiveness of that glorious
sport. Why should anyone seek to remove from

the trout-fisher all possibility of similar sensations, only less in degree?

A lure which produces sport under conditions
which render all others futile is worthy of great
respect. Consider a hot breathless day of July
when the distant air quivers above the meadows,
when the long flats are smooth as glass, save those
in which the tortured cattle strive to gain a little
comfort. The trout likewise have departed in
search of more consoling surroundings in the rippling
aerated shallows at the head of the pool; but
that is not the only reason underlying the migra-
tion. The cunning fish know that sporting over
the wavelets dance the flies, and that now and
then these lightly touch the surface, sending away
the ova on the adventurous journey of their varied
life. Some of the busy insects are cut down before
their work is completed, and even those that escape
such an untimely fate must of necessity sooner
or later fall to the stream. Then a dainty hackled
pattern suggesting the busy or spent fly will lure
many a fine trout from the waving current. The
fish are eager and the fly floats quickly past; long
and close inspection is therefore impossible, and
so the sport is merry, though the conditions drive
the wet-fly man in despair to the coolness of the
trees.

Consider also the glories of the evening rise,
the delight of the dry-fly man, the irritation of
the wet-fly fisher. The stream flows lazily onwards; the melody of the woods is silenced; the
air is still and quiet save for the persistent hum of
innumerable gnats; the hills are bathed in the
red glow of the west. The gay spinners have

awhile been busy, but their life is over, and now the pool is covered with their exhausted forms. The water is dotted all over with the tiniest rings, caused, however, by the heaviest trout, and over them the wet-fly angler casts his team of flies, delicately enough it is true, but how utterly unavailing is all his skill his silent reel and uncurving rod plainly show. One after another each promising mark is reached, but the result is ever the same; the trout continues steadily to suck down the plenteous feast, until an angry or a clumsy cast sends it in terror to the depths.

Let him change to a simple hackled fly, light and airy, touch it with oil, and dry it thoroughly; then let him lay it softly on the water perhaps a foot beyond a dimpling rise; let him watch it closely, very closely, for it may vanish silently and mysteriously without even a floating air-bell to mark its going. The answering strike must reach the trout just after the fly has disappeared from view, more slow than usual must the action be, for the fish are more leisurely than they are under a brisk breeze ruffling the water. If all has gone well, he may prepare for a long and thrilling struggle which will, if fate is kind, terminate in the dipping of the net to enfold a trout that never would have fallen, at that time at any rate, to any sunken lure.

Perhaps he will have time to make another conquest before the fluttering sedge-flies fare forth. Then the trout are not in such deadly, sober earnest; they are quite as keen but not so quiet; they are in joyous, exuberant spirits, splashing over the flies, smacking the water in their glee, pur-

suing the restless insects. A change to the Corncrake or the Cinnamon Sedge, whichever the waters
indicate, keeps the angler in excitement. If he
will but curb his haste, concentrate on one fish
at a time, get his fly into the eddying water at
once, keep his eyes from wandering—and very
difficult it is to do all this—he will have a totally
different kind of sport, fast and furious, not sedate
and serious. The wet-fly will in these circumstances account for a fish or two ; but a floating
sedge will assuredly produce a trout, or at least
a rise, at every cast that is accurately delivered.

Often the loch is covered most liberally with
Olive Duns, and yet only a trout here and there
will take one. Now the angler might be seriously
tempted to persist on such an occasion with the
dry-fly ; but, when it is so apparent that the trout
are not feeding on the surface, he should conclude
that they are on the look-out for something else.
As a matter of fact the dry-fly kills better when
no flies are about, than it does when flies are
plentiful but are not being taken. Accordingly
he should decide that the trout are feeding on the
ascending nymphs and, fishing the wet-fly, he will
usually do well enough to convince him that the
deduction was correct. When the hatch is completed, the floating feast is attended to by the
trout, and the dry-fly comes again into favour.
Both lures are necessary, each having its special
uses, and it is easy to determine when the dry-
fly will be acceptable and when it will not, but
it is much more difficult to say when the wet-fly
will meet with satisfactory response.

A rising trout of worthy dimensions hooked

on an ordinary wet-fly assumes at once an expression of ineffable disgust. It apparently concludes that it has reached its dotage, that it has entered upon its second childhood, and it yields to the pressure of the rod, coming to the net like any fingerling. It has no desire to live, having been found guilty of such arrant stupidity.

On the other hand it is easy to observe the confident look of anticipatory delight, with which a trout comes to the dry-fly, change to one of profound astonishment when it discovers the barb. It knows that it has been deceived, but the knowledge does not fill it with despair ; it argues that any trout, even the monarch of the stream himself, would have had no suspicions, and it fights a glorious fight that it may escape, and, by explanations and excuses to its fellows for the momentary lapse, regain its reputation for caution and wariness. But it does not always escape. So the dry-fly takes the best-conditioned fish and the fight they show is to the maximum of their powers.

CHAPTER V

The Rod

THE most serviceable rod for all-round dry-fly fishing in burns, waters, rivers, and lochs is one of ten feet. It should be light on the wrist, because much casting is necessary, somewhat stiff because it is required to lift a heavy line neatly off the water, to deliver a fly lightly and accurately to any desired spot in calm and gale alike, and to stand well up to a breeze. Provided that it answers these requirements, it may either be of greenheart or split-bamboo, and rods specially designed for the work are readily obtainable.

After the beginner has made an attempt with the rod he already possesses, and has satisfied himself that dry-fly fishing is both within his powers and capable of great results—these facts will be apparent after a very short trial—he should procure the best weapon his means will allow. It is a sound investment. Our own particular favourite is of built-bamboo, ten feet in length, and with it we have killed thousands of trout up to $3\frac{1}{2}$ lb. in weight. It shows not a flaw, does not deviate to the extent of a millimetre from the straight path, and appears fit for many more years of service. We have never addressed one single angry word to it, though together we have spent many trying days and more very pleasant ones.

The Reel

Any sort of reel will serve the purpose, provided that it is in good working order, ready to answer a strike with the minimum of delay. It is of considerable advantage to have one specially for dry-fly work, though not essential, and we can thoroughly recommend one about three inches in diameter of contracted pattern and well-filled with line. This enables one by reason of its quick-winding properties to get immediately in touch with a hooked fish.

The Line

It is absolutely necessary that the line be of waterproofed silk, and fashion decrees that it be tapered. In length it need not be more than thirty yards, and therefore to it should be spliced sufficient undressed line to fill the reel entirely. A satisfactory line is expensive, but with reasonable care it will last for years. After use it should be taken off the reel, dried by exposure to the air, and then rubbed down with *Cerolene*. This preparation not only preserves it, but gives it other desirable properties which will be mentioned in due course. The weight of line must depend on the rod, but one which will generally give complete satisfaction is a double-tapered line of medium weight, i.c.i. that is ·02" at point, ·04" in centre.

Gut and Casts

It has for some years been exceedingly difficult to procure gut of high quality, a fact which is extremely unfortunate, as such is of the utmost importance. We might manage to content ourselves with other items of our fishing equipment being of inferior quality, but we could never persuade ourselves to go on loch or river, unless we were amply provided with good gut. Nothing irritates the angler so much as the loss of a good trout caused by inferior gut, and therefore he should take particular pains to obtain it of the very highest class. On no account should he buy a cast, but should make his own ; they are the most reliable, and their manufacture adds greatly to the joys of preparation for an expedition.

The dry-fly fisher will find most satisfaction in drawn gut, of which he will require five strengths, from 5x to ix. From a supply sufficient for his needs he can make casts suitable for every purpose. All dry-fly casts should be tapered, as by this means accuracy in direction and delicacy of alighting, both highly desirable, are very materially assisted.

To tie two lengths of gut together, there is no knot which can compare in any way with the blood-knot, of which we give an illustration. It would be difficult to say too much in praise of this knot : it is very neat when finished ; the ends of the gut are in the centre of the knot and consequently protected ; it is the best knot for either fine or stout gut ever invented. If it is desired to have a dropper-fly, then one of the ends put through the centre can be left long for the purpose. After a time it will be found that the amount of waste is infinitesimal. It allows of repairs to a cast being made with the greatest ease. Facility in tying the blood-knot comes only after practice, but, though it took hours to acquire, it would still be worth all the trouble, for it is one of the most valuable possessions the angler can have.

We should gladly acknowledge the source of our indebtedness; but we have been using the blood-knot for so many years that we have completely forgotten how it was introduced to us. Every angler to whom we have shown it has become enthusiastic over it, and adopted it to the exclusion of all others. We have seen a large company of anglers and boatmen squatting on an island of Loch Lomond all industriously engaged in practising the blood-knot; that was on a day of dead calm when it was more pleasant to be ashore among the trees than afloat under a merciless sun.

How to tie the Blood-knot.

1. Put left over right. (A over B.)

2. With the fore-finger and thumb of the left hand hold the strands firmly at their intersection; pass A over B twice, meantime holding B tight with the right hand, and pass the end over strand A and under B as shown.

3. Hold with the forefinger and thumb of the right hand the knot as far as made; keep strand A tight with the left hand; pass B behind and over A twice and place end of B from behind into the loop; the ends of A and B will point in opposite directions.

4. Moisten the whole knot slightly and pull all tight.

N.B.—The gut must be well soaked beforehand.

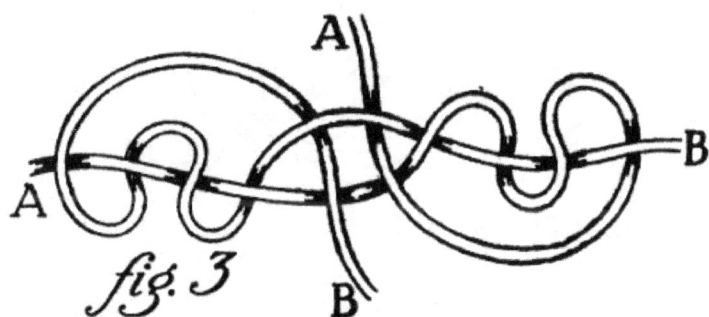

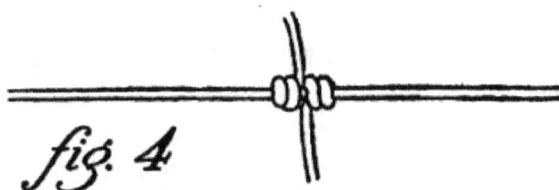

HOW TO TIE THE BLOOD-KNOT.

In making up a tapered cast with this or any other knot, it is obvious that no thickness should be omitted, that is to say, for instance, 5x cannot be tied directly to 3x; the intermediate 4x must be included.

The length of cast we recommend is one approximately the same as the rod, a small difference in either direction being immaterial. We refer now to general requirements. In special circumstances, for example when it is necessary to project the fly into the teeth of a gale, a much shorter cast is an advantage, being much more easy to manage. The angler, having regard to certain parts of his own particular favourite river, can devote much

Loop on cast

time and study to the making of casts, experimenting with gradual and steep tapers, but he will find a cast made up as follows will usually satisfy all his wants. The lower half should be parallel, all of one thickness, viz., the finest the trout demand or his skill permits, while the other half should be made up from the other strengths.

Gut as sold nowadays is usually stained, and many are the different shades required to meet the demands of the fastidious angler. We prefer to have it only faintly stained, a kind of misty shade, and think more of it after it has been in use for a few hours. After alternate exposures to the water and sun, the stain disappears, and the gut, we imagine, acquires invisibility and consequently greater deadliness. When we settle down to attempt the downfall of some particularly good fish, we never put on a new cast, but one that has already several victories to its credit.

Hooks

There is no part of the apparatus deserving of more attention than the hook on which the fly is dressed. If the angler wishes to catch trout, and refuses to be content with merely raising them to his fly, then he must give his careful attention to his hooks.

A dry-fly hook should be light and strong, tempered so that it will not break readily or bend to the weight of a heavy trout; it should have a wide gape so that it will hook and not only scrape the mouth of a fish; it should be long and very sharp in the point, and have great penetrating power; it should be straight and unsnecked in the wire so that it floats on an even keel; it must be eyed.

This question of hooks has received of late much consideration from tackle-makers, and now most of them stock a special type of hook for dry-fly work. The result is that the angler is now able to procure hooks which have many, if not all, the requirements mentioned above, and he should take care that he gets them.

The correct size of hook for each particular

pattern of fly should also be obtained by the angler, and that can be determined at once by consulting the plate of artificial flies. We should like to specify the size exactly by number and name, but we cannot do so without mentioning the name of some maker or dealer. Our objection to doing so is that we might seem to be claiming for a hook a superiority that it does not possess; we have not tested all makes, though we have tried many, and there may be a series better than any we have used. The guidance to size which the plate gives should prove sufficient.

Knot for Eyed Fly

1. Hold hook with eye upwards between the forefinger and thumb of the left hand.

2. Push the gut from the right through the eye of the hook.

Knot for eyed fly

3. Pass end of gut behind the main strand, over in front, behind and into loop B.

4. Hold end at X. Pull on main line, passing A over B and over eye. The knot is formed at X.

It is quite unnecessary to cut the end of gut short, as it is inconspicuous amongst the hackle or between the wings of the fly.

The knot should be retied whenever the gut shows the least sign of wear.

Floating Agents

It is necessary to anoint a fly with some preparation which will enable it to remain on the surface of the water. In olden days we used for the purpose, vaseline, paraffin, and even butter from the lunch sandwiches, when we chanced to leave both the former behind, but we now have much superior materials. Many years ago we were introduced to *Natare*, a mixture obtainable everywhere, we should imagine, and so perfectly has it always done its work that there is no need for us to try any other floating agent. It is possible that *Floatane*, *Duxoyl*, etc., have the same composition. *Mucilin* is also highly recommended.

Beginners frequently ask how often it is necessary to make an application of the agent. Those of the liquids mentioned above that we have used are very lasting in their effects, being in fact almost, if not wholly, permanent; but a good practice is to wash, dry, and re-anoint the fly immediately after it has made a capture. It should be noted, however, that at times an absolutely dry-fly is much more enticing than one which, though it still floats, is somewhat water-logged. It is well, therefore, to dry the fly thoroughly before offering it to a rising trout, and also when changing from one pool to another. *Amadou* is recommended for drying the fly, and after much trouble we procured some, but it is not one whit better than filter-paper. It is a very good plan to treat with *Natare* all dry-flies as soon as made, or received from the tackle-maker. They are then ready for use at any moment.

The line must also be made to float, and to effect this we have always used *Cerolene*. Other preparations like *Mucilin* and *Floataline* may be equally good, but of them we have no experience. A dressing of *Cerolene* must be given fairly frequently in the course of a day; the angler will see plainly for himself when his line is calling for treatment.

Opinions are divided as to whether or not the cast should be allowed to sink. After much ex-

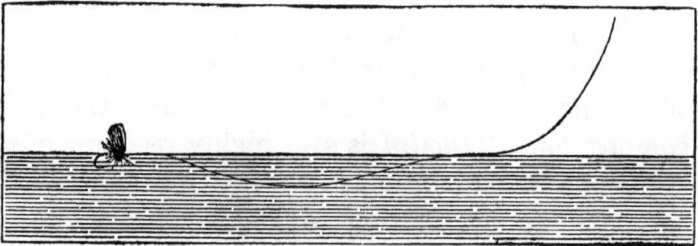

THE DRY-FLY CAST SINKING.

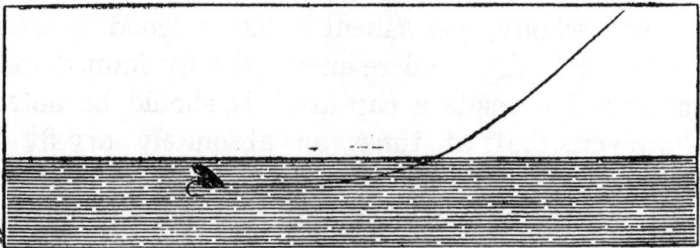

THE EFFECT WHEN THE BACK-CAST IS BEING MADE.

periment we have reached the conclusion that it should be rubbed down with *Cerolene* to within a foot of the fly or flies. A moment's consideration will show that, if any part of the line or cast is beneath the surface, the action of the rod in making the backward cast must pull the fly under. A few experiences of this kind must have a very injurious effect on the fly, loading it with water, neutralising the care expended on its construction, and very probably reducing its efficiency. It would appear, therefore, that the whole cast ought to float, but, whatever it may be to the trout, a floating cast is alarmingly conspicuous to the angler, who is apt to feel that it removes all possibility of success. Accordingly, we leave undressed the foot of gut next the fly. If a dropper-fly is used, then a length of gut on either side of it should be allowed to sink. The length of the water-trip undertaken by the fly is thus reduced very considerably, and at the same time the gut in the vicinity of the fly does not offend the eye. The arrangement is, of course, a compromise, but in practice it works so well that we have never felt inclined to hold it responsible for failures.

A line-greaser, such as is now procurable anywhere, is convenient both for carrying and applying the *Cerolene* ; it is really an indispensable part of the equipment.

Creel, Landing Net, &c.

When the angler goes out fishing with the dry-fly, he is rather more likely to require a large creel or bag, and a strong, capacious landing-net than at other times ; but he should content himself with his present possessions, until he discovers for himself that they are inadequate for his purpose or unworthy of the lure.

The subject of flies, being both large and important, will be dealt with in a subsequent chapter.

CHAPTER VI

LITTLE ENTOMOLOGY

THE modern angler expends much time in the study of his beloved pastime; he realises that there are joys in fishing beyond the mere capture of fish, and the results of the interest he displays in everything in the slightest degree connected with the sport are evident all around.

Very few are now content with what used to satisfy thoroughly their forefathers. Consider the vast improvement that has been made in rods; the dainty weapon of the present day is but a toy in comparison with the long, heavy, unwieldy rod of our ancestors, and it is capable of giving more efficient service and in addition infinitely greater pleasure than its cumbrous predecessor. Reels and lines have been improved almost out of recognition, while there has been a refinement in casts and flies and tackle generally which is obvious to anyone having a few years' experience of angling. These changes have been partly necessitated by the advancing education of trout, a consequence of the ever-increasing popularity of angling as a sport; but they are also largely due to the angler's demands for comfort and enjoyment. He objects to use implements which call for an excessive expenditure of energy; but what principally receives his disapproval is the fact that even a heavy trout hooked on coarse tackle makes but a feeble resistance ; he desires no humiliating triumphs.

The great majority of fishermen now concern themselves with matters to which their forefathers gave only the slightest attention, e.g., with the artificial rearing of trout, stocking of waters, provision of new forms of food and care for existing supplies, prevention of pollution, destruction of unwelcome aliens that prey upon the more desirable trout, or consume the food intended for them, suppression of predatory birds. By a judicious arrangement of stones and boulders they form new streams and pools and so convert barren stretches of a river into fine trouting water ; they acquire new reservoirs, stock them, and thus add very considerably to the sport-giving capacity of the country. They rear aquatic flies of various kinds and transport them to new waters or to such as are deficient in certain species. There is no limit to their activities.

It is very difficult at the present time to find an angler who is not intensely interested in the life-histories of the flies on which trout feed and of which he is accustomed to make copies wherewith he seeks to deceive the object of his search. The entomology of the river and loch has the power to interest anyone, be he angler or not, for a more fascinating study does not exist.

For the angler it possesses additional attractiveness in that, no matter how great his dexterity and manipulative skill may be, his success must to a high degree depend on his intimacy with the flies of the waterside

Many are deterred from the study by the forbidding nomenclature, but the scientific names are really necessary to avoid confusion—the same popular name is applied to different insects in different localities, e.g., the term May-fly is given to the Green Drake, the Stone-fly, and the Grannom, all flies that differ from one another as much as they possibly can. However, as we shall take other means to prevent confusion, we intend to use in our discussion the scientific appellations only for the different orders.

All flies, which go to sustain trout and which therefore concern the angler, may be roughly divided into the following orders :—

Order	*Ephemeridæ.*	*Trichoptera.*	*Perlidæ.*	*Diptera.*
Wings	Upright.	Pent-shaped.	Long, flat, parallel.	Short, flat, diverging.
Representatives found on most Scottish waters	Duns and Spinners. Olive, March Brown, Iron Blue.	Caddis-flies. Cinnamon Sedge	Stone-flies. Needles.	Gnats and Midges. Black Gnat, Gravel-bed.
Artificials	Olives of various shades. March Brown, Red Quill. Iron Blue, Blue Hen. Black Spider.	Corncrake. Black Sedge. Grannom. —	Needle-brown. — — —	Badger Spider. Black Midge. Gravel-bed. —

It is impossible and certainly unnecessary to examine in complete detail all these flies ; in fcat they have not all been thoroughly investigated ; but we shall give a brief life-history of each order that is typical of that order.

The *Ephemeridæ* enjoy a varied life, the greater part of which is spent beneath the waters. The duration of the winged state is infinitesimal as

compared with that of their aquatic existence.
The egg soon hatches into a larva which, according
to its species, may burrow in mud, crawl or creep
among stones, swim from one
shelter to another. All larvæ
alike prey upon minute or-
ganisms, until for each the
appointed time arrives for its
transformation. The period
required for the full development of the larva varies, and
it may be delayed by untoward weather conditions or
hastened by favourable circumstances ; but, when it
passes, the larva reaches the
air, in some cases by ascend-
ing to the surface of the waters, in others by moving
towards the bank.

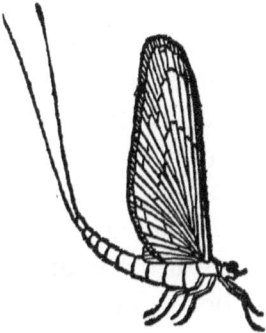

Olive Dun.
(Ephemeridae)

Species which adopt the latter method afford the
angler the best opportunities for observing the
emergence of the winged insect. By turning over
a few stones close to the edge of the stream, he will
soon be rewarded by finding on the underside of
one of them a larva or nymph on the point of undergoing its metamorphosis. He will know when
to prosecute the search by noticing fully developed
flies resting along the margin of the stream. The
large Evening Olive, a conspicuous fly on the
Tweed in July, is one species which is easy to
observe, coming as it does to the gravelly shores
for the purpose, and spending quite a long time in
the process, of extricating itself from the nymphal
envelope. Some which rise direct to the surface,

are apparently able to emerge without effort and almost instantaneously.

The newly fledged insect is known as a dun or subimago. It is not yet fit for long flights, but is keen to test its wings. Those which do not require a grip of dry land before they can enter upon their aerial life, sail quietly down stream, their wings gently quivering the while, presumably preparing for the great adventure. The voyage is fraught with danger from the hungry mouths below; but always some escape all perils and rise into the air.

Naturally the duns are always borne down by the current. Why, therefore, does not the lowest pool of the river, the loch or the sea, in time receive all the flies and consequently also their myriads of eggs? We have often thought of this problem and frequently have determined to note the progress of the flies down the stream and the subsequent behaviour of those that survived the dangers; but the sound or glimpse of the rising trout has invariably succeeded in diverting our attention from the flies to the spreading rings. The flies must, when they do take wing, head upstream, or our rivers would be without a single representative of the *Ephemeridæ*.

The dun has not yet attained to completion. It has still to suffer or enjoy another transformation. Alighting on some convenient spot, the insect withdraws from its already beautiful form an infinitely more delicate model of itself even to the filmy iridescent wings and tender setæ. It is then termed a spinner or imago, the perfected fly. The pale watery duns, which in their thousands throng our lochs and reservoirs on quiet, still evenings of

summer, afford one the most frequent opportunities of observing this final emergence. They
settle anywhere and everywhere, on stone and rock,
weeds and gravel, and even on the angler's person.

The fragile spinners have but one care and one
occupation, the perpetuation of the species ; they
cannot feed, but spend all their time in airy dance
and visits to the stream for the purpose of laying
their eggs. When these duties are over, they fall
exhausted, lifeless on the water, but the whole
wonderful cycle has begun, and in due course the
duns and spinners will greet us by the river.

To the *Trichoptera*, the flies of the hairy
wing, belong the sedge-flies and caddis-flies.
They likewise spend a life of infinite variety
and stirring change. They are found in
every type of water,

Cinnamon Sedge.
(Trichoptera)

running and still, and no one can have failed to
observe the fluttering clouds of flies so plentiful
on summer days and evenings, or the curious abodes
of the larvæ or caddis-worms, as they are called.
In one respect the larvæ of the many species are
alike in that they manufacture for themselves
tubular homes which they decorate on the outside
in fashions distinguishing the various species with
sand, gravel, shells, or straws, and so cunningly
are these tubes constructed that by reason of an
ingenious admixture of materials their density is
only slightly greater than that of water. The
larva protrudes its head and its six feet and moves

freely about from place to place, dragging behind it what is to all appearance a huge burden.

In time the larva pupates or enters into a period of rest preparatory to changing into the winged state. During this time it does not feed or move about, but, being still alive and wishing to remain so, it must breathe and also protect itself from its enemies. It effects this double purpose by closing up the entrance to its home by means of a sieve or grating through which water carrying the requisite oxygen can freely pass, but by which irritating foreign matter and predaceous creatures are excluded. After awaking from its sleep the larva, by its own characteristic method, sets out for the air ; there it undergoes the great change and emerges fully fledged. There is no intermediate stage corresponding to the sub-imago of the *Ephemeridæ.*

Though many caddis-flies rejoice in the gloaming, and some are even more nocturnal in their habits, others again select the full light of day for their aerial adventures. They are none too strong upon the wing ; some flutter bravely enough, while their relatives seem to find all necessary pleasure in crawling over or remaining quiescent on old wood beside the water. They are never far from the edge of stream or loch, and all lay their eggs on the water, therefore trout know them well.

It is quite possible that some species of sedges have a flavour that is not to the trout's liking. There is a sedge-fly commonly seen floating on Loch Leven ; the boatmen call them " hornies," probably from the long antennæ which distinguish the order *Trichoptera*, and some at least declare that trout absolutely ignore them. Whether it is true or not we cannot say, but we have certainly never seen trout taking them. In this there is an assumption that trout have a memory for flavour ; but no one who has seen the avidity with which they rise to the Iron Blue duns, and the accuracy with which they single the little morsels out from amid other flies, as well as the suddenness of the fate of the first arrival of a hatch, can doubt that the supposition is justified.

Many anglers will associate the sedge-flies with the few hours of semi-darkness in June and July, and will no doubt recall happy times spent on smooth-flowing shallows, when the trout quietly stopped the progress of the slowly-moving flies and valiantly fought to regain their liberty. The dry-fly fisher has these memories ; but he will content himself with them and not seek to renew them, for he has all the sport he requires in the full light of day or the grey of gloaming, when he can follow the fate of his fly and answer every wile of his plunging captive.

Members of the *Trichoptera* are readily recognised by the long pent-shaped wings drooping over the body.

The *Perlidæ* or stone-flies are relatively of small importance to the dry-fly man. They inhabit quick-flowing strong streams, not one species, so far as we have observed, selecting still water for its habitation. By far the best known is *Perla maxima*, a deadly

Needle Brown.
(Perlidae)

bait on the great majority of Scottish rivers. It is interesting because it is a denizen of the water and forms a valuable food which rapidly brings trout to the summit of their excellence, making them all the more desirable to take later in the year by means of a small floating fly.

The larva is known as the creeper, also a favourite bait for trout and grayling, and a terrifying creature to handle for the first time. It prefers steep gravelly shallows and broken water generally, which it leaves at the call of the air for the stony bank. There it enters the winged state, but it hides and scuttles among the stones, either unwilling or unable to indulge in flight. The flies venture forth more freely at night, when they may be collected easily by means of a lantern. We have that only on the evidence of other anglers, for we have never considered them worth the trouble. Of course, we have proved the deadliness of the Stone-fly; but even in the height of its season we prefer to use, and find it good to use, a small floating copy of dun, sedge, or midge.

The smaller members of the order are known to anglers as Needles, and their development, we expect, for we have not studied them as we hope yet to do, is similar to that of the most important species. All are recognisable at once by the long, flat, parallel wings extending down the body. Yellow Sally and Needle Brown are two of the commonest lesser stone-flies, and in certain districts are abundant enough to merit some attention from the angler.

Diptera, i.e. two-winged flies, are an innumerable class. Those which have an aquatic origin or live in close proximity to the water, are full of interest, including, as they do, gnats, midges, smuts; the gravel-bed, a crane-fly, belongs also to this order. These undergo a complete metamorphosis, that is, they are found in larval, pupal, and winged states.

The gnat (*culex*) delights in stagnant backwaters of the river, in which the larvæ display their wonderful ways and from which on assuming wings they reach the haunts of the trout. The larva hangs vertically in the water with its tail end at the surface absorbing oxygen, while its head swings about below in the eternal hunt for food. On being disturbed it sinks into safety, but recovering courage or being forced to come up for air it gains the surface again.

Feather Midge. (Chironomus)

The feather-midges (*Chironomus*) frequent still or slow-running water. They are known to everyone by their delicate plumed antennæ and are often seen dancing in columns within the shelter of the hedge-rows or in quiet corners of the garden. The larva receives the name of the blood-worm, for which its shape and colour are responsible.

The *Diptera* which concern the angler are slender-bodied flies, while some are so extremely small in every respect, that they are generally termed motes, or smuts, or curses. These extraordinarily minute insects are numerically very strong and therefore form an important and, to all appearances, a favourite food of the trout. Their life-history would doubtlessly prove an absorbing study, if one possessed the requisite patience and leisure ; so far we have contented ourselves with attempts at imitations or rather suggestions of the tiny creatures in their winged state and in endeavouring to lure trout with these creations.

There are many reasons why the angler should study the development of aquatic flies. As is only too well known, there are some days during the season that are not good fishing days, even though the lure employed be the floating fly. Sometimes the trout from one cause or another unanimously resolve to abstain entirely from food ; fishing can then be weariness indeed and, when that is so, surely it is pleasant to turn the attention to something else of interest, the food of trout, for example, the other living creatures of the water. The time passes quickly and perhaps profitably, for something may be learned which may be the means of ensuring sport on another occasion, possibly at some later period of the day, for few days are wholly blank or hopeless.

In time the angler will acquire a vast store of knowledge which will always be reflected in the sport obtained under any conditions. He will at least learn to distinguish the various orders of flies and, when he goes to purchase, for example, a stock of sedge-flies, he will unhesitatingly refuse to accept, though it is not unlikely that he will be offered, specimens adorned with the upright wings of the *Ephemeridæ*. He will know, with a fair degree of certainty, what species he should meet on the river when he goes in pursuit of the trout. Though no sign of life comes from the stream, no indication that one fly is going to be preferred before another, he will decide the species that is due to arrive or has just departed, lay it upon the water, and find his judgment not at fault.

CHAPTER VII

FLOATING FLIES

OF floating flies there is such an immense variety that the beginner in the art of dry-fly fishing must be perplexed and discouraged, when he is confronted by the almost endless array of patterns laid out for his inspection in the tackle-shop.

He cannot tell what to accept and what to reject; he may not know which specimens represent living insects and which are copies of purely imaginary flies. He is at a loss, and is forced to ask advice from the dealer. The latter will say regarding a particular pattern either that it is a good killer or that he sells a lot of it, one of which is perfectly true, for there are only two types of dry-fly, viz. one which appeals to fish, and one which attracts fishers.

The unfortunate beginner is therefore not assisted much towards a selection, and probably acquires a large stock, the majority of which he will never use.

The hosts of flies which are at home on our rivers, or pay them unpremeditated and undesired visits, have all been more or less faithfully counterfeited; but not content with these, some anglers have set their ingenuity to work, given their imagination free scope, and designed flies unlike anything in nature. The products of their skill are artistic creations very pleasing to the eye of the inexpert, who is charmed with the neatness of the workmanship, delighted with the colour scheme, and is apt to feel that at last he has within his reach the means which will render impossible an empty creel.

On putting to the test any one of his possessions, no matter how much it differs from any known insect, he will find that, provided he has oiled it and has not selected a day during which the trout have unanimously resolved to abstain from food, it will bring him at least a little sport, for the simple reason that the fish will see the fly on the surface, the place where they expect to see flies.

Almost any combination of silk and feather which floats will deceive a fish or two; but that fact, instead of justifying the invention of new patterns, shows its utter futility. A copy of the fly that is on the water, or was there yesterday, or would be if the conditions permitted, will prove far more acceptable than the most ingenious improvement upon nature ever designed, and therefore one who has little knowledge of dry-fly fishing should restrict himself to a few patterns such as are described below. When he becomes expert he will find them adequate for all his requirements.

We shall deal in the first place with the *Ephemeridæ*. As these flies of the upright wing exist in two distinct winged states, the sub-imago or dun, and the imago or spinner, it would appear almost necessary to have four artificials for each species in order that the two sexes in each state may be represented. If such detail were essential for every species, then the total number of patterns required by the angler would be formidable. As a matter of fact, however, many species exhibit only minute differences, and the sexes of the same species show so little variation in general appearance that the trout of the streams we have fished have not yet learned to distinguish between them. Their brethren of other rivers and countries may be more discriminating, but for some years to come, even on the most frequented Scottish waters, a copy of the female fly, dun and spinner, will satisfy the trout and all anglers, except the ultra-purist.

It is as impossible as it is unnecessary to manufacture an exact imitation of any fly. Can we ever hope to obtain anything even remotely approaching the soft, delicate, segmented body of the dun, the quivering, iridescent wing of the spinner? Can we give any artificial the tremulous movement of the living fly? Does not every capture we effect show that the trout must have ignored, though it could not have failed to see, the indispensable addition of hook-bend and barb? Will a fish overlook such a conspicuous attachment and object to some slight error in shade or size?

In an artificial fly we must content ourselves with a superficial resemblance to the real insect, a suggestion rather than a facsimile. There is no reason why we should not strive to attain perfection, even though we know that much less will suffice. We can aim at eradicating obvious defects; but as long as a hook must be present we cannot eliminate them all, and therefore it seems superfluous to provide copies of male and female of the same species when the difference between them is so insignificant.

The artificial sub-imago is usually dressed with

double wings ; that is to say, the wings are composed of four folds of feather, not, be it understood, because the natural fly possesses two pairs of wings —one pair is much smaller than the other—but for a totally different reason. A dry-fly built with single wings is, after a few casts and under-water trips, a very different object from what it was when new ; the wing is now a collection of individual fibres, and that fact, while it might convert the fly into a very effective spinner, renders it comparatively useless for the purpose for which it was expressly designed.

A fly dressed with double wings lasts for a longer time and accounts for a larger number of trout than one with single wings. After a fish is captured, the fly should be washed, dried, oiled, and dried again—for an absolutely dry fly is at times infinitely superior to all others—and then the fibres of the wing should be gently stroked into position. Such flies are mostly of use in spring and autumn, but on any cold day of summer a fleet of sub-imagines may be seen sailing down the stream, when of course the angler will at once take the hint.

It has been fashionable for a few years to imitate, or rather suggest, the wings of spent spinners by means of hackle-tips fastened on horizontally at right angles to the hook ; for some time we contentedly used these extremely delicate lures and spoke in praise of them ; but now we consider that there is a serious defect in their construction.

When the female imago has completed its life's work, it falls spent and exhausted on the water ; its transparent wings lie spread out, in contact with and flat on the surface. In fact, they are invisible to an angler on the bank, but he will see them easily if he wades out and looks vertically down upon them.

The cock-hackles, which support, as they should, the imitation dun high in the water, cannot, however convenient it might be, accommodate us now by refusing to do likewise with the spent spinner ; the wings cannot lie on the surface if the generally recommended cock-hackles are used. A careful application of the floating agent to the body and wings, but not the hackle, might make the fly a much more satisfactory lure ; but it is difficult to prevent the liquid spreading to parts where its presence is not desired.

After a fairly long trial we have found a fly dressed in spider-fashion superior to the hackle-point spinner. Such patterns are very effective during the evening rise and also in low water in summer. The majority of spiders we have seen err in having too much and too long hackle, some of them, March Brown spiders particularly, being excellent miniatures of the brush of a chimney-sweep, but very unsatisfactory attempts to imitate a fly.

The conclusions arrived at are that, so far as the *Ephemeridæ* are concerned, the duns should be dressed with double wings and single cock-hackle, the spinners without wings and short, soft hen-hackle.

The hackle of a dry-fly is of extreme importance, because it serves at least two and sometimes three purposes. Not only is it intended to represent the legs of an insect, but it is mainly on the hackle that the dry-fly floats.

Here we have an example of the difficulties atten-

dant on any attempt to produce an exact imitation.
The angler imitates a hexapod, but he must give
his artificial many more than six feet, or its power
to float will be negligible. There is, however, no
necessity to go to extremes, and that is precisely
what is generally done. The minimum quantity
of hackle that will float the fly should be the aim
of the fly-dresser ; to use more is to detract
seriously from the virtues of the lure.

The third purpose of the hackle is to suggest
wings, and very admirably it succeeds, if one may
judge by the reception given by trout to the deadly
spiders. Some anglers would give the hackle a
fourth use ; it rectifies a mistake in casting, or
overcomes the difficulty they have in so delivering
the cast that a winged fly will sit on the water
with its wings cocked. They use spiders exclusively, and their trouble ceases to exist.

Simplicity of construction is advisable in a dry-
fly. We possess some very elaborate specimens,
with bodies divided up into different shades, most
wonderful replicas of the sub-imago of the Olive
Dun. A nearer approach to an exact imitation is
scarcely conceivable, but we are perfectly satisfied
that they are not at all superior to a simple pattern.
We have fished the simple and the complex simultaneously on the cast, giving them alternately
the tail position, and at the end of a long trial
against the wary trout of Clyde we could not
declare either the superior of the other. The basket
was by no means empty.

No matter what fly should unexpectedly appear
on the water the angler need not be taken unawares.
If he will but carry with him a selection of silks

and an assortment of hackles he can in a few minutes dress a fly which, while perhaps not a superb example of the fly-tier's art, will yet meet with a ready acceptance from the trout.

Of all the numerous varieties of dry-flies offered to the nimble trout, by far the most popular with Scottish anglers is the redoubtable Greenwell's Glory. It is an indispensable pattern, useful at any time of the season and often invaluable ; probably every angler uses it, while some are with difficulty persuaded to entrust their fortunes to any other. Its mere presence on the cast inspires the confidence which begets success.

Though originally made in imitation of one of the darker Olives, it owes its deadliness, we imagine, to the fact that it bears a superficial resemblance to many duns rather than a striking similarity to any particular species.

In accordance with the earlier method adopted to suggest segmentation, the body is usually of waxed silk closely ribbed with the finest gold wire. For this purpose quill is now almost universally employed, and certainly it succeeds in giving a more life-like appearance to a fly. Consequently we have dared to modify the dressing that Canon Greenwell prescribed for his great invention, feeling certain that he also would have used quill for the body of his fly, had that most satisfactory material been known in his day. Experience has amply demonstrated that the alteration is beneficial.

As a general fly, always reliable and often extremely deadly, it has no equals. When rising trout are nowhere in evidence, and one is forced to " fish the stream," or remain idle, no more profitable fly than the Greenwell Quill, as it may be called, can be laid upon the waters.

Following it closely and challenging its proud position as first favourite is the Medium Olive. Under that heading are classed together several species differing from one another to such a negligible extent that for practical purposes attention to individual characteristics is wholly unnecessary. Fortunately they select for their arrival various periods of the year, and are to be found on practically all waters, so that this fly likewise is of general application and must find a place in the dry-fly box.

Sometimes in spring the angler will encounter a hatch of dark Olives, and then his Greenwells will look after his welfare satisfactorily enough, but a special pattern is desirable. In summer a pale variety appears on many waters in such numbers, moreover, that the angler who is not provided with copies may be left lamenting the loss of a great opportunity. It happens to be one of our particular favourites, for many a fine basket it has brought us on Loch Dochart in July.

We have formed a high opinion of a fly, for the introduction to which we are indebted to G. E. M. Skues, author of *Minor Tactics of the Chalk Stream.* It is named the Rough Olive, and with it we have killed many trout in every month of the season both on loch and river, the best basket being one of 10 lb. from the Clyde in May. We have never failed with it, and if there is no indication from the waters as to which fly will prove acceptable, we often use it on the cast as an experimental pattern.

For early fishing the March Brown is requisite. It enjoys but a short season, yet while it is on, it attracts to itself all the attention of the trout, and therefore the angler cannot afford to ignore it.   The welcome it receives is rapturous.   Some anglers never see it, either owing to misfortune in their choice of day or to the fact that they are timid to venture on the river before the balmy days of May. In either case they miss what is probably the most glorious and thrilling sport of the whole trouting season.

It is good to be on the river in April ; there may be one or two days of disappointment, but persistence will surely meet its reward—a strong westerly breeze, sunshine and cloud, and a hatch of the gay March Brown.   As the tempting flies are blown before the wind on to the sparkling pool the river awakes from its winter sleep ; too long has the surface remained unspread ; at length the feast is prepared and the trout rise in glee, splashing over the drifting flies in ecstasy.   Soon all is quiet again, but the fish are on the watch, and the artificial, deftly delivered at the tail of the stream, will delude one into thinking that the forerunner of the next shower has arrived.

A really good pattern of March Brown we have not yet seen, and we are not completely satisfied with the dressing recommended below.   At the most we manage only one day per annum on the river when this fly is in evidence, and in some seasons we miss it altogether ; so that it takes a long time to investigate the qualities of an artificial.   Therefore the pattern is still in the experimental stage to a far greater extent than the majority of the others ; but nevertheless it will meet with considerable acceptance from the trout.   Possibly exactness is even less necessary in a March Brown than in any other fly, for the fish at that season are ravenous, waiting not to inspect—there are too many eager mouths farther down the pool—and they throw themselves upon the floating lure. Perhaps we should not take too much advantage of their impetuous, unreasoning haste ; but not far ahead lies the time when they will chasten us with their indifference.

Soon after or even before the March Brown passes away, that ever-welcome tiny atom of the dusky wing, dainty yet hardy, the Iron-Blue Dun, appears. It revels in cold and rain, though it avoids not April sunshine, but later it renders cheerful the most dismal day, and never does greater fortune attend the angler than when a fleet of these miniature representatives of the *Ephemeridæ* sets out for a voyage on the river. Some have declared, and we have had reason to believe, that the trout show an unmistakable preference for them by picking them out to the exclusion of even larger duns that may be in company with them on the surface. The flavour of the Iron-Blue must be surpassing sweet.

We have seen many attempts at an imitation of this succulent insect which bore not the slightest resemblance to the natural fly or to one another. We have a very fine pattern of this fly which has done great work on many waters and at widely separated periods of the season ; but we have like-wise proved that a simple Black Spider is the superior of most of the numerous variations. The trout take this spider well when the Iron-Blue is up, and so it seems reasonable to conclude that they take it in mistake for that fly.

Neither p.... .... from the

fly-box, as when the natural fly is on the water something closely resembling it is indispensable ; the winged variety will be preferable on the streams, the hackled pattern on the pools. The latter is also a useful lure to throw at a venture before or after the rise. Even in midsummer, whenever the weather is cold or boisterous, and again in September, when there is a hatch of *Ephemeridæ* so similar to Iron-Blues as to be indistinguishable from them, we do well with both these flies.

One of the best known dry-flies is the Red Quill, which was in all likelihood intended originally to represent the female Olive imago, but the heavy, opaque wings of the artificial, its customary dress, are not at all comparable with the marvellously delicate wings of the living insect. Consequently we have had the wings removed altogether, and now we have a fly which is certain to deceive many fine trout during the earliest part of a fine summer evening.

We have now arrived at the period of calm, bright days and warm, still evenings, when the water is generally at its lowest level and the trout at the height of their wariness. Spinners or imagines are usually alone in evidence, and it behoves the angler to use none but his most delicate lures.

Winged flies may now be discontinued altogether or limited to rough streams and to occasional days of northerly or easterly winds and low temperature, when slight hatches of duns already mentioned may occur; and in their stead under more probable conditions the dainty hackled flies will keep the angler happy. Of these we give the place of honour to the Blue Hen Spider. It is an intensely fascinating fly to look at ; the trout as well as the angler find it so. Its construction is of the simplest, but its seductive powers are of the greatest. Natural hackles of the correct shade are somewhat difficult to obtain, but a dyed feather will serve equally well, though on that point it would be very difficult to convince a Tweed fisher.

This fly resembles a number of small spinners which are on the river in June and July, and it is also a particularly good copy of the female imago of the Pale Watery Dun, the appearance of which on loch and reservoir formerly indicated to many anglers that all expectation of sport had departed. With this beautiful pattern in his possession no one under such circumstances need give way to despair ; but instead a great feeling of hopefulness should steal over him, because there is then presented the possibility of an hour of intensely interesting sport among eager cruising trout, and a probability of great reward to silent, careful manipulation of delicate tackle.

It is almost impossible for anyone to have a stock of flies sufficient to enable him invariably to deal successfully with rising trout ; but, as we have already pointed out, a fly which will assuredly bring a few fish to the creel, no matter what unfamiliar species of dun or spinner arrives, may be made in a minute or two from a hackle and an inch or two of silk, carefully chosen to suggest the general characteristics of the type occasioning the rise.

Once during a yellow spate on Clyde we were aroused from weary inaction by the startling announcement that the trout of Newton Flat were rising madly. The fly that was producing this phenomenon was a large dun and, curiously enough, there were in the box three specimens with snipe wings, badger hackle, and light quill body which were almost a faultless imitation. During the few minutes the rise lasted we killed two fine trout. We did not lay in a stock of these Gray Quills, as the tackle-dealer called them, and we have not seen again a hatch of these light duns, though ten years have passed since that unusual experience of fishing dry-fly during a flood.

Having now given a list of upright-winged flies quite sufficient for all but exceptional occasions on all the Scottish rivers we have visited, we proceed to the discussion of other orders, the members of which, however, are so numerically strong that it is possible to deal only with the most important.

We consider the best of these is the Sand-fly of Clyde, or, as it is better known in other districts, the Gravel-bed, and there are good reasons for thus conferring distinction upon it.

Making its first appearance during hot weather towards the middle of May, it is likely to be found on the water for a period of three months whenever the temperature is sufficiently high to tempt it forth, for it is essentially a fine-weather insect, revelling in warm breezes and brilliant sunshine.

On hot, thundery days we have seen the gravel absolutely covered with them, but again, under conditions to all appearance identical, we have failed to observe a single specimen, so that it is impossible to predict when setting out for the river that the Sand-fly will be in evidence. Nevertheless, the angler must be prepared for its advent by having in his possession a plentiful supply of good imitations, for the trout are very fond of it and lie close to the gravel on the windward bank of the pool waiting for a shower to be wafted to them.

When fishing for trout feeding on sand-flies a very little carelessness will result in an empty basket. The fish will naturally be where the flies are, and that as a rule is in shallow water near the edge of the gravel. The angler should therefore select only such reaches as have stretches of sand and gravel along the bank from which the wind is blowing.

If he chooses the easy cast down-wind, he will find that an unseen approach is impossible to accomplish, and that the sole result of his efforts will be a series of furrows caused by the hasty flight of trout from the shallows to the depths of the pool. Consequently the cast will generally have to be made from the water beneath the opposite bank, and therefore also more or less against the wind ; but if these points are attended to excellent sport can be enjoyed with the artificial sand-fly.

We find that Webster's dressing—viz. black silk body, black hackle, and wings from the hen-pheasant tail, is quite satisfactory, but we do not approve of the split wing he advocates. A few fibres of feather tied in, without division of any kind, so as to lie low along the hook, give a much superior wing for a floating pattern. The hackle should be of black cock, stiff and long, for the natural fly floats high in the water.

We have proved that a Black Spider is not altogether ignored when sand-flies are on the water, and on one occasion in July, when we learned for the first time that a strong hatch of these welcome insects could occur in that month, we killed seventeen splendid trout with a Blae and Black, the nearest approach to the fly in demand that the box could then furnish.

We are of opinion that trout do not obtain a clear view of the wings of a floating fly, and these experiences just noted, as well as many others of a similar nature, strengthen the belief that the body and hackle are the points which should receive most attention from the fly-dresser.

The Blae and Black, or the Black Midge as we now prefer to call it, since the name suggests at once the insect it is intended to represent, is as fine a pattern as one could float in July and August over a feeding trout. Not only so, but the Clyde grayling seems to prefer it beyond all flies, real and unreal, and great is the execution we have done with it.

Of the smaller diptera, so exceedingly minute in some cases that all attempts at imitation seem foredoomed to failure, trout appear to be particularly fond. Webster's Black Mote and Halford's Black Gnat we have invariably found quite ineffective when trout are feeding on the tiny flies of the dark body and white wing. That may be due to persistent bad luck, but we have deceived or at least attracted many a good fish indulging in a display of this annoying habit, as it is frequently considered, and that, too, by using a very simple fly, the simplest of all, namely, a Badger Hackle.

This feather has a black centre and white tips, and two or three turns of it on a bare hook of small size are all that is required to suggest to a trout the natural insect. A short body of black silk (not that it is necessary) may be added to allay the qualms of the angler and so induce him to give it a trial.

This pattern will give a good account of itself when the little watery duns are out on quiet evenings on loch and reservoir. Many an angler has given up in despair and disgust on seeing his efforts entirely ignored by " smutting " trout, but defeat is by no means a foregone conclusion ; in fact, it may readily be converted into victory if the Badger Hackle is laid quietly on the smooth water and floated over the rise.

The *Trichoptera* or sedge-flies are a numerous family, forming a plentiful supply of obviously agreeable food for the trout, and therefore they deserve more attention from the angler than they usually receive. They are well known to the night-fisher, most of whose death-dealing deceptions are intended to represent these insects of the wonderful life-history, and while it is true that many of them love the night and are therefore of little interest to the dry-fly man who finds himself under no necessity to fish in darkness, some rejoice in the brightness of daylight, and others again are most active in the gloaming hour.

These caddis-flies float much lower in the water than do the *Ephemeridæ*, and therefore the artificials should be provided with short, soft, hen-hackles. Unlike some other flies, they are seldom, if ever, at peace on the water ; apparently they do not enjoy being borne quietly onwards by the current, but skate about the surface until, sooner or later, a trout rises to terminate the voyage.

The Corncrake, the Cinnamon, and the Black Sedges are all patterns likely to prove useful from time to time. On Loch Dochart the Black Sedge is plentiful ; but there we never happened to see the trout taking them ; on the other hand we found the trout of the River Cairn, a tributary of the Nith, very keen on them in the month of August, the rise being most pronounced and general. As we had nothing better at the moment, we offered them a Black Spider, and it was well received. There seems to be no limit to the usefulness of that pattern, but a superior imitation is easily made.

The light Corncrake and the Cinnamon Sedge are both very good. The former has brought us a few fish on sunny afternoons under the most difficult conditions, while the latter is a splendid fly for a late evening of summer. We have fished the Cinnamon on the Clyde in the gloaming and under moonlight (a delightful experience !), and with it have taken some grand fish, not many, only a brace or at most two at an expedition, but almost invariably superb specimens ; also with it we hooked what would probably have proved our record trout had misfortune in the form of sunken wire not intervened.

The Grannom is an indispensable pattern on many rivers, and like all sedge-flies should be dressed with low-lying wings ; it is not a member of the *Ephemeridæ* as the majority of fly-dressers seem to imagine. Due in May about the same time as the Gravel-bed, it sometimes occurs in such prodigious numbers that the angler finds it hopeless to enter into competition against so many. Though year after year we have been on the river at a time when this phenomenon might have been displayed, we have never been privileged to witness it. Such accidents will happen to anyone who is not so

fortunate as to reside on the banks of a river; but
should we ever encounter the hordes of the Greentail
we shall proceed up or down stream away from the
vicinity of trees to places where only stragglers are
likely to penetrate.

There still remain the *Perlidæ* or stone-flies. With
the exception of the Stone-fly itself, *Perla maxima*,
which few would trouble to imitate when the natural
flies are so easily available as a bait, the members of
this order are not worthy of more than passing
notice. We have seen Yellow Sally, Needle-Brown,
etc., many and many a time, but only on one occasion
did they excite the trout to activity. That was on
the Endrick in early October, when the Browns
were so numerous as to annoy the angler by their
selection of a resting-place. The trout were taking
them down quietly and steadily, and had we not
been provided only with rod and tackle suitable
for bigger game, we should have been pleased to try
the effect of a hackled pattern. Anglers who fish
the Endrick frequently would probably find a copy
of this fly a valuable addition to their stock.

The Green Drake or May-fly of the English angler,
which would be accorded first place in many lists,
is not included among our indispensable dry-flies
for the very sufficient reason that its occurrence in
Scotland is confined to a few waters. No one can
fail to recognise at first glance the large, handsome
fly which arouses so much enthusiasm across the
Border, but we have never heard of any district on
this side where the fly, natural or artificial, is seriously
used.

Our list may be considered somewhat meagre,
but in actual practice it will generally prove exten-

sive enough, as it provides for all but unexpected events.

DRESSINGS OF THE PATTERNS

No. 1. GREENWELL QUILL.

Body : Dark quill.
Hackle : Red with black centre, often termed "cochybondu hackle."
Tail : Dark olive.
Wings : Hen blackbird, upright.
Season : Reliable all through the season.

No. 2. DARK OLIVE DUN.

Body : Dark olive quill.
Hackle : Cock's hackle, dyed dark olive.
Tail : Dark olive.
Wings : Blackbird, upright.
Season : April.

No. 3. MEDIUM OLIVE DUN.

Body : Medium olive quill.
Hackle : Cock's hackle, dyed medium olive.
Tail : Medium olive.
Wings : Snipe, upright.
Season : May, and occasionally thereafter.

No. 4. PALE OLIVE DUN.

Body : Light olive quill.
Hackle : Cock's hackle, dyed light olive.
Tail : Light olive.
Wings : Starling, upright.
Season : June and July.

No. 5. ROUGH OLIVE.

Body : White swan herl, dyed olive, ribbed with gold.
Hackle : Cock's hackle, dyed medium olive.
Tail : Medium olive.
Wings : Starling, upright.
Season : Useful any time, very good in April and September.

No. 6. MARCH BROWN.

Body : Brown quill.
Hackle : Cock's hackle, dyed olive.
Tail : Dark olive.
Wings : Hen-pheasant wing, upright.
Season : April.

No. 7. IRON-BLUE DUN.

Body : Black quill.
Hackle : Cock's hackle, dyed dark olive.
Tail : Dark olive.
Wings : Blackbird, upright.
Season : April and May, cold days during summer, and September.

No. 8. BLACK SPIDER.

Body : Black quill.
Hackle : Black hen.
Tail : Black.
Season : Useful at any time.

No. 9. RED QUILL.

Body : Undyed quill.
Hackle : Ginger hen.
Tail : Ginger.
Season : Evenings of June and July.

No. 10. BLUE HEN SPIDER.

Body : Yellow quill, ribbed with brown silk.
Hackle : Blue hen (light dun).
Tail : Blue hen.
Season : Evenings of June and July, when Pale Watery Dun is up.

No. 11. GRAVEL-BED (CLYDE SAND-FLY).

Body : Black quill.
Hackle : Black hen's, long and fixed on top of wing.
Wings : Hen-pheasant tail, few fibres only, tied flat along the body.
Season : Second fortnight of May to end of July; in warm weather.

No. 12. BLACK MIDGE.

Body : Black quill.
Hackle : Black hen.
Wings : Speckled hackle points dyed olive, projecting on each side of body.
Season : Warm days of summer.

No. 13. BADGER HACKLE.

Body : Black silk, very short.
Hackle : Badger, black centre, white tips.
Season : Warm, calm weather when trout are " smutting."

No. 14. CORNCRAKE SEDGE.

Body : Broad yellow quill.
Hackle : Red hen hackle, continued down the body.
Wings : Corncrake, pent-shaped.
Season : Afternoon and early evening in July.

No. 15. CINNAMON SEDGE.

Body : Hare-lug.
Hackle : Dark brown hen.
Wings : Brown hen, pent-shaped.
Season : June and July evenings.

No. 16. GRANNOM OR GREENTAIL.

Body : Light hare-lug.
Hackle : Pale red, hen's hackle.
Wings : Inside of soft part of hen-pheasant wing, pent-shaped.
Butt : Peacock, green.
Season : May.

No. 17. BLACK SEDGE

Body : Broad black quill over silk.
Hackle : Black hen.
Wings : Black hen, pent-shaped.
Season : August.

No. 18. NEEDLE-BROWN.

Body : Brown quill.
Hackle : Natural brown cock.
Season : From August onwards,

CHAPTER VIII

INSTRUCTIONS

THOUGH comparatively very few anglers have become dry-fly fishers, it is probable that a great many have given the floating lure a trial; but it is generally after many weary hours of fruitless casting on an unfavourable fishing day, when everything else has proved of no avail, that they suddenly remember the existence of a little box of dry-flies stowed away in some corner of the creel.

They proceed to put them to the test, having heard of their infallibility, but they are in the worst humour for fishing after long-continued disappointment, and they cast without care or interest. The result in all likelihood is further failure; the efficacy of the dry-fly is declared a myth, and its devotees are denounced as unmitigated exaggerators, or the equivalent in words of fewer syllables. They make a general deduction from one particular isolated case, but fail to see that, if they apply the same sort of reasoning to all their experiences of the day, they must conclude that the wet-fly, or the worm, or whatever lure happened to be in use, has absolutely no power to capture a trout.

Now the dry-fly on its trial should be used under conditions which seem to predict a successful issue, that is to say, at a time when trout are feeding on the surface. It is not fair to judge it by the response it elicits when the living fly is either absent or ignored. We do not estimate the worthiness of the trout by the fight it displays in December, or assess the value of the grayling from its April form; we do not decide that the wet-fly is a useless lure because it brings little sport in July. Accordingly we ask the beginner to postpone his attempt and withhold his opinion of the floating fly until the advent of an auspicious day.

Success with the dry-fly is not inevitable at all times; but on certain occasions it is, and often, very often, when the invitation to use it is far from clear, it may be truly astonishing. Even in some cases when used as a kind of forlorn hope, it has succeeded beyond the wildest expectations, and the lucky angler has been converted at a stroke into an enthusiastic dry-flyer ready to throw away his assortment of wet-flies and bait-tackles; but such a pleasant experience is given to few and deserved by none.

The dry-fly can and sometimes does prove very attractive, when fish are not rising or taking any form of food, for the very good and sufficient reason that, resembling as it does a living insect, and probably one, moreover, that is well known on the stream, it may arouse within a trout not any distrust but rather a desire to eat. However, such a reception cannot be depended upon in these circumstances, and therefore, as we earnestly desire the beginner to come to an honest and correct conclusion regarding his new lure, we hope he will select for the occasion of his first ventures the conditions already suggested.

Before he sets out he should prepare a cast according to the following plan, knotting the lengths of gut together by means of the valuable knot illustrated on page 48. Let us suppose that each strand of gut is sixteen inches long. Eight of these will be required, four of 4x, two of 3x, and one each of 2x and 1x; they should be carefully selected from the hank, round, smooth and without flaw, and put into slightly warmed water for at least an hour to soften. In making up the cast, the end of strand 4, where it is joined to strand 3, should be pulled out to about three inches, and then the knot drawn tight. This is the most convenient and satisfactory method of attaching a dropper-fly; not only is the fly easily, quickly, neatly, and securely fastened, but it stands out beautifully at right angles to the cast. The wet-fly fisher on loch and stream would do well to adopt this method.

It will be apparent that we are recommending the beginner to fish two dry-flies on the cast, and this advice will be considered so very extraordinary in certain quarters that it is necessary to give reasons for daring to oppose recognised authority.

The reasons are as follows :

1. As already explained in Chapter III, it requires a great effort on the part of the wet-fly fisher to reduce his three or four or more flies to a single unit at one fell swoop. Many Clyde and Tweed anglers still use a cast carrying as many as ten flies; it will be difficult to convert them to the dry-fly.

2. The cast has two points of suspension, and therefore the flies are not so readily dragged under the surface by the cast and line, when the latter begin to lose the power to float. The life of the fly is prolonged, and a willing trout is not deterred by unnatural behaviour of the fly.

3. The cast falls more lightly and more horizontally on the water if it carries two flies. At least we imagine it does and, seeing that the hackles do tend to lessen the speed of descent, it is reasonable to suppose that, by doubling their number, the fall will be rendered still more gradual. If the surmise is correct, surely the advantage is of value to anyone and especially to the beginner.

4. In water ruffled by wind or current, it is sometimes difficult to discern a fly. If two are used, one may be easily seen, and then the other can be picked up at once. In dry-fly fishing it is most essential to watch the flies carefully.

5. Often we have caught a trout on the tail-fly, when there could be no doubt that the dropper-fly had previously passed over the fish. When both flies are alike in pattern, or even if they are different, and the first causes no alarm, then one is justified in concluding that the trout was interested by the first and therefore fell to the second, or alternatively that it imagined a hatch had taken place, and that it was time to get busy. The result might be the same if we were to use a single fly and cast it twice, but we would require also to know of the trout's existence and be sure of placing the fly on the right line. We assume, of course, that there is no rise to guide the cast.

6. In practice we find—or perhaps it were better

to say we think we find, for there is no certainty in fishing—that two flies are superior to one, when rising fish are not in evidence, and we are casting at a venture.

There are objections to the use of two flies:

(1) One fly may interfere with the other's free progress down the stream.

(2) One may catch up in weeds while a trout is being landed.

Neither of these accidents is possible in the pool or flat where we intend the beginner should make his early efforts. Weeds, eddies, and all difficulties will be assumed to be non-existent; but, after some expertness in the art of manipulating and delivering a floating fly is attained, he will not avoid such difficulties. He will expressly seek them, and he will find soon enough that in certain places one fly is better than two. He will remove the dropper-fly, but not necessarily the dependent gut, whenever he finds it advisable; for example, when he tries some tricky corner, and also when he seeks to accomplish the death of an uncommonly good specimen. He does not require to be told that the prospects of victory are much enhanced if the attention is undivided.

There is one event made not impossible by the use of two flies, neither calamitous nor objectionable, but in every way glorious, viz. a double capture, and we sincerely hope that such fortune comes to the dry-fly fisher on his first day. We have had that thrilling experience dozens of times, and every time it comes we are as delighted as with the first; it can never become stale for the issue is uncertain, until the pair of beauties lie side by side high up the gravel. So fine a bit of sport we refuse to make impossible, and whenever we encounter an easy flat we affix again the dropper-fly to the cast, if perchance we have just previously been poking about cunning nooks of the stream.

Now the angler who is after fish and nothing else does not want to capture two trout simultaneously; it would mean for him loss of time and opportunity during a good rise. But he, who desires sport above all, will welcome the hooking of a double and enjoy himself to the full, even though he lose one or both in the landing.

The beginner's lesson is being rather long delayed by discussions which he may not clearly understand, but we hope that he will yet appreciate these digressions.

Let us imagine the day all that could be desired— a fine day in May, with sunshine and cloud, a cool upstream breeze, conditions which suggest the probability of a good hatch of duns occurring from time to time and causing the trout to be lively. He should pass on up the river, neglecting even tempting places and ignoring rising trout— it is only for one day that he is asked to undergo such hardships—until he arrives at a flat of moderate depth, varying from one to three feet, having a nice gentle current well spread over it and a sparkling stream at the head. Perhaps if he knows his river really well, he can go to such a place without delay or much consideration. We are stipulating the easiest of conditions; but such places are easy to find. We could name dozens of such flats on both Clyde and Tweed; but it is unnecessary, for those who fish these rivers will think of them at once, and those who know them not would not benefit by the list.

In a damper he should have his cast ready for work; but, before he begins operations, he should first determine the species of fly on the water. He should wade quietly out, at a part he does not intend to fish, and intercept one or more of the flies floating down. If trout are rising, he will be rather unwilling to do this, being more eager to fish than to catch flies, but the process will occupy but a few minutes, and the confidence

Line to loop

it will give him to know that he is using a fly the nearest approach to the natural insect he can find in his box will stand him in good stead. Confidence in his tackle is the best part of his whole equipment. Of course, if he has much experience, he may be able to name the fly correctly after a single glance from a distance, but sometimes the expert requires to make a close examination. Doubt will not enter his mind, if he really knows the species of fly.

He should now put up his rod, rub down from five to ten yards of his line with Cerolene, tie on his cast, and to it attach two flies bearing as close a resemblance as possible to the insect he has just captured. The flies should be fixed by means of the simple but very reliable knot described and illustrated on page 51, dipped in *Natare*, and dried with filter-paper. A drop of this liquid or a little of the line-dressing should be taken between the finger and thumb of the left hand and applied to the whole cast excepting a foot on each side of the dropper and a similar length at the tail. *Natare* must not be allowed to touch the line, as it has a solvent effect on the waterproof dressing.

Everything being now in order, he should enter the water quietly about the middle of the flat, where will be a good wave caused by the wind blowing against the current, and when knee-deep turn to face upstream. We cannot tell him the correct length of line to use because that varies with the individual. He should pull off about a yard at a time from the reel, make a false cast in the air when the slack line will run out, and continue to do this until he has the length with which he has been accustomed to do his finest casting with the wet-fly.

He must not on any account dip the point of the rod in the water and give it a sudden jerk to get out the line. This is a trick practised by hosts of anglers; but it is none the less a most unnecessary proceeding at any time, and fatal when dry-fly fishing, because it removes most effectively the benefits conferred by the dressing applied to the line.

He is now ready to begin casting the dry-fly, and first and foremost he must remember not to aim directly at the surface, but at an imaginary point a yard vertically above the water. It is very difficult to avoid making this mistake, especially when a trout happens to rise just within casting distance. Everyone knows it is wrong, but many omit to remember the fact at the right moment and, just as the golfer must tell himself to keep his eye on the ball while making his stroke, so the angler must advise himself not to aim at the water or the rise.

By so doing he allows the parachute-like wings or the soft spreading hackle of his flies time to act, and they lower the lures softly to the water. Lightly they will touch, and their most natural appearance, as they float onwards, bobbing to every wavelet, is sure to delight him, and make him feel that success in the shape of an answering rise cannot be long delayed. The first casts should be made straight upstream, the flies allowed to float not more than a yard before they are lifted off, and, after a false cast in the air to throw the water off them, they should be replaced with as much care as he can command. It is highly dangerous to allow them to float farther after an upstream cast—in actual practice it is quite unnecessary—because when he lifts preparatory to the next venture he may, if the flies are too near him, succeed in hooking himself.

It is quite possible that he has heard that, for every cast that is laid on the water, at least a dozen must be made in the air, in order to ensure the flies being thoroughly dry. He may even have seen dry-fly fishers practising these graceful evolutions with the rod and line. These are the timid

anglers, terrified to catch a trout, and therefore
they reduce the possibility of such a catastrophe
to the vanishing point; it is only after they have
gained the requisite courage that they venture
to put the fly on the water. One false cast is all
the fly requires, and even that can be dispensed
with, if the angler is in a hurry.

Very soon the beginner will begin to feel that
he is picking his flies off the water and laying them
on again. He may now vary matters somewhat
by casting at various angles to the current, even
straight across it. When doing so he may allow
the flies to float much farther than before, without endangering his person, and he is sure to
observe that after going a certain distance they
are retarded or accelerated in their progress by the
line. He is being introduced to an elementary
form of "drag" which is the greatest difficulty
the dry-fly angler has to contend with, but the
successful circumvention of which gives him one
of his greatest pleasures.

As a matter of fact, every angler, no matter
what his special predilection as to lure may be,
has many of his efforts rendered failures by this
same trouble; but in their case its existence is
seldom suspected, as its effect is not so clearly
manifested on other lures as it is on a floating fly.
"Drag," and the methods of overcoming it, will be
discussed after the elementary principles of dry-
fly fishing have been mastered.

It will be remarkable if, by the time the feat
of laying a fly neatly and delicately on the water
has been fairly satisfactorily accomplished, not a
single rise has resulted. If, however, that should

be so, there need be no despair or doubt regarding the virtues of the new lure, for such a thing should not be expected if, as is assumed, the trout are not rising, though he will certainly feel surprised that his life-like fly riding the stream so naturally should not have elicited some attention.

He should now return to the bank, dry and oil his flies, dry and re-anoint his line, and wait for the mysterious appearance of a sub-imago, the precursor of the next hatch. Sooner or later, very soon on such a day as this, it will arrive, to be followed immediately by dozens more of the same species, whose presence will at once arouse the trout into energetic action, and hearty rises will be the outcome.

Out again into midstream he should go, lengthening line on the way, and now he may be so eager to cover a rising trout that he will forget the injunction not to aim at the surface of the water. If a fish breaks water up in front of him, he will, if he is like most other anglers, pull off a yard or two of line and throw over it. The cast will be clumsily done, and probably the line will fall heavily where the tail-fly should have alighted softly. The first effect of a rise is to make the angler lengthen line. It is rather curious, but very common. He does not consider whether he can cover the trout with the length of line already out; he takes it for granted that, because it is a rise, it must be far away. He should try first with a false cast whether it is within his distance, and he will find very often that it is; if not, he should step forward a yard or two preferably to handicapping himself with a line he cannot fully command

Another point to note is that the boil made by a rising trout travels downstream, and therefore, if the fly is cast for the rise and not for the trout, it will fall short of the fateful place. If the fish cannot be attended to at once, its position should be marked by some object on the bank; it may be rather far off for immediate investigation.

Now the beginner will want to know how he should attempt to cover a rising fish. Some authorities will advise him to place his fly a yard or more beyond the trout and allow it to float freely downwards without any movement of the rod. This may serve in some waters; but in the rivers and streams of Southern Scotland, which are fished every day in the season by many accomplished anglers, the trout are inordinately gut-shy. Therefore we advise that the tail-fly be placed not more than a foot beyond the trout, and that only in streamy water; in calm, currentless water it should be placed as neatly as possible exactly on the rise.

Owing to the suspicion with which these trout view even the finest of gut, the cast should not be made, except in a few instances, straight upstream; instead it should be delivered up at an angle of 45° to the current, when of course little gut will traverse the field of vision of the trout, and none at all will pass over it. An upstream cast is necessary or advisable when the trout is lying in very fast water, either at the neck of a pool or under the angler's own bank, in a narrow, curving corner, or wherever obstacles prevent a cast across.

There are three matters arising out of these con-

siderations that call for explanation. We advise
the beginner to make his first practice casts with
the dry-fly straight upstream, and then tell him
that such a cast is to be resorted to only on exceptional occasions. In the first place he is practising,
not fishing, but a more important point is that a
cast directly upstream, though not a good raising
cast, is a grand hooking cast, that is to say, only a
few trout will be raised, but of these few a large
proportion will be hooked. He is, therefore, not
likely to be subjected to many disappointments in
the shape of unaccepted offers ; but on the other
hand might easily make a capture, an event highly
desirable at the initiation stages.

The second matter requiring elucidation concerns
the statement that trout, which are much sought
after, become very suspicious of, and are readily
alarmed by, floating gut. In apparent contradiction
we have related that a trout may accept the tail-fly
after allowing the dropper-fly to pass by untouched.
We would not expect such a thing to happen in
quiet water of gentle flow, but we know it to be
quite common in streamy broken water in which, it
is natural to expect, the gut will not be conspicuous,
and that is, from necessity, the type of water into
which our flies are most frequently cast.

Thirdly, it will be obvious that, though two flies
adorn the cast, aim is always taken with the tail-fly.
Theoretically the dropper should not be present,
but anglers are not infallible and, as we have good
reason to know, frequently overestimate the distance
of a rising trout. The dropper-fly very often succeeds in correcting such a mistake. Moreover, in
our Scottish streams, trout are numerous and in

certain bodies of water are congregated close together. A fish may be observed rising; but it is not by any means the only fish within a circle of a yard in radius; there are plenty more near it ready to take a fly when the chance comes, and one of them may succumb to the dropper.

Meanwhile the pupil has been industriously casting, gradually working his way up the flat, but taking care, however, not to move forward in the act of delivering the flies. He should keep his line waving in the air while he takes a step or two, and only after coming to rest again at a new position should he make a cast. Obviously, if he acts otherwise, the line will not be so tight from rod to fly as it might be and must be, if offers are to have their most welcome ending.

He is certain to have discovered that his flies will not always oblige him by falling and floating right side up after the manner of a living insect. It is customary to say that they do not float with wings cocked, which is perhaps a more picturesque way of phrasing it but which is correct only if the fly happens to be a copy of one of the *Ephemeridæ*. A cast high in air, as already recommended, will usually result in the fly alighting as intended, and an underhand cast will almost always succeed in laying it down correctly. To execute this cast the rod should be held out horizontally across the stream, the line flicked sharply backwards and then brought forward, but the rod should not be allowed to pass farther upstream than the angler. It is an easy cast to acquire, useful for the purpose mentioned and also in any shallow water, rippling or still, where a trout may readily catch a glimpse of a waving rod; but accuracy in direction with this cast is attained only after much practice.

Also it is very probable that he will be startled by a sharp report, whenever he removes his flies from the water preparatory to making a cast. This phenomenon denotes that he is rather energetic with the backward cast, that in the process he is pulling his flies beneath the surface and then plucking them out, and it probably also means that the line and cast are crying out for another dressing of the floating agent.

If his movements have been quiet and deliberate, and his casts fairly satisfactory, it will be surprising if the reward of a rise is still delayed. If all goes well, a rise is certain, and a fight with a goodly trout will end in him netting the first victim to the floating fly. He is sure to admit that the capture has afforded greater satisfaction than it would have given, had the lure been one to which he has been long accustomed. That is largely because the fly, the rise, and the strike are all visible ; but, in addition, the trout is almost certain to be a good one for the river, far better than the average that falls to the ordinary wet-fly.

A capture, however, presupposes a rise, an almost certain event even at an early stage, and also a successful attempt at a strike, a much less certain occurrence. Frequently, far more frequently than we really care to admit, a trout hooks itself. This statement may be unpopular, as it takes away from the angler a great part of the satisfaction he feels ; but, however unpleasant, it is nevertheless true. We are unwilling to believe it, but we must, as the evidence is so conclusive. Anyone who cares to withhold his hand when out dry-fly fishing will soon be convinced that it is often unnecessary to assist a trout in securing a fly, but just as surely he will learn that a fish, as soon as it takes the artificial into its mouth, is aware of the unreality and that it has the faculty of expelling at once the fly which has not been forced securely over the barb by the movement, complicated or simple as the case may be, of the trout as it regains its station. Therefore, because it is sometimes necessary, it is always advisable to strike.

To give clear and explicit instructions on the art of striking is beyond our powers. It seems to us that directions must depend on the individual, his rod, length of line, and the offering trout, that is to say, on many factors all very different and all highly important. A trout rises, the eye sees, the hand acts, the line tightens, the fly responds; many things have to take place and the time required for an answer to each stimulus varies throughout the sequence; if there is delay at any point, the final response must likewise be retarded.

One angler may generally carry through the sequence more quickly than another but even he will not invariably complete it in the same time, because his form changes, winds do not blow always at the same pace and belly out the line to the same extent, the rising trout is not always the same distance away, the fly does not float at a constant rate. It takes a long time for the motion of the wrist to be communicated to the fly, and the time varies with the wind, place, trout, and the conditions.

We have fished on Loch Leven and many other lochs, sharing the boat with many friends, and we have noted the rise to the other rod, marked the strike, and waited for the coming of its effect ; it was slow. We have asked that the same be done for us, and we, who considered ourselves quick on the strike, learned that we were not. It may surprise some who do not know it to hear that the first action of the strike as usually made is to lower the point of the rod ; that adds appreciably to the time taken.

Then there is the trout itself. It may be heavy or light, lazy or agile, hungry or well-fed, slow or quick, and it may rise in many different ways. We have been recommended to count six slowly and then strike. If we carried out that advice on Loch Dochart, we should usually be striving to hit a trout that was anything up to fifty yards away from the fly that had deceived it. We suspect that those who so advise us are in the habit of fishing for trout which rise slowly to intercept a fly and roll lazily over it. We know trout of that kind, and we hook them by lifting the rod slowly until the line is tight, commencing the movement as soon as we see the rise. We are well acquainted with trout which are so agile that, unless the line is straight all through and unless we strike as quickly as we possibly can, we are bound to miss them. Many of these we have hooked by the tail, and that shows that we were rather slow and the trout not quick enough.

We fish all kinds of water, sluggish and swift, running and still, inhabited by trout varying in weight from quarter of a pound up to more than three pounds, and exhibiting all the variety that the race is capable of, and we know that instructions of a definite nature cannot be given. We might attempt a rule, but it would have so many exceptions that the rule would be lost. Each rise must be treated on its merits, and that demands a lightning decision, often wrong perhaps, but sometimes right and frequently very lucky. In flowing water we endeavour to strike as quickly as possible any trout that appears under a pound in weight; with heavier fish the whole action is more gentle. In still water we may have to respond at once or wait for the trout, everything depends on the way it comes at the fly. As a rule, heavy fish are more leisurely than small ones, but even a salmon can snatch so suddenly that it cannot be answered in time, unless the line is stretched taut down-stream, when reply is unnecessary.

Other anglers may find these methods useless; our quickest action may be to them slow and so each must for himself solve the problem of striking.

In dry-fly fishing the rod should be held in striking position, viz. about 45° to the vertical, and all striking should be done from the reel. It is easier to regulate a reel than it is to apply just the right pressure with a finger to a line.

While the angler must find out for himself whether he is too quick or too slow on the strike, and be able to come to a decision on the spur of the moment regarding any particular fish, he must remember that, when fishing with the dry-fly, he often knows when to expect a rise. This simple fact is equivalent to a gain in speed and must be taken into account.

Many people seem to imagine that " quick " and " forceful " are convertible terms. A strike should never be forceful; it must be gentle although quick, and the reel should give at most but one protesting

click or two. Some like to hear the reel sing out
its wild cheering notes to the hills around, and
glorious music it is when accompanied by a wild
headlong rush for liberty. Then it is not only sweet
but safe, because it starts more softly. Even a
smoothly running reel has some inertia which must
be overcome, and that may not be done if the call
is too sudden ; hence the strike must be administered
gently.

Our pupil has now received so many instructions
and listened to so much discussion that he must be
able to cast a floating fly, raise a trout, and strike
it correctly. Of course he has long known how to
land it. When the fish has been duly admired and
laid to rest in the creel, the fly should be washed
to remove any blood or slime that may be adhering
to it, and dried. It may be oiled again, but that
should not be really necessary. Time should be
taken to examine the flies in case they require to be
re-tied to the gut, and the wings should be adjusted
or stroked into position.

He will naturally enough desire to go further
upstream, to try his fortunes elsewhere, possibly in
some slightly more difficult flat or pool. His
ambition is excusable, his enthusiasm exactly as
we expected, and we do not wish to restrain him in
any way ; but we must inform him that one of the
greatest mistakes a dry-fly fisher can make is to
cover a lot of ground in the course of a day's fishing.
Not only is that unnecessary, but it may even be
the means of converting what might have proved
an excellent day into a mediocre one.

A hatch of flies, it should be remembered, is
almost invariably a local event ; that is to say, it

does not occur in every pool and shallow of the river at the same moment, a fact almost too obvious to mention. The angler, in his anxiety to make the most of his time, may hurry from pool to pool hoping always that the next will show him a fine rise in progress and witness his success; but instead he may miss the hatch everywhere by arriving at each pool after the flies have passed off or leaving just before they appear.

There is nothing to be gained by this procedure on a river, though in a small water in which the trout are always, more or less, on the look-out for food it may sometimes pay. We call attention to it because this hurrying over the pools not only tends to spoil the sport of the individual offender, but also that of others who may be on the river. A comparatively short stretch is capable of giving all the sport required, provided that it is carefully fished and duly rested.

The angler may consider it rather monotonous to go over the same pool or series of pools again and again, and so it may be; but it is far less dreary than wading miles of a river and receiving only a slight return or none for hours of casting. The main point is that he must find himself at a really good part when the rise begins and, having made the most of his opportunities, he may then satisfy his desire for change of scene by wandering up-stream; but we feel rather confident that he will be only with difficulty persuaded to leave the place that has already treated him so kindly.

When trout are rising well, progress up a pool should be very slow indeed, and it will be found that, after the entering stream is reached, the trout at

the tail are ready for another offensive. In discussing this question, we admit that we are thinking
principally of Clyde and Tweed, the trout in which
are so much fished for and are so accustomed to
the sight of man that they resume feeding very soon
after interruption ; but in smaller waters and in
rivers less frequented we know that a longer stretch
is required for a day's fishing.   Still there is nowhere
any necessity for much walking, and the angler
will find that his sport depends on the thoroughness
and care with which he fishes a few pools, rather
than on the amount of walking exercise he under-
takes.

CHAPTER IX

TACTICS

THE dry-fly fisher quite early in his career will learn that success depends not only on the delicacy with which the fly is delivered, but also on the direction of the cast. When a trout, rising to the natural fly, happens to be within his casting distance, he may cast to it from the post he at the moment occupies, or he may change his point of attack, not necessarily in order to approach nearer to the trout, but rather for the purpose of putting himself into a more advantageous position relatively to the fish and the current.

He should review the situation, make his decision as soon as he can—after a little practice and experience his movements will be made almost unconsciously or, rather, will appear automatic—and the result will be reflected in his success. In fishing, every cast should receive all the thought it requires. The spectator who watches an expert industrious and keen during a good rise may conclude that fishing is an easy business requiring no thought, but only a certain manual dexterity; but that is simply because he fails to observe the little changes in position, action and delivery which distinguish the complete angler from the ordinary performer.

For example, a right-handed angler will find it
expedient to move so that the rising trout is upstream to his right rather than to his left, for
when a cast is made to the left his view is liable to
be obscured by the rod, a not unimportant point.
A cast straight upstream must result in "lining"
the trout, that is to say, the gut must fall above
the trout and float down over it ; some fish, as we
have already seen, know only too well its significance.   If, however, by reason of a strong current,
broken or clouded water, the gut is not perceived,
a rise is a certainty provided the fly falls nicely,
and a successful strike follows almost as a matter
of course, because the line is tight.

In a deep broad pool having a strong current
flowing down the centre, a cast straight across is
the best of all for raising a trout if the flies alight
on the current, but only a very small proportion
of the raised fish will be hooked, unless of course
the fact is known and certain precautions taken.
Such a pool is full of trout, partly because so few
are taken out.   The wet-fly man, who fishes it
precisely as he does other pools, finds in it little
reward, unless fingerlings be counted reward, because his flies alight in the slack water on the far
side, his line in the centre, where it comes under
the influence of the steep current and sucks out the
flies at extraordinary speed.

The dry-fly fisher will meet with the same fate if
he adopts the same tactics, but he will raise a
trout at almost every cast if he lays his flies on the
current.   However, these rises come to nothing,
because the wind blowing up or down stream puts
such a curve on the line that the strike is invariably

late ; often a trout may be got, but, if so, it is fairly certain that the angler did not fix the hook.

In a stream of the kind under review, trout will rise within five yards of the angler, who, therefore, should use a very short line, cast it straight across stream, allow the flies to fall on the quickly flowing water and to float not more than a yard, when he should take one step forward, cast again, and so to the head of the pool. For this work we consider two flies infinitely better than one. This is the sort of place where natural rises are often scarce, and yet dozens of trout are waiting and willing. If a rise is missed even with this procedure, a further shortening of the line may bring the welcome resistance at the next offer, but restraint in the power of the answer is required, for, when the line is short, the strike is quick.

For the majority of flats and pools, the most profitable direction lies between these two casts, as it combines the advantages of both and reduces their undesirable features. When a fly is presented accurately with a cast up and across stream to a rising fish, little of the gut passes over it, hence the trout is likely to offer and, if the fly has not been given a long journey to perform, this offer should be accepted.

Often the angler will see a trout which is rather beyond his powers to reach, and depth of water may make it impossible for him to reduce by a direct advance the distance between it and himself. Perhaps it is accessible from the opposite bank, and if so, he should, after marking its position clearly, proceed in search of a ford ; he may then assail it from close quarters. If this involves a

loss of time or expenditure of energy, or is open
to any objection, there is another course open to
him.

He should try his hand at " shooting the line."
If he will pull off another yard from the reel, hold
it between the forefinger and thumb of the left
hand, and make his usual cast, he will at a certain
moment be aware of a distinct pull on the slack
line. Had he released his grip at that moment,
the line would have shot forward. This is one
of the easiest tricks to learn and the secrets of success
·are: Cast as usual, let go when the line asks for
it, and do not attempt to shoot the maximum all
at once. In this way the flies can be neatly placed
one or two yards beyond the usual distance—
experts can shoot several yards—and on occasions
facility in this art may prove valuable. As it is
possible to deliver more line than may be held up
by the rod, the part shot must be recovered by
hand before the back-cast is made. For obvious
reasons, the angler when wading must be content
with less distance than he who fishes from the bank
can command; anyone can cast farther from a
height than from the water and, moreover, slack
line long enough to reach the water cannot be satisfactorily shot.

Under the heading of tactics we may examine
another item of advice that is not uncommonly
given to the dry-fly fisher. He is recommended
to recover his fly at once if it does not fall correctly,
that is, right side up, and deliver it again. A fly
floating in an unnatural position may awake suspicion in a trout, but a fly plucked off the water,
however gentl~ ~~ ~~ ~~~~ ~~~~ ~~~ ~~~~ ~~~vinced,

succeed in thoroughly alarming it. If any angler can make his fly leave the surface in the same delicate way that a sub-imago takes wing, then doubtlessly he will make use of his superlative skill ; but ordinary mortals will succeed equally well, if they fish out the cast and then repeat it.

Similarly, if the angler makes a mistake in his aim at a certain trout, he should temporarily ignore that fish and allow his fly to complete its voyage. By so doing he may conceivably lure another trout ; but he has less chance of scaring the one that induced him to cast, and it will be waiting for him at the old place when he has finished the unexpected, perhaps undeserved, fight. We have seen, and most anglers have seen, trout rising so close together that the rings intersected as soon as formed and passed down stream in company.

All the time the dry-fly fisher is at work he should be exercising and cultivating his powers of observation, and thinking out his plan of campaign. Many parts of a river capable of producing many trout to a thoughtful angler may yield nothing to another.

As an example, let us consider those little corners which are found in so many waters. The rivers turns almost at right angles to its course ; the main body of water pours along one bank into the next pool and strikes against the opposite bank, while a certain amount trickles over a thin gravelly shallow into a backwater, scooped out in times of flood, fairly deep, practically motionless, very calm, and generally weedy. Such a place, the backwater, is sure to be tenanted with good trout intent on feeding, but very shy and cunning.

If the angler lays his fly according to custom

beyond a rising fish, it will, as it floats almost imperceptibly along, be subjected to the most careful scrutiny, and in all probability the invitation will meet with a point-blank refusal. He should therefore stand in readiness until the fish rises again, and at once without a moment's delay he should put the fly on the mark. Accuracy is the supreme requirement; delicacy is not so essential. The fly should not alight in front of the trout but as close as possible to it on one side or another, or even behind it; the fish is aware that something has again arrived for it and turns to snap at it without hesitation. As soon as hooked, the trout bolts for the strong rushing neck, so leaving the back-water and its occupants undisturbed, and it will be surprising if only one victim is secured from such a troutful place. We have deceived very many fish in this way which, we are perfectly convinced, would not have been taken had any other tactics been employed.

Sometimes trout, especially those which delight to lie beneath the shadow of a high bank, can rise with exceeding quietness, so very quietly indeed that some would fail to observe the disturbance of the smooth surface, so faint it is. Not only so, but if they did mark the slight effect, they might be surprised to know how great its cause. The trout—and any one which rises in this quiet fashion is generally a grand specimen—seems to raise itself gently to the surface and suck down water, fly, and air, all together. The fly vanishes, but marking the place where disaster overtook it, appears a floating bubble, which may remain stationary for a long time, if the water is still.

The angler, knowing the cause, should watch for these effects, as he proceeds up the pool or arrives at a new one. If he observes an air-bell floating within the shelter of the bank, he should send out his fly to investigate whether it has been left there by a feeding trout. Frequently such a sign has invited us to switch a fly across, and often the raising of a fish has proved—to our satisfaction at least—that our deductions had been correct.

Though it is a rule that a dry-fly must be cast up, or up and across stream, there are notable exceptions. Of these we have already pointed out one, but there is another. Sometimes a trout will take up its feeding station in an awkward, curving corner, or so near a piece of rough water that an upstream cast is foredoomed to failure. A dry-fly can be floated down to a trout by means of a downstream cast, and a very interesting cast it is to execute, highly successful too, if there is sufficient depth of water to afford the angler concealment. Naturally it is of limited application, but nevertheless many a trout has succumbed to these tactics.

Thus it is that dry-fly fishing can never become dull. Its practice induces, encourages and repays study of all the moods, peculiarities, and surroundings of trout. Every day brings its own problems, and in their solution the angler finds much of his happiness.

CHAPTER X

DRAG

IF the wet-fly fisher, who believes in fishing downstream, casts his flies across a pool of uniform flow, they float onwards for a time freely in answer to the current, but in course, as the cast becomes tight, their progress is checked, they begin to swing round, and finally they are directly in a straight line below him. If he repeats the cast with a dry-fly he will see the fly, after a short journey undertaken exactly as a living insect would perform it, turn aside from its path and at rapidly increasing pace plough across the surface of the water towards the centre of the pool. He will then understand what drag is and learn also how his wet-flies behave under water; he may even realise the cause of his frequent failures at midsummer.

Drag is the greatest trouble of the dry-fly fisher; but the problem of its avoidance is not unwelcome, for, necessitating as it does the exercise of thought, skill and ingenuity, it adds materially to the interest of days spent beside the waters. That being so, we shall not take away from him all his pleasure by solving all his difficulties; in other words, we make a virtue of necessity, for it is quite impossible for us to enumerate and examine all examples of

drag ; almost every day on the river a new problem
is set us to solve, and often we devise new tactics
in the hope of at last overcoming an old stager of a
trout that dwells secure in some ungenerous corner.
The examples we take are therefore to be considered
as illustrative and the solutions as merely suggestive.
We point out the difficulty and so enable the angler
to perceive it, before he ruins his chance of sport
by proceeding, as if none existed ; we indicate
methods of surmounting it, but leave it to him to
select that which most appeals to his particular
style or to modify it in any way that his previous
experience pronounces advisable.

Whenever the artificial fly leaves the course that
a natural fly, unaffected by a breeze, would take,
or has its pace influenced by some force other than
the current, it is said to drag. This usually fatal
effect can be produced (1) by the sinking of the line,
(2) by the action of the wind on the line, (3) by
the influence of the stream itself.

If the cast or line begins to sink, it will gradually
pull the fly along the surface and finally beneath
it. This movement can be appreciable only in a
dull, still pool or a loch and scarcely requires consideration, for it simply means that the line is calling
for redressing. It may occur when the fly has been
allowed to remain where cast for a comparatively
long time, and that is occasionally a means of
bringing up a trout in deep, calm water, but, when
the effect of this little trick is being investigated,
precautions should be taken to guard against the
fly dragging.

Some anglers object to the trouble involved in
drying and re-treating the line, possibly because the

seriousness of the inattention has not been pointed
out to them. Some have fished the dry-fly for
years and have never floated cast or line. It was
a long time before we could tolerate the sight of
floating gut, but, having happily got over our
aversion, we now know that more offers go unaccepted by reason of the line being submerged
than from any other cause.

Let us consider what happens in a pool devoid of
current, when a good breeze is blowing. The natural
fly, when it alights, does not remain stationary,
though perhaps quiescent, but is wafted along
before the wind, just as any floating body would
be. An artificial fly is attached to a line, and
the wind acts on the line, waving it about, with
the result that the fly makes rapid and erratic
changes of position. Trout accept the living insect
but refuse the dragging imitation. On certain
streams, trout are said to be rather suspicious of
even a living fly that is not floating at rest in still
water or freely down a current, but we have seen
no instances of the kind. On the contrary, we
have watched March Browns buffeted about by
a strong wind, and seen the trout chasing them
eagerly and throwing themselves upon them. But
the artificial fly must not indulge in similar antics.

The action of the wind must be counteracted.
Obviously the less line that is exposed to its action,
the less will it be affected, but to reduce the length
influenced the only device available is to lower the
point of the rod. Unfortunately that involves a
loss of striking power, but the handicap must be
accepted as being the smaller of the two evils, and
the angler must do his best to fix the hook by a

sharp downstream strike or a quick raising of the rod.

We now proceed to the most important cause of drag, and that which necessitates the greatest study, viz., the stream itself. If the fly and any part of the floating cast or line are in currents of different strengths or of different directions, the fly will be retarded or accelerated in its progress down the stream. The effect may take a long time to manifest itself, as in the type of water chosen for the beginner; but in little places here and there all over the river the fly may drag immediately it alights. Therefore the angler must study the methods of avoiding it, if he is not to remain content with easy casts and admit the finest trout beyond his powers.

In the diagrams which follow, variation in strength of current is indicated by variation in the distance between the lines, i.e., the closer together they are, the stronger is the current; the angler is easily recognisable; the trout is always heading upstream. As one fly is quite sufficiently difficult to manage in water of the description now to be discussed, and as the angler must now be an enthusiastic dry-flyer, seeing that he has advanced to this stage, the dropper should now be removed.

First, as it is one of the places most beloved by trout and therefore of surpassing interest to the dry-fly fisher, we propose to consider the " hang " of the pool, that part at the tail where the water swells, before it breaks into the leap for the next pool.

Here the trout is in comparatively slow water, while between it and 1 the flow is very fast. If the usual cast is made direct to the trout from the usual distance, the fly will fall on smooth, slow water and the line on a rapid current. The consequence is that the fly, as soon as it alights, is torn along the surface at the head of a fearful furrow, and the trout flees in terror to the deepest depths of the pool.

If a good upstream wind is blowing, the angler may wade forward—it is generally possible in such a place to do so—allow his line, shortened to the length of his rod, to stream out before him and dap the fly just in front of the trout (see Chapter XIII). If the wind is downstream or too light to permit of dapping, he may move to 2 and make a horizontal cast partly across country, or he may from 3 try the effect of floating a fly down to the fish (see page 113). One of these methods is sure to be better than either of the other two, and he must decide, after an examination of the particular place and consideration of the other conditions, e.g., direction of wind, depth of water, which it is. Care must be taken that as he moves to 2 or 3 he does not betray his presence to the trout.

The diagrams show a pool such as is described on page 110, viz. one having a brisk current flowing down the centre ; but in this case the trout is rising in quiet water outside the rapidly moving stream.

If the angler casts as in Fig. 1, the current will act upon the line, carrying it downstream, and sweeping the fly at great speed away from the point where it fell ; Fig. 2 shows the probable position of the line and fly after a second or two, and it will be observed also that the trout has vanished.

Let us suppose, however, that this fatal cast has not been made. The angler has then several alterna-

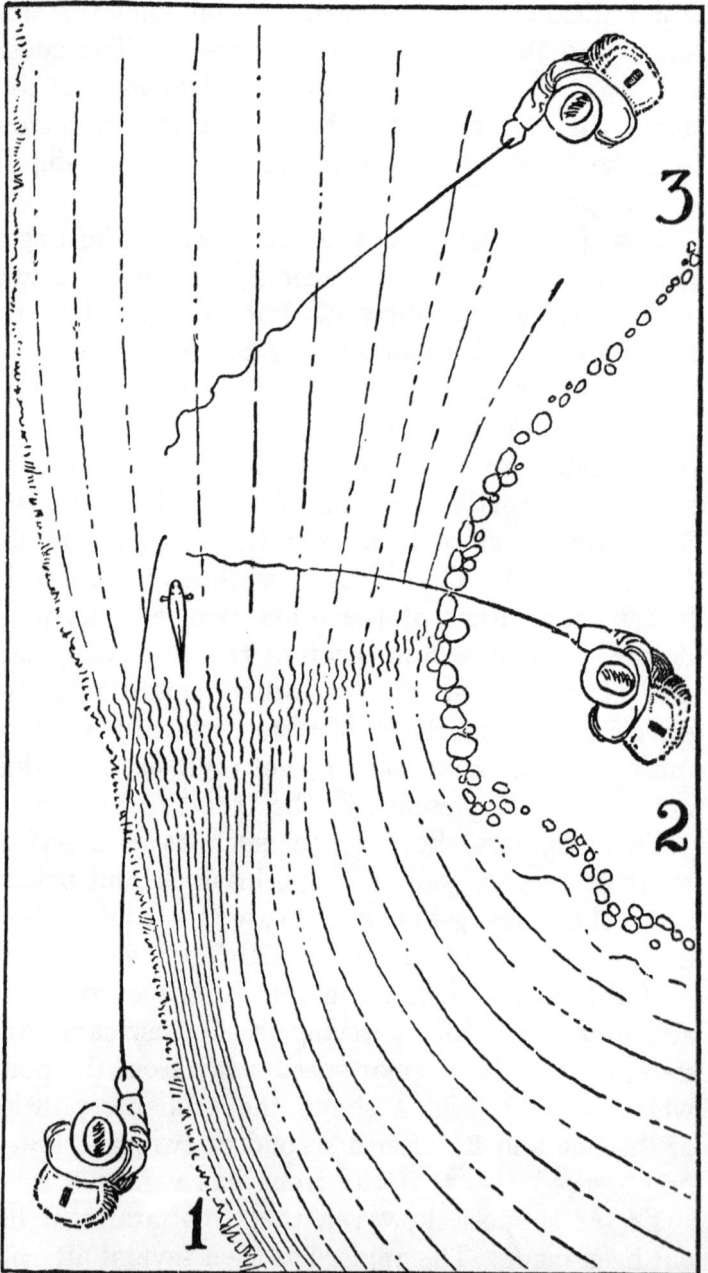

CASTING TO A TROUT IN THE "HANG" OF A POOL.

tives from which to choose.   He may try a cast
such as is shown in Fig. 3.   On paper, and to those
who have not tried it or seen it done, it may appear

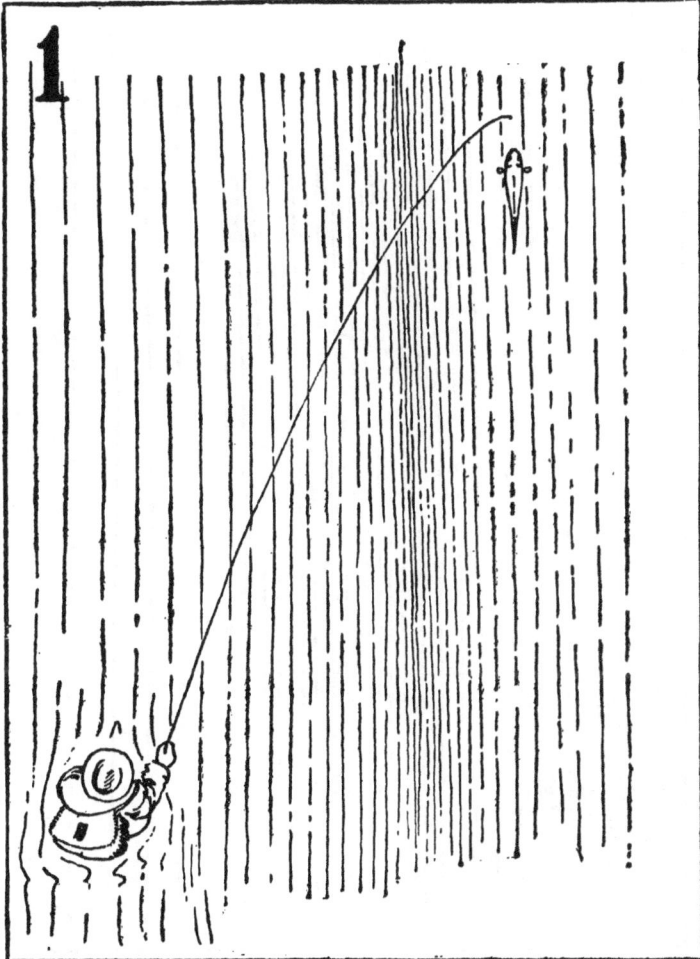

A STRAIGHT CAST ACROSS A FAST STREAM.

an impossible sort of affair ; but it can be executed,
only after considerable practice certainly, by holding the rod horizontally across to the left and

switching the fly upstream. He should by all
means try it, for ability to do it well is a valuable
possession on such an occasion as this, and on

THE EFFECT OF THE PREVIOUS CAST.

others also ; unless he overcasts, there is no harm
done. The concave curve on the line has to be
removed before the fly begins to drag and, if luck

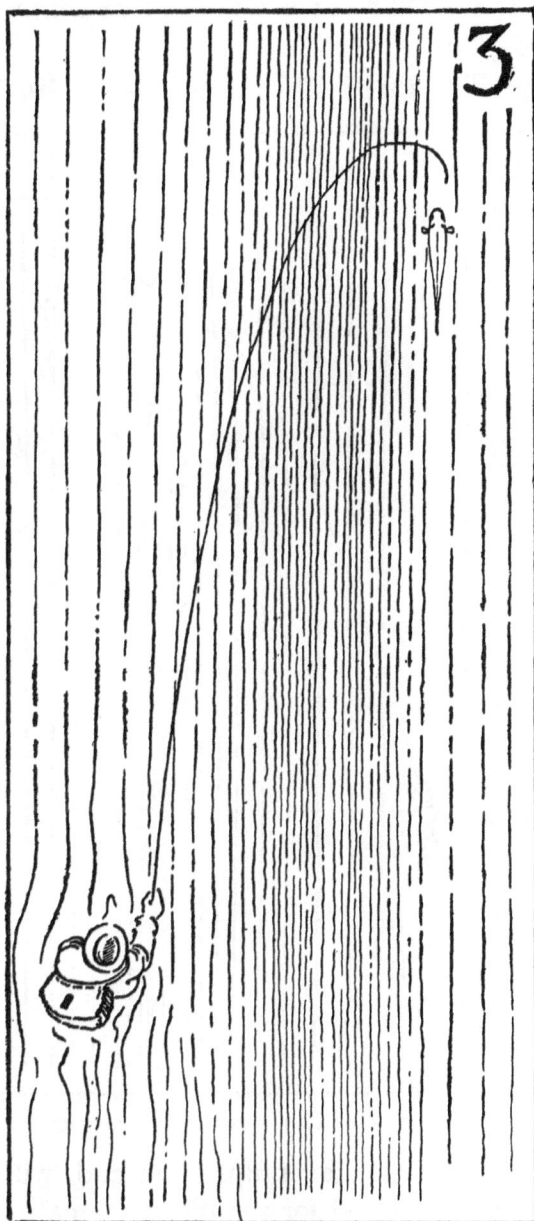

THE BACK-HANDED CAST FROM THE RIGHT BANK.

attends, it will reach its objective without arousing
suspicion.

He may prefer to try the much easier cast shown

A SLACK CAST ACROSS A FAST CURRENT.

in Fig. 4. He moves upstream and, with a longer
line than required for the distance, makes the usual
cast ; but as the fly comes forward, he checks the

movement of the rod momentarily and then lowers
it to its accustomed position. Possibly this cast
is more easily accomplished when one desires to do

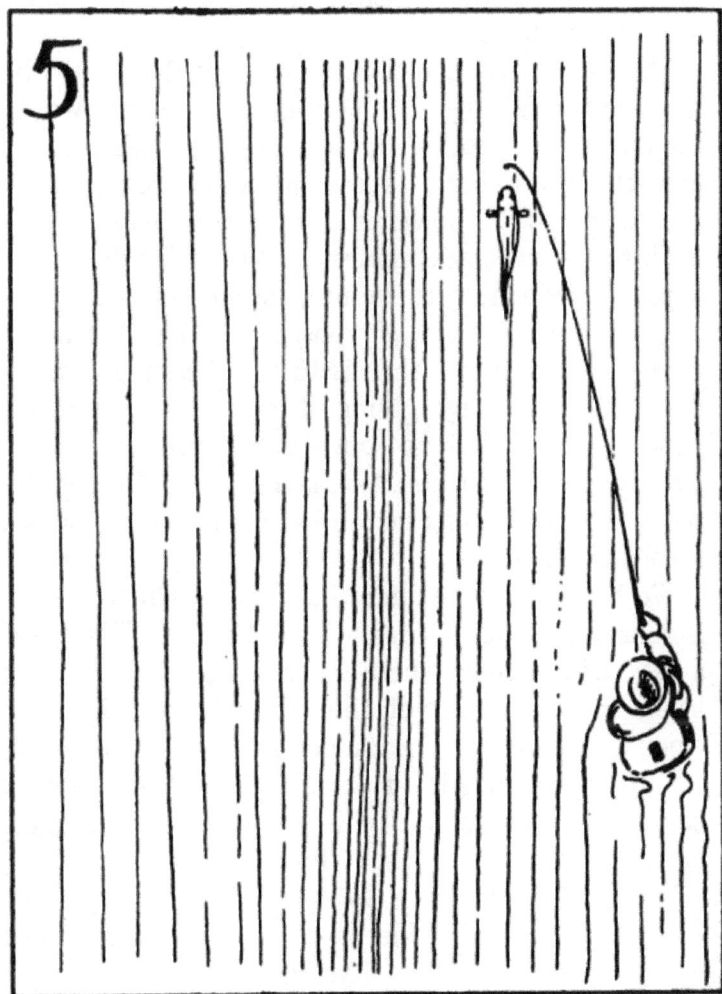

CAST AVOIDING THE FAST CURRENT.

something else; many a time, when the angler
endeavours to deliver a nice straight line, he casts
one beautifully adapted for such a situation. The

line does not extend itself fully, but lies in a snaky wriggle across the surface, and it has to float a considerable distance before it can exert any influence upon the fly.

The favourite solution when possible may be that shown in Fig. 5. The angler walks down to the tail of the pool, wades across to the other bank, and tries the effect of a cast up and across stream. The trout may, however, be rather close to the bank to be an easy conquest. When all other casts appear foredoomed to failure, he should endeavour to place the fly, from any position he likes, straight to the trout's nose ; that is to say, he should make drag impossible by giving it no time to develop because the fly has no journey to perform ; it has already arrived at its destination and often it receives a hearty welcome and sometimes, of course, a cold reception.

We have still to examine a case in which the fly is retarded in its course. The diagrams illustrate a bend of the river where the fast flow is along one bank, the remainder of the water being relatively quiet and gentle. The angler who casts direct to the trout, as in Fig. 1, will find that his slowly moving line keeps back his fly, which is dragged into the slack water, as in Fig. 2.

What he should have done was to move up as in Fig. 3, and try the underhand cast or switch across to the opposite bank. The line falls in a convex curve, and therefore the fly moves freely for a considerable time. We rather like this cast, finding it highly successful, but we do not move up all at once ; we proceed gradually upstream, casting all the time, estimating the distance and strength

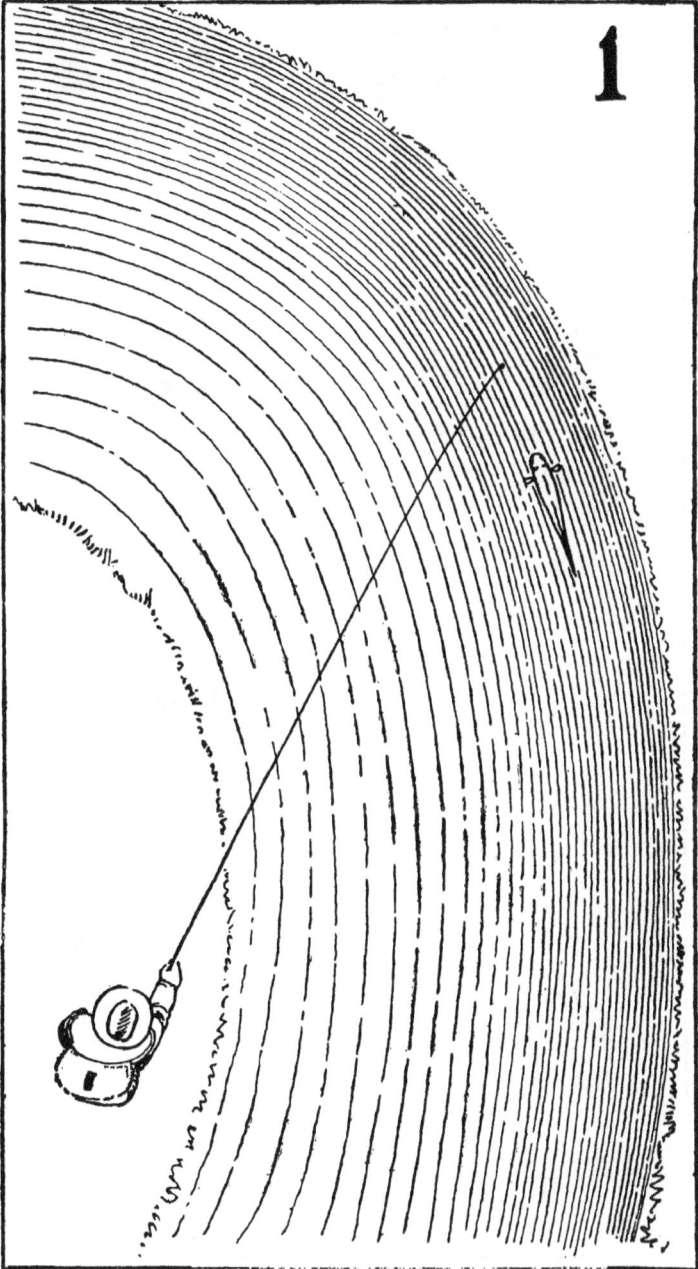

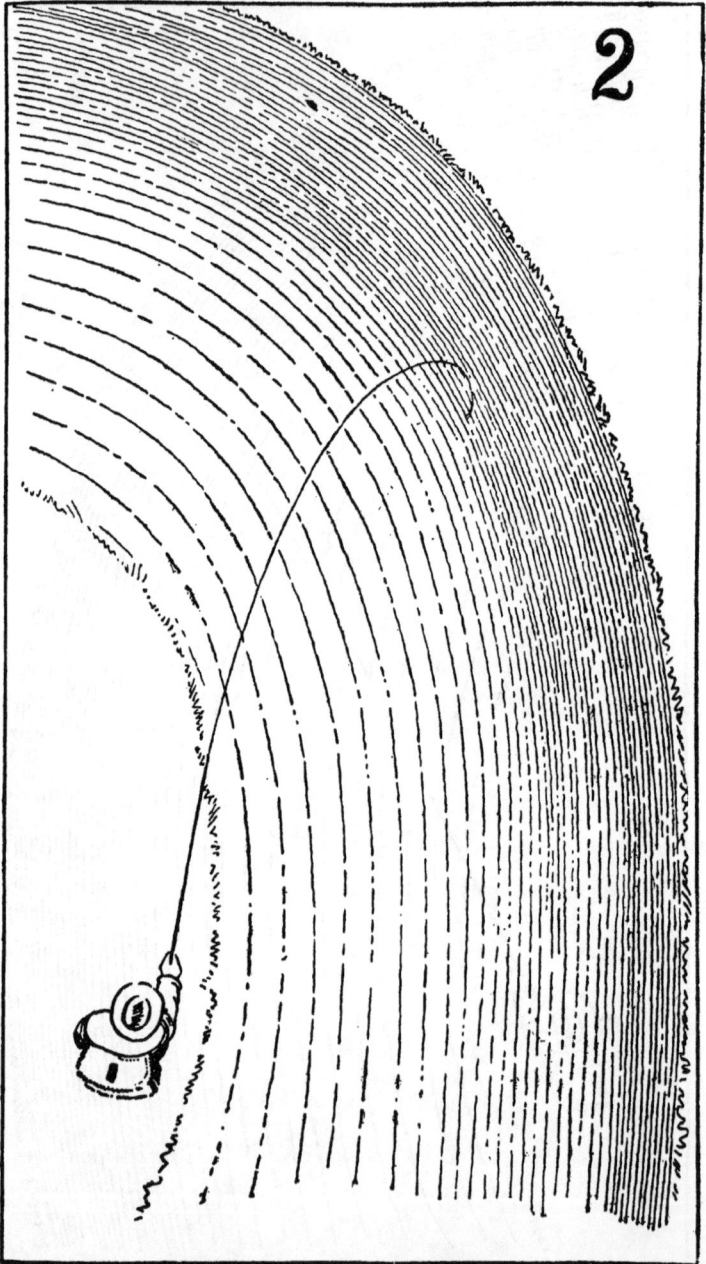

THE EFFECT OF THE PREVIOUS CAST.

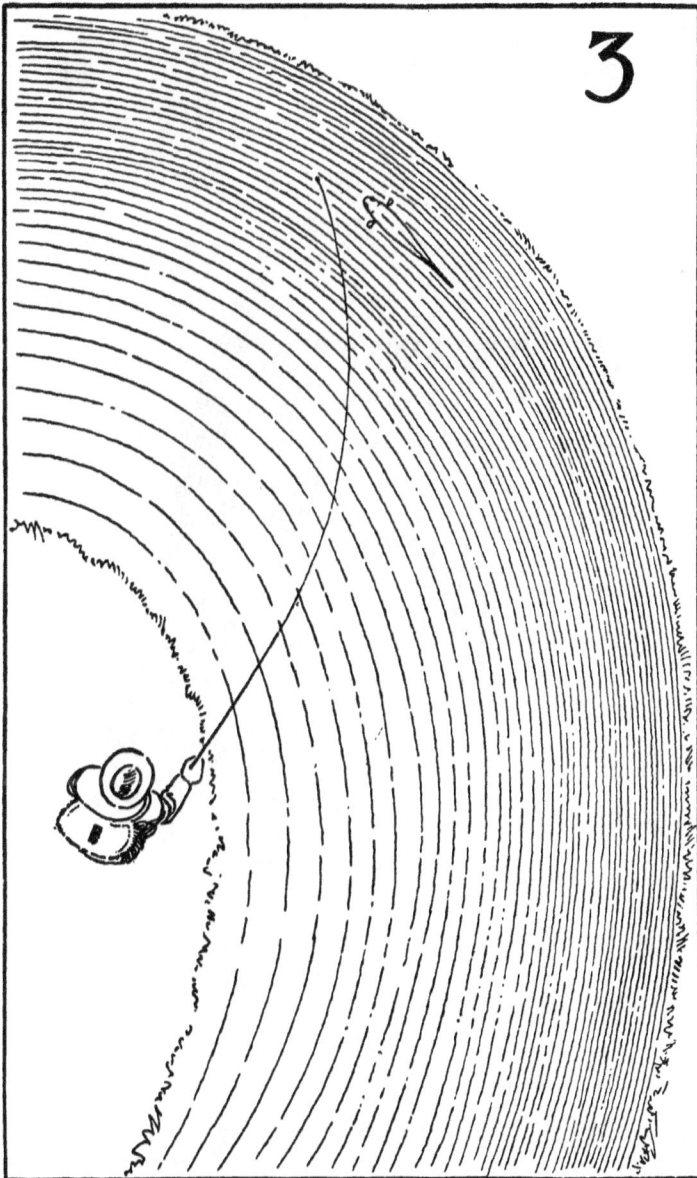

THE UNDERHAND SWITCH FROM THE RIGHT BANK.

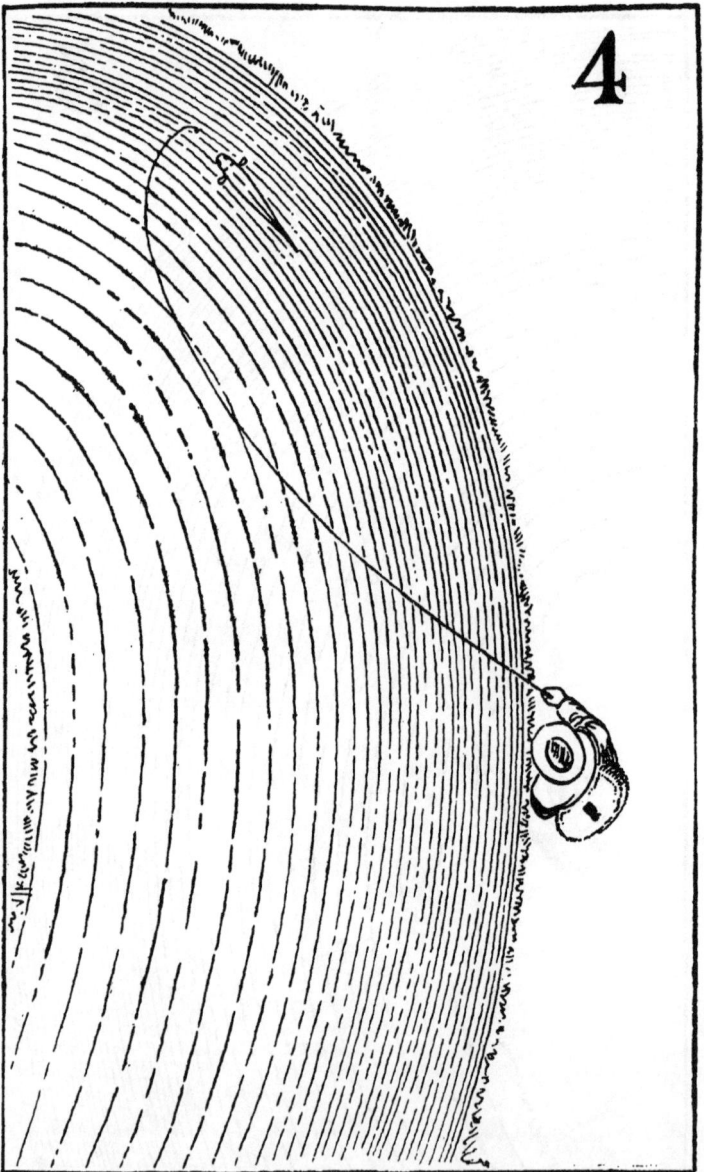

THE BACK-HANDED CAST FROM THE LEFT BANK.

required.   As an alternative, the angler may select the method of Fig. 4, which is simply a repetition of the switch from left to right shown in Fig. 3 of the previous set of diagrams, but in this case the cast is made from the opposite bank.

In all cases where the angler anticipates that drag will occur, he should consider carefully whether success would not be likely to follow an attempt to dap a fly either from the water or from some point on the bank.

Though we have not gone into the problem of drag very deeply, yet we have tried to suggest means of avoiding it, and therefore it may surprise some to know that we at times endeavour to cause it.   The River Clyde, which, we hasten to say for the benefit of those who are so unfortunate as not to know its magnificent attractions, is inhabited by a race of highly educated trout, is characterised in its highest reaches by stretches of water, such as are shown in the diagram opposite.

The water is deep and of smooth flow, the angler's bank is low and gravelly, while the opposite bank along which the trout lie and rise with infinite gentleness, is high and grassy.   Many a time, in such a place, we have floated a fly perfectly over a trout and received a flat refusal.   Accidentally, we admit, we once discovered that these annoying trout, which delighted in ignoring our best efforts, were attracted by a dragging fly.

Our method is to cast a wriggly line, so that the fly falls a yard, or sometimes more, above the trout, allow it to float down straightening out its coils, until the fly is just on the point of dragging, and then to push the rod forward.   The fly at once

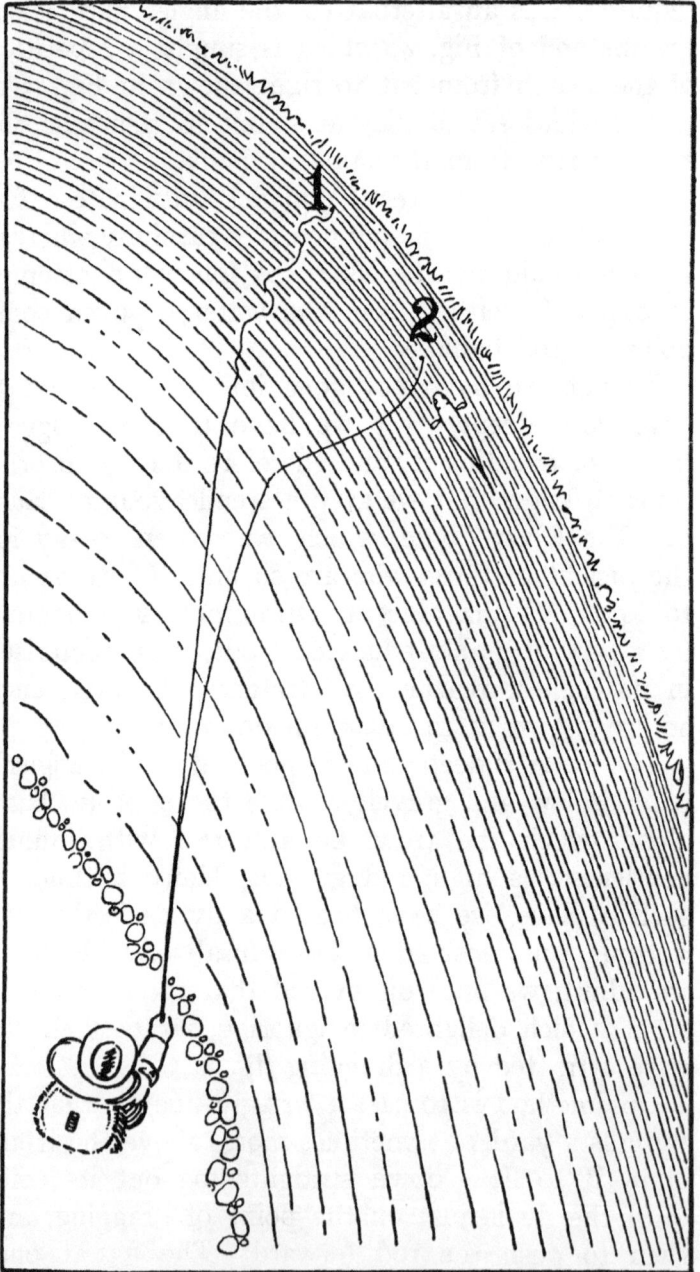

TO PRODUCE DRAG.

skips across the surface, and the trout snaps at it, making no mistake in aim and securely hooking itself. We can offer no explanation, unless it be that the trout imagines that the fly is making a desperate effort to escape. We always try first to float the fly correctly down, and if that fails we repeat the cast as described ; we have killed dozens of trout in that way, none heavier than ¾ lb., but many of them half-pounders ; and other anglers, who can believe that this is no fishy story, may care to try their luck with such curious tactics.

CHAPTER XI

ON WADING

FOR every individual angler there is a certain length of line with which he can execute his neatest, most delicate, and most accurate casts, and, whenever he observes a trout rising, he will naturally want to bring himself to such a point that the distance between him and the rise is that at which he is most expert.

He understands, of course, that every yard of line used outside that favourite length imposes upon him a handicap with which he would much rather dispense. Sometimes he can arrange matters to his liking by a cautious advance upon the bank, but even the greatest care will often not prevent his discovery, whereas by wading he can in the majority of cases reach the spot desired, and reach it, moreover, without giving the trout a hint of his presence and intentions.

It may be taken as axiomatic that no pool or stream in a river will fish equally well from both sides at the same time. The two banks are never precisely the same ; the current usually sets to one side or the other and the water is not of uniform depth all over. On one day the trout may be feeding on the shallow side, on another in the depths below the high bank ; they may be in the centre of the pool, at the tail, or at the neck ; their situation depends on the type of food which is available.

When they are expecting the gravel-bed fly, for example, they are congregated near the edge, especially in such pools as chance to have the gravelly bank on the windward side. When creepers are assuming the winged state, the trout crowd the neck of the pool. If the day favours the hatching of duns, the shadow of the high bank and the rippling entering current are greatly favoured, while if a good breeze is blowing, and nothing in particular is expected, the tail of the flat is sure to be well tenanted. The angler, therefore, desirous of the best sport possible under the conditions, must know where to expect the trout or discover, by observing the rises or other means, their whereabouts, and plan his campaign accordingly.

If the trout are not confined to any particular area, but are rising in all parts of the pool, he need not even then conclude that it is immaterial which bank he fishes from ; one side is almost sure to be better than another in that it offers an easier approach. There may be a bush to provide cover, or it may be that the background of one bank confers invisibility. As the day progresses, the superiority of one side may or may not be continued. It may be transferred not so much because the sun may throw the angler's shadow up the stream ; but because, owing to the water being differently illuminated, the trout are enabled to learn that they are being attacked. Still we know pools, mostly narrow pools, fast-flowing and broken, which invariably fish best from the same bank, not the one that would be selected by an angler desiring easy wading and casting, but the opposite bank, high and crumbling. The reason is that the trout always lie at the tail or in the strong current among the masses of grass-topped earth torn from the bank, and it is quite impossible from the shallow side to float a fly over them without drag.

The conclusion, therefore, is that the angler must wade, no matter how small may be the stream he is fishing, in order that he may cross from one side to another, whenever knowledge of the water or his experience of other waters tells him that it is advisable to do so. He should, of course, exercise some care in the selection of a ford, and have regard for his own sport and that of others.

There are objections to wading, and certainly waders can be abused, but abuse is due to thoughtlessness, not to design. An angler wading carelessly up a stream can ruin for an hour, and in some waters for many hours, the sport of anyone following after him; but so can one who fishes from or even walks upon the bank. That fact does not excuse anyone, and we should say that of the two the wading angler is the less likely to disturb the water. Frequently we have had trout rising immediately behind us and within a yard or two on every side, which seems to prove that quiet wading upstream does not alarm the fish. Splashing about in the shallows will, however, send the trout fleeing in all directions, and being quite an unnecessary proceeding, it should be dispensed with; it entirely removes all possibility of success from everyone, including the offender himself.

When the angler enters a pool he should imitate his fellow-angler, the otter, and slip stealthily into the water, taking care not to raise a wave before him. It is possible to capture trout in absolutely calm, shallow water, both during the day and in the evening, if precautions are taken not to give the trout a hint of the presence of an enemy. Even to walk on the gravel is fatal; they must be fished for from deep water on the opposite side, and very pretty sport it is, giving the angler every reason to be well pleased with himself, if he scores a triumph; to assail them from the top of the far bank is to invite defeat, in fact victory is then quite impossible.

There is no question that wading may easily be and often is overdone, some anglers apparently counting it their greatest happiness when they find it just within their powers to withstand the force of the current or the uplift of the water. It may be very picturesque, but, except in very rare instances, it is wholly unnecessary. If they reached such dangerous depths only after searching thoroughly the water nearer their own bank, they might be excused, but some are actually in the habit of commencing operations from mid-stream. The trout do not all lie under the far bank; there may be anglers coming on unfurnished with waders, and it does not put them in a hopeful frame of mind, when they see their flies alighting where another man has just been floundering.

It is mostly the downstream wet-fly fisher who is guilty of this offence as, by putting a large body of water between himself and his intended victims, he hopes to keep his presence unsuspected; but this he would effect with much greater comfort to himself and less annoyance to others, if he would turn about and face upstream. As we have indicated above, quiet wading seems to have little or no influence on the trout round about; but it is somewhat difficult to believe that, no matter how often they appear unconcerned, and therefore, since an angler who has lost hope is unlikely to gain success, we think that the practice could well be discontinued to the advantage of everyone.

Wading is not unattended with danger; an incautious step may lead to disaster and a sudden termination to a spell of good sport. It is more probable that one will omit to take care when things are going well than when the trout are dour and look without favour on the flies. Attention is in such circumstances directed entirely upon the great opportunity, and other matters are neglected.

Some of our rivers are characterised by ledges of rock on which one may walk easily and in comfort for many yards on a smooth surface only a few inches under water, but the path is narrow and its end abrupt; black depth awaits a hasty step. In other rivers there are other perils, chief among which is yielding gravel. On the Clyde there are many deep pots whose sides are steep, almost vertical, and the gravel surrounding them is small, loose, and crumbling; on the Earn there is at least one such place. It is well to know them and treat them with respect, but the angler in his eagerness is apt to forget, until his feet begin to slip from under him.

In summer, when the streams become low and the stones assume their slimy slippery deposit, wading is far from comfortable, and every step must be carefully undertaken, but we forget all troubles whenever a good July trout sucks down the floating fly and splashes wildly about, while we inelegantly scramble towards the bank, the better to answer its wiles.

The numerous drains, that bring water from the hills to lochs and reservoirs, form traps for the unwary angler. Usually they are cut far into the still water, and generally they are filled up with soft mud ; it is easy for him to see and avoid them, when he is not intent upon other things ; but a trout, rising just out of reach down the bank, may hasten his steps, and a drain may stop them with unpleasant suddenness. Still, we all take risks gladly, and it is wonderful how often our eyes happen to look downwards just when they should; we shudder, and retire, and carry on again.

Waders may prove useful in unexpected ways. They may enable the angler, for example, to retrieve a fly, the killing pattern perhaps and the only one in his possession, consequently of infinitely greater value than all the remainder of his varied collection if, by some momentary awkwardness, or by an unlucky cast in a place bristling with difficulties, it should be firmly hung up. Again they may be the means of securing for him a goodly trout firmly hooked and almost beaten which, in its final burst for liberty, contrived to get to weed, a trout that may prove to be his record fish.

We know no disadvantage in waders ; they are hot, heavy and uncomfortable. but we are quite unaware of it, while we are engaged in fishing; it is only when we are condemned to walk in them a mile or two on the road that we notice these unfortunate features. Seeing that they are so valuable to the angler, he should take care of them, drying them inside and out as soon as possible after a day's fishing, and they will last for several seasons.

Therefore we counsel the angler to wade, but to remember at the same time that the pool that is yielding him sport can yield him more, if he will exercise as much care over his wading as he does over his casting, and that following in his wake are other anglers who also hope to find happiness beside the river.

CHAPTER XII

TROUT-STALKING

THE trout is a wary animal, extremely suspicious of the human form, and when, as in the height of summer, he is well-fed and therefore under no compelling necessity to accept anything which arouses within him the slightest doubt, there is no creature of the wild more difficult of approach or more ready to take alarm.

In certain streams, smooth and placid, whose banks are much frequented, trout may, it is said, become so accustomed to the sight of man that they remain totally unperturbed by his presence, and will enjoy, with the utmost indifference to a crowd of spectators, a banquet of flies or nymphæ. The merest glimpse of a waving rod, the slightest flicker of light from gossamer gut, the least deviation of a fly from the true path will, any one of them, suffice to tell these trout that danger in the form of an angler has arrived, for, despite their seeming nonchalance, they are fully alive to the perils that surround them. They are even more difficult to lure than their brethren of the wild moorland solitudes, who, though they recognise an enemy in every man, and are therefore to be approached with the greatest caution, are not quite so well versed in the angler's wiles or so able to distinguish the signs of his dangerous presence.

At times, as in the chalk-stream so in the distant burns, the headwaters of rivers such as Clyde and Tweed, and in their lesser tributaries, fished the whole season through by appalling numbers of accomplished anglers, trout must be carefully stalked if they are ultimately to find their way into the creel.

A more interesting or pleasant sport than trout-stalking has never been devised. Not only must the angler's presence be concealed from the fish, those referred to above being alone excepted, but his purpose must likewise always and everywhere be unsuspected. The inherent shyness of the quarry, their power to read unerringly the meaning of a wave across the pool, and determine the cause of any vibration of the bank, their ability to see with excessive clearness within a field which, though somewhat circumscribed, is still all too large in the angler's estimation, all combine in their defence and render a successful attack a matter of supreme difficulty.

Nor does the attractiveness of the sport end there. It is conducted under summer skies blue and bright, amid the riotous confusion of the water's edge where every living thing is happy. The cuckoo may mock at our defeats, but the curlew's lonely call cheers and bids us try again ; the sandpiper runs along the gravel, as if to give warning of our coming ; the kingfisher flashes past, a sunlit jewel. We have but one enemy among the birds, the tantalising water-hen, who from among the rushes watches us sink stealthily into hiding, and then, laughing, scuttles out across the pool.

We lay down the following requirements which seem all to be demanded, before one is entitled to consider himself engaged in the fascinating sport. The approach and concealment must entail some departure from ordinary procedure; the water must be at lowest summer level; the individual trout sought after must be a rising fish and a worthy specimen of long experience; the surroundings must call for care and study in the accurate placing of a fly, and will in general favour the trout more than the angler. The latter may, if he can, and must if he is to achieve success, remove by the adoption of certain tactics the disadvantage under which he is placed. A big take will not denote that the angler is possessed of extraordinary skill; rather will it signify that one at least of the necessary conditions has been absent.

In our larger rivers, broad and deep, it is generally necessary for the angler to wade in order to reach a feeding trout; the depth of water from which he must operate will place him beneath the range of vision of a trout, and therefore it is ridiculous in such circumstances to talk of stalking. The term is wholly inapplicable. It is not even essential to fish upstream in these rivers, the breadth and depth of the water being sufficient to ensure the obtaining, without thought or effort, of the first requirement, viz. the concealment of the angler. Of course, even in the largest river there are tricky little corners, inhabited by fine fish, whose excessive cunning can be overcome only by the greatest skill; but these are exceptional places. Since we have laid it down that the trout-stalker must exercise great care in approaching the water, and experience difficulty in reaching his casting position without the trout suspecting his presence, we decide that the art is confined to the smaller streams.

On the River Ardle in Perthshire, above the Bridge of Cally, there is a truly delightful piece of water, a long pool formed by a cauld built diagonally across the stream. On the deep side heavily bushed the trout lie in a gentle current. They are not large, a pounder being most exceptional, but they have a fair experience, that being a function of age rather than of weight, and are therefore well worthy of capture. On our first visit up the stream we saw them, confident and secure, rising lazily to take down flies and generally conducting themselves after the manner of two-pounders, and they at once acquired great importance. We found that an attack from behind the tall bushes was impossible to carry out, that the water at the lower end was too deep to wade, and that walking along the top of the cauld exposed us to the view of the trout.

Next day we transferred our position to the bottom of the stony bank, and thus failure was converted into success. We waded through the white rushing water, gradually lengthening line as we advanced and as the pool broadened out, until we were able to slip over the cauld into shallower water, from which we fished out the pool to the neck. On that occasion and thereafter, as a result of these tactics, we took out an astonishing number of trout, of a size much above the average for the water, from which we concluded that parts at least of the pool were seldom, if ever, fished, and that the trout had not learned to suspect a floating fly. It was a curious experience casting into water so much above the accustomed level, and reaching up with the net for trout at the edge of the overflow also presented difficulties.

In the Clyde, a short distance above Elvanfoot, where the great river is still only a small stream, we once captured a beautiful pound trout, of which at the time we felt extremely proud. We were progressing quietly upstream, casting the dry-fly at a venture, when we became aware of the fish rising regularly at the tail of the next pool. It occupied what we should even yet consider a difficult position, namely the last yard of a steep swelling glide immediately before the break into the headlong rush. There was no cover available on the bank that seemed sufficient, and in any case it would have proved useless, because it was obvious that if we cast to the trout as usual, the moment the line touched the water it would sweep down the fly with a drag certain to strike terror into the heart of a two-year-old.

We left the water, and after a detour entered the pool far above the industrious trout. Wading cautiously as deeply as we dared and crouching low as we moved forward to our selected post, we switched the fly across and down at the end of a very slack, well-fatted line ; the gentle current slowly straightened out the line, and the fly approached ever nearer and at increasing pace towards its goal. Direction of the cast called for no attention, as the waters gradually converged to the narrow channel where the trout waited. At the critical moment the fatal drag threatened to intervene and swamp the fly, but by reaching forward with the rod we managed to prevent disaster. All unsuspecting the trout took the fly, and the reel broke the gloaming silence. The fact that the light had begun to fade no doubt contributed to the trout's downfall; but satisfaction was nevertheless completely justifiable, for the incident occurred many years ago, when we were first learning to know and respect the trout of Clyde.

The situations dealt with are uncommon; but they serve to illustrate all the more clearly that trout sometimes take up positions which render it imperative for the angler to adopt special measures to ensure that neither his presence nor the character of his lure will be disclosed. At all times it is necessary for him to remain invisible to the trout, until and even after the hook is home; but occasionally, especially on smaller streams, concealment is difficult to arrange. Not always will he find the required protective covering on the bank, though, whenever it is at hand in the form of bush, rock, or clump of rushes, he will probably accept it without further thought. We have, however, strong objections to the elevated position of the bank, and much prefer to be on or below the level of the water.

Whenever we get the opportunity, we like to work along the base of a high right bank, as we imagine that the background of grass and exposed soil confers invisibility. The rod, when not in actual use, should in such a case be carried pointing downstream. The left bank is equally good for those who are ambidextrous. If, owing to depth of water and absence of any foothold, such a procedure is impracticable, then it is necessary to conduct the stalking from the top of the bank or from the opposite side. In most cases we select the former.

By crawling along about a yard from the edge, one may approach so closely to feeding trout as to be able to observe their every movement—and very exciting it is to see a big fish daintily selecting its food. The rod, however, is a source of danger. If the ordinary overhead cast is used, the scaring of the trout is almost inevitable, but the underhand cast, in the execution of which the forward movement of the rod is stopped when it points out horizontally across the stream at right angles to the bank, will very frequently produce the desired result. Much practice is required with this cast, before one can lay with unfailing regularity a fly on a given mark; but perfection in the art is a valuable possession, worthy a large expenditure of time and trouble to acquire.

The great trouble often experienced, the losses incurred, in attempting to land trout caught under unusual circumstances should be considered as adding to the excitement of the sport. We have known of anglers who leave certain corners untried, because they are deterred by the difficulties, or convinced of the impossibility of bringing a trout to the net. They should solve each problem as it arises, and the first is the hooking of the fish; the second may solve itself. One single success might conceivably convert a forbidding place into a favourite cast.

In some waters there are long smooth flats only a few inches deep which yet contain very fine trout. To take a specimen from the inflowing stream is an easy matter, almost a foregone conclusion, if a rise is in progress; but to lure one from the tail of the flat, where the surface is as glass and the current barely perceptible, is a worthy ambition, and not at all impossible of realisation. Some of the older authorities on angling advise the fisher to pass over such places as being utterly hopeless; but no one should accept defeat without a trial. A rising fish can be caught by anyone possessed of the necessary skill, and that skill will never be acquired, unless it is developed by careful attempts to capture trout from unpromising places. The angler who will accept that as true, and refuses to be discouraged even by many defeats, will in time find himself enjoying most glorious sport in water which he used to consider could not yield a trout to the greatest expert.

It is admittedly difficult to lay a fly on shallow, flat water with delicacy sufficient to bring forth agreeable response; but frequent practice will make it possible. The fact that the water is always to some extent disturbed by a rising fish assists the angler, who should place his fly at once and exactly on the rise, not some distance beyond it, as he would in a deep or fast-flowing stretch. The answering rise, if it comes at all, is instantaneous; the strike should follow as quickly.

There is another difficulty. If the angler blunders up the gravel to the water's edge, then long before he comes within his casting distance the trout become aware of his presence and flee for refuge to their hiding-places under the bank or in some deeper corner of the pool. Any skill he may possess is now of no avail. He should instead survey the scene from safe range, study the rising fish, mark clearly the most desirable, and set himself the pleasant task of attempting its downfall. As at most only one capture is likely to be effected in such thin water, why should it not be the best ? He may make a mistake in his deductions from the spreading rings, but his satisfaction will be in no wise diminished, for he will probably remain in ignorance of the error.

His selected victim will in all likelihood be rising close to the bank, as that is the position favoured by big trout. If that bank happens to be the right, he should lay his fly lightly on the grass or rock overhanging the fateful mark, and then, after an interval of a few seconds, he should bring it to the water, not, however, by any raising or other movement of the rod, but by gently pulling on the line with the left hand. The fly may refuse to leave the grass, in which case the pool is lost, as he will probably be unable to retrieve his fly without exposing himself to view.

Should the trout occupy a station under the left bank it is a less easy conquest. The fish in such open flats as we are discussing will see the angler, unless he is immediately behind them ; that is to say, he must be on or close to the same bank as the trout. He who is able to cast left-handed will adopt the plan already recommended ; almost anyone is able to execute this cast sufficiently well if he will assist his left hand by supporting the extreme end of the rod with his right. If he does not care to try this, a lucky back-handed switch may land the fly where it is wanted, and bring him fortune.

In stalking trout in deeper and also faster water, there is another matter of paramount importance, one which might not occur to the angler, and that is the moment which he should select for presenting his fly. Many consider that the sooner the fly reaches the mark the greater is the prospect of success, and that is certainly sometimes true, as seen above, but more usually no greater mistake in tactics can be made. This unreasoning haste is the direct, though often unsuspected, cause of many defeats, not that it results in a clumsy cast, which is not unlikely, but because the fly alights where the trout is not, or when it is not engaged in watching the surface.

Few, who have even an inconsiderable experience of Loch Leven, can have failed to discover that the trout there frequently behave in a manner which at first may prove rather disconcerting, but which, after it is understood, adds largely to the interest of their capture. Indulgence in the habit is manifested principally when surface food is present in fair, not superabundant, quantity. The trout travel quickly, not directly against the wind but diagonally up and across it ; they rise at intervals on their route, and as a rule are easy to lure. They do not select calm weather for the display, as some might suppose ; it is more likely to be seen while a fine fishing breeze curls the water. If the angler places his flies across a rise, the fish is not there to receive his offering, but a yard or two farther on its course ; he must therefore not aim for the mark, but for the point where he imagines the trout is due to arrive.

In quiet pools of rivers trout at times similarly roam about ; but they are decidedly leisurely in their movements ; they do not travel at so great a pace nor so far as those of Loch Leven. It is generally only when they are sampling tiny diptera or watery duns that they set out on a cruise in the circumscribed area of the pool. The angler who decides to test his skill on these particularly worthy trout—we hold the cruiser in the highest esteem—must be prepared to exercise to the full the patience with which anglers are supposed to be endowed beyond all other mortals.

He must not be rash in taking cover : the object of his desire is not a stationary trout but a rover. It is consequently more difficult to stalk, as it may, at some point of its circuit, catch a glimpse of the incautious intruder. If he succeeds in remaining invisible, he has scored one victory, itself praiseworthy ; but the other, and by far the greater, will never be his, if he lays his fly over the rise ; he must judge where the trout will next arrive, that is to say, his fly must reach the water at the right spot and before the rise.

An hour or two spent on a bridge over a streamy pool when trout are feeding is time well spent ; but anglers are generally, in such circumstances, more anxious to fish than to acquire knowledge that will add to their sport during subsequent rises.

There is a great deal to see and to learn. A trout
raises itself towards a fly floating overhead, backs
downstream in close proximity to it, till finally,
a foot or more from its original position, it takes
courage and gulps down the struggling insect. It
then returns to its post. The angler's lure placed
on the rise will be unseen, but, if cast above it,
it may succeed in bringing the fish up. It is obvious
that the fly may be delivered too soon.

Another trout discovering a fly some distance to
one side shoots forward and seizes it. If the artificial fly covers the rise while the fish is on the
return journey, the rise will not be repeated. Moreover the cast will more than likely fall over the
returning trout, effectively scaring it. A few
seconds' delay in such a case is advisable. Of
course, movement of this kind, which seems to be
confined to brisk streamy water, cannot be clearly
seen when one is engaged in fishing, but under
certain conditions of water and sky it can be
detected, and it can always be guessed.

In the strong current at the neck of the stream
a fish hurls itself upon a fly, is thrown off its balance,
and is carried down for quite an appreciable distance. It must be allowed time to recover its
position before another fly is offered. It would
appear that the fish concentrates all its attention
on securing its prey and cannot at the same time
retain its place. From these considerations we
conclude that in streamy water the angler should
be slow rather than quick to send his fly out, and
that he should place it from one to two feet, according to the strength and nature of the current
beyond and above the point indicated.

In still or gently gliding pools trout, except when 'cruising, seem to prefer waiting for the fly to be brought to them, and selecting only such as give them the minimum of trouble to secure ; they are not so violent in their attacks, rising quietly, and sometimes scarcely disturbing the surface at all ; they do not move to one side or another as they do in faster water. We find, or think, it pays best to lay the fly on the rise or only a few inches beyond it ; but again it is well to consider whether it should be done at once or delayed. We have, not once but on numerous occasions, seen a trout rising with such regularity and at intervals so small that the rings from consecutive rises interfered with one another. In such a case the fly could be delivered at any time, as the trout must be poised very close to the surface, but to succeed the artificial would have to be a very good imitation of the natural insect on the water. In more usual circumstances it is better to postpone presenting the fly, so that the fish may have time to sink to its position, that is until it is again on the look-out.

It will often be noticed that when the *Ephemeridæ* are hatching they arrive in comparatively small detachments. A good trout will secure for itself the best position its prowess can command, and collect as many specimens as it can while the hatch lasts ; it then descends to swallow and digest. The angler should not enter into competition with the flies, if they are numerous, or lay siege to the trout while it is busy taking down the insects. He may ; but, as suggested in the preceding paragraph, his success will largely depend on the excellence of his pattern. He should wait, if he can, until he sees the next company coming along, and arrange that his fly is at their head to show them the way.

Again, on a breezy day on the moorland, trout similarly receive their food in a series of courses ; they are not particular as to species, welcoming anything that the wind may chance to bring along. The angler likewise need not concern himself at all about the pattern on his cast, but he will find it a very good plan to delay sending it forth until he sees the next gust waving the grass of the holm, driving before it a varied assortment of moths, midges, froghoppers, and the rest.

The successful stalker, who has marked down his fish, reached his chosen stance without betraying himself, identified the accepted species of fly, delivered his copy lightly on the surface at the right place and at the correct moment, raised, struck and hooked his trout, is liable to come forth from hiding in order to finish the conflict. In so doing he is guilty of two mistakes. He ought to remember that a hooked trout is more easily managed, less inclined to bolt for shelter in weeds, if he remains invisible. Also he should think not exclusively of his captive, but of the other trout the pool contains, one or two of which he may yet hook, if he studies to keep the victim away from their vicinity and himself concealed from their keen eyes.

CHAPTER XIII

DAPPING

SOMETIMES the trout-stalker, in the course of his leisurely and happy progress up the stream, will arrive at some part where, by reason of dense bushes, low-hanging trees, or wild confusion of rock and boulder, casting in the ordinary sense is impracticable. He need not pass such places by, as so many of his predecessors have done : there are trout there that remain comparatively ignorant of the wiles of man, have profited by his timidity, and being unmolested have waxed fat and careless. They can be caught by any angler who will not shirk difficulties, and who will practise the art of dapping an artificial fly ; that is in ordinary words, laying it lightly on the water without any assistance other than that conferred by a friendly breeze.

Dapping with the natural fly has long been practised. The stone-fly fisher impales the living insect, a female preferably, on a series of two or three hooks arranged with cunning purpose to protect the principal points of attack, and using a line only a little, if at all, longer than his rod, he searches thoroughly the type of water in which these flies spend the major portion of their existence, viz. rough stony stretches and necks of pools. Most adepts believe in keeping the fly on the surface ; but others declare that it is most effective if sunk a little, in which case it must, we think, be indistinguishable from a creeper. When a good upstream breeze is blowing—and that is what the stone-fly fisher desires—it is unnecessary to cast the bait ; the wind will carry it out beautifully. In the absence of a breeze or when it is adverse, the fly must be cast, but very lightly, if it is not to be thrown away altogether.

Not content with the grand sport obtained in the two or three weeks during which the mature stone-flies are about, some fishers, making deductions from their experience, search about for other flies to use in the same way. The men of Leadhills are the keenest and the most proficient at the game that we have seen. They use the " Grey " fly, a fat dipteron about the size of a Cleg, which is extremely common on the moors of Daer and Duneaton, the Daddy-long-legs, and later in the year the " Doctor," a crane fly with black body and scarlet legs. At times the ordinary House-fly and the Blue Bottle are pressed into service, and the luring capacity of all these insects, not one of which, the stone-fly excepted, is of aquatic origin, furnishes very convincing proof that trout in some streams will accept with freedom flies which are not born of the water.

A day with the natural fly is a very interesting experience ; but many anglers, holding that the satisfaction derivable from any possession varies directly with the difficulties encountered in its acquisition, consider that the artificial fly constitutes a more sporting lure, and prefer it beyond any natural bait. That is our belief, formed after an experience of all methods of catching trout, but we see no reason why the artificial should not bear the closest possible resemblance to a living insect. Hence it is that we advocate the use of a dry-fly. With the natural fly as lure we should be almost certain to catch more fish than with the dry-fly, but it is more certain that we would not derive so much pleasure. Dapping with an artificial fly is quite a legitimate method of fishing, provided that it is resorted to only when necessary, viz. in places where casting is not merely difficult but entirely beyond the angler's powers, and where drag is impossible to overcome. It can be used with great effect anywhere that provides sufficient cover, but it is allowable only in these special circumstances, or under conditions such as we are about to discuss.

There are days on the breezy Uplands when the wind is so strong that it is almost impossible to cast. The line stretches out horizontally before the rod, and sometimes the light cast is whirled vertically away, refusing to go on the water. Dapping being the only method practicable, the angler has to choose between it and an immediate return homeward. We have been treated to these conditions quite frequently, and we have never had any hesitation in making our decision. We fish, and that without any qualms, though with regrets.

Ephemeridæ may be absent ; but if the sunlight is strong, as it is usually on such a day, there are other flies about to arouse the trout. If we are on the Daer, we walk along the high bank, crouching if it seems advisable—crawling on these days is wholly unnecessary—and we allow the line to stream out in the wind. By altering the direction of the rod it is usually possible to manœuvre the fly to where it is required. Sometimes the sport is quite good, but it is difficult to prevent the line slapping the water, or the fly from being tossed about. In a more moderate breeze the basket would doubtless be much heavier, but in that case we throw off yards of line and cast over the spreading rings. Dapping is forced upon the angler, not deliberately selected.

There is one corner of the Daer, viz. the head of Watermeetings Pool, on which we seldom omit to dap a fly. There the water flows at great pace round a sharp curve, and drag is unavoidable. Now it is perfectly allowable to dap for an expectant fish as well as for a rising one; but how is one to tell whether a trout is in a state of expectation or not? If a fish is seen hovering near the surface, apparently active and alert, then we may conclude that it is on the look-out for food; but in such a place as we have under consideration a trout could not hover; it must lie on the bottom behind some protecting stone that shelters it from the great force of the strong current. Also the troubled surface effectively conceals the trout from view. The result is that we persuade ourselves that it would not be in such a place except for one purpose, viz. to obtain food, therefore we lower a fly to the water to find out if a fish is there.

With these and similar exceptions, dapping is inadmissible on bare, open streams such as those of the Southern Uplands, where nothing interferes with the freedom of the cast. Its usefulness is mostly restricted to heavily bushed streams and rock-bound pools, where the angler is so near his fish that he cannot cast to them.

The sport reaches its perfection in midsummer, when days are hot and trout in the main river are lifeless. Then it is pleasant to wander up some cool, shady glen under the trees and among the crags, peering now and then through the leaves or over a sharp ledge of rock into a deep, black pot. Almost every scramble reveals a trout poised near the surface or leisurely swimming round looking for something wherewith to satisfy its appetite; if nothing is seen, then the bubbling water at the foot of the fall is sure to conceal a good one.

Let the angler then pass his rod slowly and carefully over the rock—let it be not the favourite rod worth, or rather costing, a guinea a foot, but any old weapon of historic interest perhaps, but little intrinsic value—and push the fly over after it. Let him lower the fly gently until it lightly touches the water, and refrain to answer the almost inevitable rise until the fly has quite disappeared from view. This is more difficult than it seems, and in fact anyone at his earlier attempts is almost sure to strike before the open-mouthed trout has even reached the fly. Perhaps the best plan the angler can adopt is to allow the trout to turn, before he dares to drive the hook home, but much depends on the method of attack. It is certain that the beginner will vastly enjoy the unusual and thrilling experience of being able to witness the whole performance.

We have pleasant recollections of hours spent among the rocky fastnesses of the Blackwater as the Shee in its lower reaches is called. It was by no means easy in certain places to reach the water in safety, and consideration of the return journey, quite as difficult, was, like the landing of possible captives, deferred until the need arose. The plan we adopted was to lower away the rod, butt first, and then go after it. Of course, after the descent and ascent at any particular place had been negotiated without disaster, we thought little of the undertaking on subsequent days.

For this sport we used nothing finer than 3x gut, sometimes gut-substitute of similar strength. On hooking a fish we allowed it to run about the pool until it was thoroughly exhausted; then we caught the line, laid aside the rod, and pulled up the trout quietly and regularly hand over hand. If this was done correctly, the fish did not give a single kick. By this method we have never landed a trout over half a pound, though many of that weight; but we shall be very pleased to try it on much heavier fish. We have found it of great use when fishing off bridges and high banks. One trout per pool was the rule, and each represented a large expenditure of time and trouble, but we judged the time profitably spent, though well we knew that when we reached the open water at the head of the glen we should add to the basket at much faster rate.

Dapping over bushes introduces another difficulty, viz. the releasing of the fly. If they are not much higher than the angler, he should pinch a small lead bullet to the cast about a foot above the fly, hold the cast to the rod and the rod high diagonally over the obstruction, and then set free the fly.

The sinker will carry out the line, but, if allowed, it would swing the fly back into the bushes. Therefore, as soon as it is released the line should be pulled in quickly with the left hand. When oscillation ceases, the bullet should be allowed to carry out the line and deliver the fly straight to the waiting trout. The fortunes of the lure can be followed through the foliage, and the strike must not be hurried. A short cast not more than the length between bullet and fly should be used. Landing a trout is a serious problem, but there is often a way out. Even if the fish escapes, it has provided some excitement, and after all that is all we want; the fish is the proof required for others, not for the angler.

Dapping is a sport full of thrills, adding a pleasant variety to the ordinary routine of a day, and the angler should always be prepared with a short cast for a trout roving in fancied security within some hidden, shady nook.

CHAPTER XIV

FISHING THE STREAM

WHEN the angler goes out to the river **to** enjoy an hour or two of dry-fly fishing, he may confine his attentions entirely to trout that he observes rising to take natural flies from the surface; or he may, in addition to attempting the downfall of all rising fish within reach, cast his fly wherever his experience tells him that a fish is likely to be lying in wait. In the first case he is said to "fish the rise," and in the second he "fishes the stream."

For the first method of securing trout there is claimed a superior charm, a claim that we cannot grant, seeing that it is not easy for us to believe that the part is greater than the whole. The angler who fishes the stream lays his flies as delicately on the water and takes as much advantage of a natural rise as he who fishes the rise; but the former knows, or is rapidly learning, something that is difficult to learn, something that the latter does not know or scorns to apply his knowledge of, viz.—the art of reading the unseen bed of the river, its inequalities, the little pockets between rocks, the deep channels between sunken clumps of weed.

Many people can tell the meaning of a rise, and some can tell whether a rise is caused by a trout or grayling, sea-trout or eel, but not so many can point out the spot where a rise would occur, if a fly should chance to alight upon it.

The purist will probably admit that the other man catches more fish, but he will maintain that the more enjoyable sport is obtained by stalking the rising trout. No man can measure the enjoyment of another. On one day of which we have clear recollections, and an accurate entry in the diary, we killed seven pounds of trout with the dry-fly, and throughout the day we had not one single opportunity of covering a rise. Had we restricted ourselves as the purist suggests, we should not have had a happy day. If an expert in the use of the clear-water worm had been out on that same day, he might have had eight pounds. Would he believe that his sport was less enjoyable than ours ?

We would rather have seven pounds to the dry-fly than eight pounds to the worm ; but his ideas may be quite the reverse. The only logical conclusion seems to be that the heavier the basket an angler takes by his favourite method, the happier is he. We, ourselves, prefer the dry-fly to all other lures, and with it we fish the rise when there is a rise to cover, and the stream when there is not.

W. C. Stewart, the author of *The Practical Angler*, who did more to popularise fishing and to educate anglers than probably any other writer, occupies a position in the history of angling between the old-fashioned school of down-stream wet-fly fishers and the modern class of dry-fly anglers.

One of his best known statements is to the effect
that the moment the flies alight on the surface is
the deadliest of the cast. This dictum is worthy
of a little consideration. He fished upstream with
three or four flies on his cast, aiming carefully at a
rise whenever he had the opportunity of doing
so, and, acting up to his beliefs as in the sentence
referred to, he cast very frequently, never allowing
his flies to travel far towards him.

If he had used a single fly, he would not have
given expression to that opinion, as only accidentally would the fly happen to alight exactly where
a trout chanced to be, even though it is admitted
that he had an intimate acquaintance with the
waters and usually, if not invariably, attempted
to reach what he considered a likely spot. In that
case he would certainly have found that the fly had
very often to travel a considerable distance downstream before it was taken; but, by increasing
the number of flies on his cast, he increased likewise the possibility of one of them being accepted
at the moment of its alighting. The fly gently
touches the water, floats momentarily, and then it
would sink, but before it has time to sink a trout
looking upon it as a natural insect just arrived
from the air has sucked it down.

Stewart was a dry-fly fisher who knew all the
intricacies of the game save one: it did not occur
to him to dress his flies with such materials as would
make them float or to oil them for the purpose of
preventing them sinking. Webster, of Clyde fame,
adopted the same methods, and " fished the stream."

In broad rivers containing wide-spreading streamy
shallows and great pools, such as Clyde or Tweed

in their lower reaches, we find it quite impossible to confine ourselves to fishing the rise, and we think, but we do not declare, that others will agree.

Suppose that a dry-fly angler with all his deadly apparatus in readiness is standing on the gravel beside a fast-flowing stream of Tweed, we affirm that a dozen trout might rise between him and the opposite bank, and he would fail to detect a single one. Rises are of many kinds, and some of them are so quiet and disturb the water so very slightly that it requires very careful observation from close range to distinguish them. Some men can spot a rise when others would see nothing; it requires not so much good eyesight as trained eyesight.

Thinking that some activity is going on which is invisible from the bank, the purist may wade out twenty yards or more and take his stand, motionless, watchful, and patient as a heron; but he may stand there for an hour or a day, and there may not occur a single rise for him to see. On the other hand he may see a trout rising on the far edge of the waving stream. To arrive within casting distance he may have to wade farther out, and to avoid the fatal drag he may have to make a detour and, such is the variation from moment to moment on such a piece of water, swinging and swaying from side to side with the wind, or owing to the irregularities of the bottom, that he cannot tell exactly where to place his fly. The spot may be far from the bank, and often there are no landmarks to guide him. If he casts at all he is " fishing the stream "; if he decides to wait in his chosen position until the trout rises again so that he may have the place definitely fixed for him, he may wait for ever.

We have spent many hours watching and studying the trout in a river, particularly trout whose stations we knew. It is quite a common thing to see a large fish rise once and not again for hours, even though hosts of flies continue to pass over it; all anglers must have observed this.

Why a trout should ignore so much food we do not profess to know. Perhaps it conceived a sudden notion to taste a fly and then, satisfied or disappointed, desired no more, but the greater likelihood is that these desirable trout do not readily feed during the day, but prefer to wait until nightfall, when they become less suspicious.

In the course of a long holiday by the river we discover one or two of these trout, and every day, as we move up the water, we exercise the greatest care with our cast over the fateful places. We have dislodged the original tenant, and also a successor or two from some of them, but we do not think we can claim to be " fishing the rise " when the rise was observed a week or more beforehand. A trout, no matter how large it is, will accept a fly some time, and therefore we offer one as often as we can; any day we may arrive at the right moment.

In some narrow streams easily commanded from bank to bank without wading, we often limit ourselves to rising fish, as it is a comparatively easy matter to locate exactly and get within reach of a rise fifty yards or more away in a few seconds; but in broad rivers where we may be wading only knee-deep and yet be many yards from the bank it would take us a long time to reach the place.

As a rule, therefore, we would make no effort to reach it at once; but instead fish quietly and gradually up to it, and while doing so we might be fortunate enough to see the trout break the surface again. If not, we would search the vicinity carefully and thoroughly, and we might capture not only the fish we had seen rising but one or two besides.

What the angler should note is that in a stream connected with a pool, trout collect for the purpose of feeding, not after the hatch of flies occurs, but in expectation of it. If a few trout are seen rising in the stream, the conclusion is that others would rise also, if there were flies enough; therefore the angler should cast his dry-fly not only to the rising, but also to the expectant, trout.

Now there are many ways of presenting the flies when one is " fishing the stream." The cast may be delivered directly upstream or at right angles to the current, or at any angle between these two directions.

The angler, who has plenty of time at his disposal and infinite patience at his command, would possibly take from one stance and with one length of line a number of casts between the limits mentioned, draw off a yard of line and repeat the process, and so continue until he was casting his maximum length, or, alternatively, reaching the opposite bank; he would then step forward a yard or two and go through the sequence again, proceeding in this way until he arrived at the strong rush at the neck; but such a systematic way of going about the business is beyond the powers of most mortals. There is no question, however, that a long stream searched in this way can yield an astonishing number of trout.

The secrets of success are : Cast often and lightly, allow the flies to float not more than two yards, pick the line off the water with as much care as it is laid on, beware of drag, have the rod always in striking position, watch the flies, and strike at once gently but quickly.

One essential is that the line must be well smeared with some agent whose purpose is to keep it on the surface, and no matter what preparation is used it will require frequent renewal. As the line must be dried before it may be treated, and as a visit to the bank is likewise required, the process necessitates the expenditure of time and trouble, possibly too when a healthy rise is in progress ; still it must be attended to, for neglect of it will prevent a fish taking the fly, or, if by some lucky chance an offer is forthcoming, it will render all attempts at striking entirely futile.

The angler methodically fishing up such a stream, and receiving little reward for his pains, may be tempted to withdraw from the contest, but he should on no account omit to fish the extreme top, where the water breaks over the rocks or gravel. Close into the edges of the rough water he should place his fly, as there are invariably feeding trout lying there ready to launch themselves without hesitation upon anything in the least resembling food. A short line, a quick eye, and a ready strike are all called for, but it is well to remember that, owing to the shortened line and the expected offer, the strike is apt to be too vigorous.

Let the angler fish the rise when he can, but in

the absence of rises, or when they are few and far apart, he should fish the stream. Why should he sit idle and miserable on the bank when there may be trout willing to rise whenever a fly passes over-head?

CHAPTER XV

ONE day many years ago, on a reedy tarn in the hospitable land of Islay, despair and weariness laid hold upon us, for the trout, usually keen and eager, seemed resolved to ignore all our efforts. The sun was hot, the breeze a mere zephyr, and the roar of the restless Sound two miles away could be faintly heard. Conditions were unpromising; but we had gone to fish and, if possible, to catch fish; therefore, though defeat complete and absolute appeared predestined, we refused to capitulate before a prolonged struggle. A blank day in Islay was, we understood, unthinkable rather than impossible, and now such an unhappy and extraordinary fate seemed imminent.

With a view to changing the luck we changed a fly, knotting on the ever deadly Butcher and, a little confidence and hope regained, we cast out upon the gently rippling water. The new fly floated, and we were just on the point of pulling it smartly beneath the surface when there appeared a ghost-like form rising slowly through the rich brown water stained with the peat of the moorland. Ignoring the trio of sunken lures, the trout made straight for the dry pattern and sucked it down. The reel skirled vehemently as the nimble half-pounder tore

off to the friendly shelter of a neighbouring belt of
sighing reeds, but, having no desire to lose the prize
so curiously won, we stopped the rush and steered
the fish to the net.   The fly was dried and sent out
again upon the waters ; again it enticed an equally
agile trout from the depths.

Hints such as these are meant to be taken.
Hurriedly we removed the wet-flies from the cast
and to it attached two floating patterns, a Greenwell's Glory and a Red Quill, from a little assortment
that goes with us wherever we go.   Round the loch
we worked contentedly, laying the flies along the
edge of reeds and on any open water, not in answer
to any invitation, but just as fancy decreed, and
the day that promised so badly proved to be one
of the best.

The possibilities of the dry-fly as a lure for the
loch, so clearly demonstrated on that occasion, have
since been frequently and successfully put to the
test, and the result is that a large selection of dry-
flies and all the attendant necessaries now invariably
accompany the usual impedimenta on any loch-
fishing expedition.   It has been many a time
abundantly proved that, under certain conditions,
the floating fly is as productive of sport on lochs
as it undoubtedly is on running water.   Nor is it
of limited application.   It can be profitably used
in calm and in storm, when trout are rising to the
surface, and often too when no sign of life is visible.

The trout in lochs differ in many respects from
their relatives of the stream, more particularly in
their habits of feeding.   The river-trout appears to
know that, if he allows a fly to float past, he will
not have another opportunity of securing it · there-

fore, when really intent on feeding, he may take anything and everything that comes along, intending to discard it immediately if in any way not to his liking. From the behaviour of loch-trout one is inclined, on the other hand, to conclude that they are perfectly aware that floating flies can be safely neglected, until either the subaqueous food-supplies are exhausted for the time being, or rival trout begin to seek what is on the surface. Thus necessity or jealousy is accountable for the remarkable unanimity displayed by the trout inhabiting still water. They do not know that the subimagines of the *Ephemeridæ* in time leave the loch altogether, or perhaps they know more than that, viz. that as fully developed spinners the flies must return.

We think that the wet-fly is the more consistently useful lure on the loch, and that for many reasons. It may represent so many forms of life on which the trout feed, larvæ, shrimps, diminutive fry, descending or ascending egg-laying flies, corixæ, and other denizens of the aquatic world; as it moves regularly or erratically it may suggest to a trout something striving to flee its dangerous vicinity; it may, as it turns, emit a flash from tinsel, wing, or hackle, that makes a resting fish awake to life and energy.

The trout find all around them the food they need; the larvæ of sedge and dun, that arise straight to the surface, must be very numerous indeed, when any escape their attentions; only those that seek the shores under cover of the gravel manage to elude them. Therefore the wet-fly kills well as a general rule. Sometimes it must be sunk very low —in some lochs the trout will scarcely take a fly cast to them, but will accept it eagerly if trailed behind the boat at the end of a long line—and on other occasions it must be fished high ; the method depends on the nature of the creatures the trout are pursuing. But we must not allow ourselves to be lured away from our subject by the glories and possibilities of the wet-fly.

The dry-fly often proves irresistible, if it is allowed to float absolutely at rest in calm water for a full minute, and then is suddenly jerked an inch or two by the left hand pulling on the line. The trout seems to argue that here is a fly, which it meant to attend to later, making endeavours to escape.

The time to fish the dry-fly on a loch is not necessarily when plenty of flies are in evidence, but rather when nymphal activity has ceased, and the trout turn their attentions to the surface. We have seen the loch not once but times without number covered with flies and not a trout moving to them ; we had good sport with the wet-fly amongst the larvæ-chasing fish, and then, by changing to the dry-fly when the trout began to rise to the winged insects, we continued to enjoy ourselves.

Some lochs produce few flies and others many ; but in all that we have seen, the dry-fly gets its opportunity sometimes, and then the wet-fly is almost useless. A calm is emphatically not the signal that betokens the advent of that opportunity, though that is still a prevalent idea ; flies hatch and also float when waves are high, as well as when the loch is smooth and flat, but whenever and wherever the trout rise, the floater scores.

We know one angler who, tired of casting on a trying day of May his unavailing flies over trout rising, in an Argyllshire loch, with aggravating freedom to natural flies but showing complete indifference to his, reminded himself of what he had read regarding the efficacy of the floating fly. Retrieving his cast, he anointed his trio of flies, Peter Ross, Grouse and Green, and the Zulu, and sent them out to ride the wavelets, and the result of his experiment well-nigh converted him on the spot into an enthusiastic dry-fly purist.

Peter Ross is a grand wet-fly for the tail of a cast ; but whatever the inventor had in view when he designed it, it was certainly not a fly ; Grouse and Green is a member of the *Trichoptera*, that hatches generally in August. The Zulu is probably the best bob-fly that can be made to skip across the waves of a hill-loch ; but what it imitates we cannot guess.

On the cast there was only one fly, and it was only three months premature ; yet all three killed well, for the simple reason that they were on the surface, and so resembled in one highly important particular the flies that were occasioning the rise. It is as well to add that another angler who persisted that day with wet-flies fished wet had by comparison only mediocre sport.

We could give innumerable instances out of our own experience of the dry-fly thoroughly vanquishing the wet-fly, when a rise was taking place ; but we cannot recall a single occasion when the advantage was reversed. Even at times in the absence of a rise we have done well with the floating fly, when the sunken variety would not lure a single trout.

For dry-fly fishing in lochs the cast should be made of carefully selected gut and should be as long as the rod. It should consist of 2x gut for half its length, and the other half may be tapered up to any thickness desired. That strength is as fine as there is any necessity for, except perhaps on well-fished reservoirs, in which the trout may have developed a shyness comparable with that exhibited by their brethren of the river. In judging the strength of the dry-fly cast required for loch-trout, one must bear in mind that a rise is generally expected, as the fly has probably been presented to a visible feeding fish, and therefore it is in all likelihood answered with promptitude, perhaps also with at least a little unnecessary vigour. The rise is unmistakable, the line tight, the angler on the alert, therefore the cast should be able to stand the sudden call made upon it. Some may think 2x gut rather fine for loch-trout, but as it is, with careful treatment, quite capable of dealing with all but most exceptional fish, no greater strength need be used by any angler who desires sport from the trout he hooks.

Two flies, three or four feet apart, should be tied to the cast, as the arguments used in support of that number for the river apply with even greater force to the loch. The dropper-fly need never be removed, except when the angler is poking among reeds and weeds, and unless he is terrified at the prospect of hooking two trout simultaneously.

It is possible that the beginner will feel himself compelled to use flies of a larger size than he is accustomed to use on the river, mainly because the wet-flies generally used on lochs are distinctly larger than river patterns. There is no necessity for adding to the number or size of the flies already given; in fact, one very useful fly on the loch is the smallest of all, viz. the Badger Hackle; but if a bigger fly endows him with greater confidence, he should by all means obtain exactly what pleases him. At the same time, we think he will not please the trout any better.

The remainder of the apparatus recommended for the river, the treatment of the line, cast, and flies suggested, will serve perfectly for the loch. If the angler proposes to fish both wet-fly and dry-fly according as the conditions inform, and, if he is sensible, he will confine himself to neither the one nor the other, he should provide himself with two rods, reels, and lines, or at least with an extra reel and line. The dressing that he puts on his dry-fly line makes it unsatisfactory to some extent for wet-fly fishing, because at times it is very necessary to make the wet-flies sink deeply in order to reach the trout prowling about the lower depths in search of various subaqueous creatures. The floating agent can be removed; but frequently he will desire to change from dry-fly to wet and back again, and he will sometimes be annoyed at the loss of time involved in attending to his line.

The angler will observe that there is one great point of difference between the loch and the river. On a running stream he casts his fly as a rule at least a short distance beyond his prospective victim and allows it to float down, but on still water he endeavours to place it right into the centre of the rings formed by the rising trout, where he may leave it for a considerable time. Then drag can trouble the loch-fisher; the shorter the length of undressed gut or line, the longer will the fly float naturally. As on the river so on the loch, wind acting upon his line will affect his fly, but drag caused by the water itself is unknown, therefore difficulties are very much reduced in number.

To fish a loch satisfactorily from a boat one should have the sole use of it, as otherwise, while he may have congenial company, he handicaps himself to a considerable extent and loses many glorious opportunities. Of course one of the great attractions in loch-fishing lies in the fact that it is possible to be in close proximity to a brother or sister angler with whom may be shared the joys or sorrows of the day, but some always, and all sometimes, prefer to be alone with their thoughts, especially when dry-fly fishing.

Frequently when a dead calm rests upon the loch, the water is dotted all over with the rings of the feeding trout, and such a happy combination of circumstances should be hailed with delight, whereas usually it occasions nothing but complaining groans. The angler should then seat himself low in the bow, instruct his boatman to row very slowly and quietly ahead—such injunctions are often imperfectly understood—and content himself with such fish as are within his reach. By so doing he will have quite an exciting time, and, provided that he is not flurried in his movements, the basket will soon acquire an agreeable weight.

If he sees what he considers to be an exceptionally fine specimen rising afar off, he is apt to tell the boatman to set off in pursuit ; both are so eager, the one with the oars and the other with the rod, that in all probability both miss the mark. Unless both can keep themselves in control, a very difficult thing to do in the circumstances, when so much is at stake and speed seems desirable, such action will result only in vexation and disappointment. It is much better to maintain the course agreed upon and to refuse to be led away from the straight path by any rise, however tempting it may be.

If, on the other hand, a fine fishing breeze is curling the water, and trout are frequently showing, the angler should be in the stern ; the boat may be allowed to drift as usual, or it may be held up to the wind. Some boatmen can work their craft to perfection, making it hover over a fruitful spot, while the angler gets many chances of laying his flies exactly where they should be placed, and men of that type deserve the major portion of the credit for the day's spoils.

The flies should not be cast straight down wind, unless a fish rise in the track of the drifting boat ; they should rather be sent out between the boat and the wind, at an angle of 45° perhaps, because they are thus more readily kept tight to the line and the rod, making a strike more certain of success. Above all things, the angler must remember not to aim for the surface ; a trout rising within his distance unexpectedly is very likely to make him forget for the moment the great necessity for delicacy in the fall of the fly.

In lochs where such a thing is practicable, dry-fly fishing from the bank is by far the more interesting method. The monotony of the drifting boat is done away with, and the variety of the ever-changing coastline is agreeable. How easily the hours slip past as one wanders round, casting the flies out upon the water, raising even only an occasional trout, with now and then a greater success.

So far as we can recollect we have not fished from the bank if a boat was available, except on a very few occasions when gales were tossing the waves about and making a voyage highly dangerous. As it happens, we have no knowledge of the sensations produced by an attempt to search the waters of our largest lochs without the assistance of a boat, but we imagine that, while a lucky choice of a really good point might result in satisfactory sport even on Loch Lomond, the insignificance of the little area within reach in relation to the immense extent within view would have such a depressing influence upon us that we would be forced away in despair.

And yet, were we afloat, we would urge the boatman to keep the craft near the self-same shore, so that we could lay the flies across that hopeful line that separates the black from the gold. When we fish from the bank we make prodigious efforts to cast a long distance out, and when we are working from the stern of a boat, we strive to get the tail-fly close to land. Whatever is desirable is just out of reach and, conversely, whatever is even slightly beyond our powers attains enormous importance.

We prefer to fish the small loch and the reservoir from the bank, and in such the trout generally lie quite close to the shore. There will always be a few trout, very fine specimens of course, which tantalise us by day by rising just beyond our longest cast, but evening brings them nearer the land, one or two of them into the creel.

When the angler reaches the scene of his conquests, he must first decide where he shall commence operations. Seldom will he be able to fish with the wind behind, as is the practice from a boat. because,

unless the breeze is very strong, there will be a belt
of calm along the shore probably so broad that he
is unable to reach the rougher water beyond. If
he can by wading or length of line succeed in this
he should spend a long time on that shore, for such a
place, the tail of the wind, yields good results. In
Highland lochs particularly, and also to some extent
in all still water, we have found this to be true, and
the probable explanation is that the trout, tired of
nymphs, or keen to take anything, lie along that
line in expectation of flies blown off the grass and
heather. If the fish are rising freely in the calm
belt, even the veriest beginner will have astonishing
sport with the dry-fly, because the wind will assist
him to get out a fine line and, if he holds back his
rod at the end of the delivery, he will succeed in
laying the flies so lightly on the water that a great
response is assured.

For long-continued casting he should select a
shore parallel to the wind, and fish it carefully down
from top to bottom ; he should have very little
difficulty in sending his flies straight across a strong
breeze. His main troubles will arise from the action
of the wind upon his line, but, if he casts only to
rising fish, these worries will be almost negligible.
Striking is often largely a matter of luck owing to
the slackness of the line, but if the rod is held pointing down wind and low to the surface and jerked
shorewards, rather than upwards as usual, in answer
to a rise, the hook will find its desired resting-place
with pleasant frequency.

Many anglers avoid the shore towards which the
wind is blowing and so throw away many opportunities of enjoying good sport and also of learning

to cast into the wind, an accomplishment valuable on the river. For this work the angler should prepare a shorter cast of stouter build, and he would be well advised to discard the dropper-fly. There are good reasons for these recommendations. Fine gut is not so essential in the jabble of wave, and is more difficult to cast and manipulate than a heavier quality. Even the most expert will at such times contrive to tangle up his cast, and the presence of only one fly as well as the use of stouter gut reduces very much the possibility of this annoyance occurring.

If he knows the loch well, he may, for the sake of variety and ease, wade out as far as may be and cast his flies across the waves ; and, whenever he finds a projecting point, he will without hesitation accept the chance of an easy cast in the sheltered bay. Long casting off a lee shore is unnecessary hard labour, for the trout lie very near the edge amid the turmoil caused by the incoming waves meeting those reflected off the land ; there they lurk, taking as they want them the flies swinging to and fro on the surface.

When trout are not rising, it is dreary, monotonous work casting a dry-fly at random upon a loch, unless, of course, hopefulness is stimulated and encouraged now and then by an offer accepted or missed. We find that we can remain contented for a longer time on a dour day, when we fish the wet-fly, than we can when we use its floating relative. The dr-flyy is cast, left to float for a time, lifted, and cast again ; that is all. The wet-fly, on the other hand, must be brought shorewards and may be subjected to a large variety of motions in the process : there is much that can be done with it. The beginner always wants to know how long he should keep his fly floating ; we cannot tell him. We fish the dry-fly on the loch during a rise; if there is none, we fish the wet-fly ; if it brings nothing we sometimes try the floating fly ; if that does not produce a fish in a very short time the awful weariness of it sends us back to the wet-fly or to the shore for lunch. It is all very different on the river, a fish or at least a rise being certain to come even on an inauspicious day with a frequency that keeps weariness away.

On summer evenings, calm and peaceful, the surface of the loch is often plentifully spread with minute midges and the smallest duns. The trout are accustomed to swim about scooping them up in great glee. Generally the sinking of the sun is the signal that awakes the fish to activity. The beginner, on seeing the surface seething, need not conclude that at last his great day has come, and that his creel is about to be filled to overflowing, nor need the experienced angler be consumed with despair. It is neither a hopeful nor a hopeless condition of things. Every single capture con- stitutes a veritable triumph, productive of more satisfaction than a dozen trout taken under other conditions. To attempt the luring of such trout from a boat is to invite failure ; the campaign should be conducted from the bank and the flies that will make it succeed are the Blue Hen Spider and the Badger Hackle. These are the indispensable flies for the reservoir and lowland loch in the evenings of June and July.

The angler who fishes a loch with the floating fly during a rise has both a pleasant and a valuable experience ; he obtains the maximum sport possible, learns to cast the fly with delicate precision unerringly to the mark, and, moreover, he acquires the art of casting at all angles to the wind, with it and against it, a faculty which will fit him to assail with every prospect of success the most cunning river-trout.

CHAPTER XVI

CONCERNING THE WIND

HOW is the fly-fisher's sport affected by the wind, its strength, direction, and temperature ? That question has exercised the minds of anglers of all times, and probably it will form a subject for discussion and debate as long as there remain rivers to fish and fish to catch.

Some anglers profess a strong preference for a complete absence of wind. Such a declaration must have rather a disquieting effect on great numbers, who, while able to capture many trout in the course of a season, find it impossible to extend a line at all, unless they are assisted by a friendly breeze. It need not occasion surprise to anyone to learn that what he considers a magnificent opportunity another looks upon as a hopeless condition. Many have formed the opinion that trout are not to be caught unless the surface is ruffled, and therefore they see no necessity for practising the art of casting in a calm, an art not difficult to acquire, but still one demanding training. Beliefs firmly established are not readily eradicated.

The smooth, brilliant mirror of the loch has a depressing rather than an uplifting effect on the angler. While he proceeds towards the scene of his day's pleasure, on the road or across the moor, he already feels that victory is to be denied ; for the hot, still air, the unclouded sky, the gleaming sunshine make him dispirited, and, long before he arrives, he decides that the trout will feel even as he feels. When at length he reaches his destination by the water's edge, he cannot display his wonted eagerness ; rather does he lie within the shade of leafy trees than nervously and excitedly fit the rod together. He does not show impatience at delays incurred in launching the boat; there is little likelihood that anxious haste will result in him entangling his cast into confusion.

Not a single dimple of a rise disturbs the broad expanse spreading before his gaze, and he begins to wish that the unfortunate expedition had been prevented ; but, as he watches, he feels a slight breath of air. Away to the foot of the loch he sees a black line stretching across, moving nearer and rapidly nearer towards him. Preparations are completed in a hurry ; the boatman pushes off, and the sound of the wavelets lapping is like the merriest laughter. Down the breeze the cast flies out, as the boat is driven across to the chosen drift, for the angler must do something to conceal his excitement.

Before the favoured stretch is reached, the breeze dies away, and the boat is becalmed. A pair of disappointed men discontentedly while away the time with tales of the glorious past, but their eyes silently and continuously appeal to every glen.

In the next bay the calm surface is observed to be disturbed ; oars are plied strongly for the goal ; but, in answer to the invitation of a roughening patch to port or starboard, the course is immediately changed. A fish may be picked up ; whether or not, as the water again flattens out, another race for the nearest ripple begins.

We too have chased the wind about the loch many a weary time, and we have seen others engaged at the same tiring game. Never have we been privileged to see an angler fleeing, as quickly as oars could take him, from the rippled areas to his heart's delight in the calm glassy belts.

Let us suppose, on the other hand, that the summer day is bright and breezy. Sport may or may not be good, so many other circumstances contribute favourable or adverse influences, but in every case the angler, who is at liberty to remain beside the waters, looks forward to the evening. Hopefulness is then at its highest. We always are filled with expectation, and though the joys we anticipate are not always granted, yet faith continues, and ever will continue, to be born within us despite occasional disappointments. The gloaming hour has been an uninterrupted delight, the glory of a whole season, the memory that has kept us cheerful throughout a winter. Then it is that we can almost agree with those who declare a calm is best.

If fish rise well, but not too well, in a calm we are really happy ; but should even the gentlest of breezes blow at eventide, raising the tiniest of ripples, and the trout continue to rise, then we are happier still. On the contrary, we are never so miserable as we are when not a single rise breaks the smooth placid water. As it may often on a quiet summer evening, and at other times as well, be the means of giving most crowded sport, the art of casting in a calm should certainly be learned by every angler ; but few, we think, will come to consider absence of wind a condition which ensures happiness on all, or even on most, occasions.

For the loch, the great majority of fishers, we are certain, prefer a breeze, while some we know like the wind just strong enough to make the boat difficult to manage. A good breeze makes the angler cheery, and he expects that it will have the same effect upon the trout. It helps him wonderfully, and he feels that sooner or later one of his beautiful casts is certain to be rewarded ; so for a long time, if necessary, his interest is maintained, and it is amazing how many trout can be caught by sheer hard work. In a calm, a few minutes will, if fish are not rising or not taking, suffice to put the angler in a despondent mood, whereas if he could persist as he does in a wind, he would probably have to call quite as often for the landing net.

Sometimes trout will rise very well by day to the natural fly, but aggravatingly out of reach of the longest cast. We have experienced this particular annoyance principally on Loch Leven, and very probably the trout of other lochs can similarly tantalise the angler. If the wind springs up, then the fish become a comparatively easy conquest, presumably because their powers of vision are much reduced.

Frequently and on many lochs our experience has been quite the reverse. A fine, gentle breeze, making neat, delicate casting the simplest of work, ripples the water ; hope rules high as we gently drift along, but the longer the drift the more continuous the disappointment. All the conditions seem to combine to make the day a perfect fishing day ; only the trout persistently and steadfastly refuse to make it so, treating every effort made with the same complete indifference.

The wind falls, and at once, all over the unruffled loch, are seen the signs that we most long to see. Then a floating fly is laid from long range upon the rise, and the once-silent reel is aroused to eloquence again ; that is, of course, provided that the trout does not sink to the depths at our approach, but instead accepts the offering. The wind that keeps the trout down may also bring them up ; such a contradiction appears inexplicable, unless the fact of the matter is that the wind has no effect upon the fish.

We conclude that it is on the angler that any influence is exercised ; in a breeze he is enabled, as he cannot fail to see, to give a much improved exhibition of casting ; he throws a fine straight line, lays his fly or flies lightly upon the water exactly on the mark desired, and his consistently good work continued with commendable perseverance and confidence in time, and from time to time, is well rewarded.

A rise at evening calm fills many an angler with doubts of his powers. The trout are feeding steadily and greedily, perhaps fearlessly ; some of the great swirling eddies are enough to make him quiver with excitement ; but his imperfections are so apparent that he despairs of success. What a change comes over him, if the merest catspaw of wind should steal along to help him ever so slightly ! He casts with hope, probably to no appreciable extent is the delicacy of his execution increased, and before the feathery reeds are quite motionless again he is fast in a fine fish.

On the river, a calm day need not trouble the inexpert caster very much, as he may ignore the placid pools and confine his efforts to the streams and broken water. He has less reason for dissatisfaction at his performance, for the rippling current hides from him his deficiencies; the trout may object to his clumsiness, but, as he is generally unaware of it, he is able to carry on, although agreeable response is delayed. Sometimes the fly will fall softly, occasionally before the eyes of a willing fish, but there is not the least doubt that even the slightest of upstream breezes would give him the greatest assistance.

Some anglers may prefer a calm to a downstream wind, but we most decidedly do not, except when the fish are rising very well. We object to walk from stream to stream, omitting the long flats and pools where, on a familiar river, we have had fine sport on other days, or where, on a new water, we are sure that good trout lie in wait; and that is what we feel constrained to do if the smooth surface of the water remains undisturbed by wind or feeding fish. If, however, a downstream wind causes a ripple, we can fish contentedly enough between the streams, even although no rise is in progress.

To put a fly straight across a strong wind calls for very little skill in the manipulation of the rod, therefore no matter from what direction the breeze comes, good casting and successful fishing are both easily possible. The angler faced with a downstream breeze should cast across it, and work his way gradually upwards. We have already pointed out the extreme deadliness of this cast in quick-flowing water, and again we give the warning that

its virtues will all be thrown away, if the flies are
allowed to float too far, or the line becomes too slack.
It is rather difficult to keep in close contact with
the fly as it floats down, because the wind blows
out the line ; a short journey for the fly and a low
rod-point will help the angler materially.

As the dry-fly fisher proceeds up the pool or stream,
casting across the current and the wind, he will
naturally be always endeavouring to put his fly a
short distance, at least, upstream, and it will be
surprising if he does not suddenly discover himself
to be possessed of a new power, viz. ability to cast
into the wind.   It is easy to learn to overcome a
gentle adverse breeze, and practice first under
simple, and later under more difficult, conditions
will in time make him indifferent to the wind and its
direction.

It may assist him to be told that he should lower
the rod on delivery parallel to the water, turn his
hand sharply to the right, and bring it in towards
his body.   If he can attend to these points, and do
each at the required moment, he has reached proficiency.   Great force is unnecessary, and even fatal
with this or any other cast ; the rod should never
be heard.   Some anglers like to make the rod whistle
in the wind, but such sounds merely indicate mis-
placed energy.

A gale makes fishing both unpleasant and tiresome
and, when it blows downstream, it is the torment
of the dry-fly man. As he must fish, he should
attempt to cast across it, and if his fly is blown
farther down the current than he would like he
need not worry ; he may by walking keep up with
his fly for a yard or more, before it begins to drag.

If he observes a trout rising, he should endeavour to float a fly down to it, while he himself remains stationary.

In a high wind fish seldom rise quietly, but usually hurl themselves upon the fly, taking no time to scrutinise it and accepting it greedily if its behaviour is above reproach. Sport is therefore sometimes surprisingly good, though conditions are all unfavourable to accurate placing.

Even the early writers on angling paid some attention to the direction of the wind as well as to its strength. Dame Juliana Berners in her *Treatise on Fishing with an Angle* enumerates several impediments which cause men to take no fish, and of these the last may be translated as follows: " If the wind be from the North or North-east or South-east, fish will not commonly bite nor stir ; the West and the South are very good, but of the two the South is the better."

The Master, in his Epistle to the Reader, hopes that if he be an honest angler, the East wind may never blow when he goes a-fishing. The Book of St. Albans gives the East wind as the worst of all. In addition, we have sundry old rhymes which proclaim the beneficial qualities of the South and West winds, and declare the East wind fatal to the angler's sport.

There are many anglers in Scotland who will disagree with these statements, or at least will accept them only with qualifications, and old Izaak himself, had he known Loch Leven, would probably have made a special exception of that water, which, it is generally agreed, fishes best in an East wind. Even yet the belief is very prevalent that trout will not rise well when the breeze is from that quarter ; neither, we suppose, will larvæ move about with freedom or be inclined to change their state. If any loch or river yields good results under such a condition, it is looked upon as some wonderful exception which must be subjected to examination and explained away.

Attempts have in consequence been made to account for this supposed peculiarity of Loch Leven. It has been argued that, as an East wind is not so cold immediately it leaves the sea as it is after it has traversed many miles of the colder land, and as Loch Leven is near the East coast, a wind from the East is there not harmful in its effects.

This seems to make rather many assumptions: first, that a cold wind makes trout fast ; secondly, that the East wind is warmer on the East coast than it is inland ; thirdly, that the land is colder than the sea ; and lastly, that whatever is not harmful is beneficial.

If our year was one eternal spring—we do not mean the spring of the Golden Age, when the rivers ran with milk and nectar, worse conditions for angling than any wind—three of these assumptions would be correct. A cold wind in spring does not encourage fly-larvæ to enter the winged state, but in summer it has exactly the opposite effect on certain species, and then trout feed readily. We who have shivered in St. Andrews by the grey North Sea know exactly how warm the spring East wind can be ; Andrew Lang also knew "how the keen and biting spray drives up the melancholy street," and R. F. Murray was often glad " to draw more close the old, red gown." Still we suppose that the thermometer would have declared the temperature to be a degree or two higher there than some miles inland. Also it is true that in spring the land is colder than the sea, but in summer we imagine that it is the warmer of the two. If the East wind were good on Loch Leven only in spring, we might accept the explanation, but as it is good throughout the season, we conclude that the observed effects cannot be wholly due to the cause suggested.

There is one point on which we should expect to find universal agreement, viz. that the trout in Loch Leven rise and take with very much greater freedom, when the sky is overcast, than they do under bright sunshine. Whenever a cloud passes over the sun, the boatmen are almost sure to tell the angler to work hard, for during the " dull blink," as their curious expression is, there is a good chance of capturing a trout. Wonderfully often the advice, if acted upon, produces the desired result. Why the fish of that loch should differ so much from others, which seem to rejoice exceedingly in sunshine, we really do not know, though we might hazard an opinion ; but that it is one of their chief character-istics to be most active on a dull day, or when the sun is obscured, there can be no question.

A cloudy sky is very often the accompaniment of an East wind on or near the East coast. Meteoro-logical records prove that on that coast of Scotland the greater part of the annual rainfall comes with easterly winds. So often do the always welcome cloud and the East wind occur together that a steady breeze from that quarter has become the favourite condition with Loch Leven anglers, but we think

that it is to the diminished light that their increased
success is due.

The only day we ever spent on Loch Lyon was,
curiously enough, a day of East wind, very light
certainly, but still a true wind, not a mere draught
diverted by the heights, and the basket of sixty-
seven trout to two rods just failed to be the record
catch for the year. It was, moreover, a very short
day, as the breeze in the afternoon died to an absolute
calm undisturbed by a single rise. Our best baskets
on Loch Ard have been made under an easterly
breeze ; Loch Dochart has given us many good takes
as well as our heaviest trout from it, $1\frac{1}{4}$ lb., a very
good fish for that water, when the wind was from
the same unpopular direction.

We know a small private loch on the West where,
the boatman tells us, the same conditions are desired
as on Loch Leven ; on Loch Lubnaig, a breeze
which drifts the boat into the mouth of the Balvaig
makes fishing very good, and several fine specimens
we have taken there on the dry-fly when the wind
was so favourable ; on Loch Lomond the East wind
is said to be the best that blows over the Endrick
bank. To Loch Leven it brings the cloud, which,
for some reason or other, is there required ; to the
lochs farther inland it brings the requisite sunshine,
and we welcome it wherever we find it.

East wind is the prevailing wind of the Scottish
spring. If the angler seeks the loch or the river in
April and the earlier half of May, he is more likely
to have it helping or hindering him than any other.
Since that is the case, it is probable that trout, as
well as the various creatures that form their food,
have become accustomed to the general conditions

of temperature. Unless the wind is unseasonably
cold, fishing should be good. Many fly-fishers consider the month of April the happiest period of the
year, and the largest trout got on the fly in a season
fall before the end of May. It would appear, therefore, that, if the East wind is not actively beneficial,
neither is it harmful.

The rivers on the East coast are classed with Loch
Leven, and similarly declared to give of their best
when the pools are ruffled by an easterly breeze,
the reasons being, of course, those already mentioned.
We are also of the same opinion, but we go much
farther and say that for long stretches of Clyde and
for all its tributaries entering on the left bank, the
same wind will prove exceedingly good. On these
waters an East wind is an upstream wind, and that,
we think, is the sole reason why the angler finds it
good; it helps him to cast fine and far off, and
keeps him concealed from the trout, that is, of
course, assuming that he does not persist in casting
against it.

We know practically every corner of the Clyde
from Thankerton to the source, and we have had
great sport all over that stretch in winds from all
directions; it is usually the wind that decides for us
which reach we select, and we are perfectly satisfied
that it does not matter from what quarter of the
compass it comes, provided that it blows against the
current. Many anglers, no doubt, will disagree.
We have heard their complaints against the East
wind on both Clyde and Tweed; we could not
sympathise with them, for our own basket was
satisfactory—we have never had a poor day under
an East wind on these rivers—but we could and

did advise them to fish upstream and with the floating fly.

In spring the East wind is comparatively warm,
let us grant, at Tweedmouth, and will become
slightly colder as it blows up the many miles of
Tweed to Biggar Water, while in summer it will
undergo a small rise in temperature as it performs
the same journey. Consequently, if it is always
good on Tweed, as it is commonly said to be, and as
we find it to be, its goodness cannot be due to its
temperature; that is due, we think, only to the
fact that it assists the angler by its direction. Any
wind that blows against the stream at any particular
part is a good wind for that part.

Some anglers have formed the opinion that warm
winds are necessary for successful dry-fly fishing.
In April there is, on all but the coldest days, a hatch
of flies, plentiful or scanty as the case may be, but
the March Brown may appear whenever there is
a touch of sunshine, even though the temperature
be low; in average weather Dark Olives and Iron-
Blues will also arrive to keep the trout and the rod
busy. In May, olives of a lighter shade are due if
conditions are those generally prevailing; the
Gravel-bed fly will come forth if the sun's rays are
powerful; the Iron-Blue will reappear if the day is
unseasonably cold. During the next three months,
it is on the coldest days that we make the best
baskets, best, that is, in weight and numbers; but
warm weather provides by far the most interesting
fishing. September resembles May.

Therefore, throughout the season, be the day
warm or cold, there is sport to be had on the river
to the floating fly and, however unpromising the

weather, there is one condition which will help very much to bring about the desired end, a condition that the angler can in many cases, by a study of the cloud-carry and a sufficient knowledge of the river, arrange for himself, viz. an upstream breeze. If the wind changes for the worse during the day, he should cast against it, not with it, and he will lure trout though the welcome help is withdrawn.

We need not discuss winds from North, South, or West, because we would arrive at the same conclusions. The angler should gaze upon the sky, not in order that he may decide whether he shall fish or stay at home, but only that he may be enabled to make a wise selection of the scene of his victories. After that all that is required, on the great majority of days, is a floating fly.

CHAPTER XVII

THE DRY-FLY SEASON

THE dry-fly may be used with considerable success throughout the Scottish trout-fishing season, but naturally it gives more efficient service at some periods than at others. Some anglers have become so impressed with its capabilities that they cannot be prevailed upon to discontinue it for even a short time; beginners especially, delighted with the great results obtained with their new lure, are not unlikely to persist with it, even when it is apparent that certain wet-flies would do very much better. This is not surprising, for the floating lure exercises great fascination over all who know it; but anyone, who wishes to catch as many trout as possible above a given size-limit, must be prepared to vary his lure from time to time, as the conditions indicate.

We shall, therefore, discuss the whole of the trouting season, endeavouring to point out when the dry-fly will surpass all other lures, and when it will be worthy only of a secondary place.

March

It is somewhat difficult for a trout-fisher to develop an enthusiasm for the month of March,

the mere mention of which is sufficient to call
up a picture of storm-tossed waters, leafless swaying trees, patches of snow on the hills. It does
not suggest the hatching fly, the leaping trout,
and the curving rod; but being anglers we can
all think of these things even in the depths of
winter. Therefore when we may we will go to
seek our fortune in the waters.

No doubt its chief claim to fame lies in the fact
that it proclaims the passing of the close season,
and heralds the dawning of another period of
sport; even were it without further distinction,
that in itself is sufficient to gain it a high place
in the general esteem.

Some there are who seek to take away from
it its principal glory, declaring that trout have
not yet by any means recovered from the hardships of winter, and are quite unworthy the angler's
art, even requiring his protection. Others again
would contradict that with the greatest emphasis
at their command, asserting that the pursuit of
the trout is already decidedly sportsmanlike, and
that, in fact, they are at the very height of their
condition. Two such opposing statements are quite
possibly both correct, for they are made concerning totally different localities. A close season
cannot be uniform and at the same time just,
in a country where there is so much variation in
climatic conditions due to altitude and environment.

The general condition of the trout over a number of years should determine the beginning and
end of the season for each particular district, but
at the same time it is advisable that the existing

close time be not reduced in length. Admittedly such a change would occasion trouble and perhaps create some temporary dissatisfaction. Although such a system would have more to recommend it than that at present obtaining, the labour involved is too great to admit of its introduction. Some new legislation affecting trout-fishing may yet be forthcoming and, whatever changes are made, in all probability uniformity will be retained, and the length of the fishing season curtailed, with the result that some places will lose one of their greatest attractions, and the month of March cease to have the same meaning for us.

All anglers look forward to the end of February as the time when anticipation makes way for participation ; they long for it, knowing that then at last they will be at liberty to seek the loch and the river in search of health and sport. Some, fearful of the weather, may delay. The first bright day, when the sun burns cheerily and bestows a little warmth, will see even the timid making frenzied efforts to get their fishing gear in order again. Off they start full of eagerness.

Few flies may be seen flitting about the surface, but the trout, like the fisherman, are expecting the coming of spring, and they will mistake the artificial for the real insect. If the day is really fine, as many days in March may be, development of the aquatic creatures proceeds apace, the trout become thoroughly aroused into activity, and will take the wet-fly with a freedom that may not be repeated during the season.

We never know what fortune may have in store, we are not strangers to disappointment, but we

can forget the bad times and remember the good ;
therefore let us fish wherever we are likely to find
trout fit for sport.   However, there are few waters
in Scotland in which much sport need be expected
during March, if the dry-fly is the lure used.   It
is true that a floating fly may bring up happy
recollections to a hungry trout and so tempt him
to the surface.   Still, results will be poor, and the
condition of the river-trout will not be satisfactory.
To these rules there may be exceptions, but in
any case the dry-fly fisher had better wait another
month.

There are lochs, for example, Loch Ard and
Loch Lubnaig, which can yield truly astonishing
sport in March.   The trout are then in excellent
form and take freely.   They have not yet, however,
acquired the habit of scanning the surface ; they
hover about mid-water, pursuing, whenever opportunity offers, the ascending larvæ and nymphs.
Consequently it is the wet-fly that scores most
victories, and that only when it is well sunk.

Those who must fish in March, and either with
the dry-fly or not at all, will in all probability
find the Rough Olive, March Brown, and the Greenwell Quill the deadliest patterns.   They must,
unless an early hatch occurs, be prepared to be
easily satisfied, and they must not estimate the
efficiency of the floating fly by the response to
these premature efforts.

April

The call of the waters becomes daily more clearly
heard until even the most hesitant angler must
heed and answer.   April is here, and none may

longer delay the happiness that awaits beside the sparkling river and the sun-kissed loch.

Mists may swing round the mountain peaks, weirdly rising and falling, growing and dissolving ; great storm-clouds borne on the wings of the south-west wind may bring the rain-laden squall to whip the crests from the rolling waves and obscure the wooded shores, but they will pass and the sun stream out again warm and cheery ; skies will not again during the year be so beautifully blue. The wind must fall with the blast, and before us there will be a period of an hour or more before we shall have to suspend operations and seek the windward trees, an hour of sunshine and hope when flies will venture forth, the trout will rise, and the rod will not be unrewarded. That is but one variety of April day.

There are others, glorious fishing days, warm and moist and grey, when the beauties of the scene almost pass unmarked, for sport is maintained throughout and the trout command all our attention.

Again we may experience bright, cloudless days when the water is calm and still, and the air is sharp with frost ; but these have a joy of their own. Then a trout is an event of immense satisfaction, and each capture fills us with pride of our skill. On such days we take time to go ashore for lunch, and find what we miss at other times not more happy, the awakening of all the wild. The woodland glades are flooded with the myriad blue hyacinthine bells, a vision more than a reality ; the river's brim is starred with the clustering primrose ; beneath the hedgerows the violet bids us

welcome ; while over all the birds are happy in
their joyful song.

Such is April, and not for worlds would we miss
its joys. Never is the world so fresh, the air so
sweet, or our hopes so high as we set out in answer
to the call. The broad flowing river claims us
more than does the loch, and the reasons are many
and good. So clear is the water that its depth
deceives the eye, and the very first step into it
may take us over the waders, and very cold and
uncomforting can water be ; but we can forget
even that unpleasantness, as we rejoice in the
easy working of the rod, sending out the cast of
flies across the broad flats just as rhythmically
as it did in the height of last season.

It is wonderful how every feature of the river
is impressed upon the memory ; we see and at
once recognise every pool and stream, every stone
and eddying corner where in previous years we
gained victories or suffered defeats.

Any day March Browns may hatch out, the
darker Olives are due, and towards the end of
the month the Iron Blue should arrive. If the
angler should have the good fortune to be on the
river when the last-named fly puts in an appearance, he has before him a spell of deadly, delicate
work ; diminutive lure, fine tackle, quiet rises,
and lusty fights are the features which afford him
delight. When in doubt, owing to absence of
signal from the fish as to which pattern to use,
he should try the sunken nymph ; but, if he feels
compelled to use a dry-fly because of its clearly
visible beauties or other reason, he should affix
to the cast the ever-willing, always useful Green-

well Quill, and that is bound from time to time
to excite sufficiently an expectant trout.

When we are on the river in April, we always
hope to see the Iron Blue, for that hardy little
insect, which revels in cold, ungenial weather,
happens to be our first favourite. The expectation of its advent keeps us patient, and an hour
in its company is great reward. We willingly
wander miles in search of even the shortest stretch
where the wind will favour us, for when that fly
is up we want to give our undivided attention
to the rise, we object to be hampered with difficulties of manipulation ; there must be no dis-
tractions, if we are to reap the full harvest of these
infrequent opportunities.

However bright the prospect on the river, the
angler should not neglect the loch. There are
lochs which can almost be depended upon to furnish sport on any April day, and there are others
which do well in favourable weather. The season
may be an early one, and that he cannot tell if he
remains in the city wishing his life away. Neither
should he await reports from exploring brother-
anglers, but should instead go to investigate for
himself. He may meet occasional failure ; he may,
quite as readily, find adequate recompense, and
be enabled to inform others as to where the happiness they most desire is awaiting them.

Reservoirs are now without exception in order
for fishing, and pleasant hours may be spent wandering round the banks and casting a questing
fly across the waves. These enjoy a longer rest
than other waters, which fact cannot fail to be
reflected in the general well-being of the trout

they contain. Undisturbed for so long a period, the fish forget the lessons learned in the previous season, and do not at once acquire the extreme wariness which later in the year will be their characteristic. They are as a rule well advanced in condition, within casting distance of the bank, not too saucy or discriminating, and they have not as yet regained their old annoying habit of fasting all day in preparation for a gorgeous banquet at an hour when the angler must usually be elsewhere.

April holds many attractions still to be enumerated. The waters are not so crowded as they will be later, but perhaps we are only deluded into thinking that is so, because, the river being full, each stretch takes longer to fish, so that more anglers can be accommodated. The larger body of water affords greater concealment, which is a great advantage, but for ourselves we would much prefer to have the river low and clear so that we could approach within deadly distance of every tiny, tricky corner. We might reach the goal desired, even if the water were full, by lengthening of the line, but every foot beyond each individual's comfortable distance involves a sacrifice of efficiency, a handicap we at least would rather not concede. In smaller streams the case is entirely altered, but the larger rivers we like to see at summer level.

Possibly the most outstanding feature of an April day beside the river lies in the manner in which sport is provided. First there is a long period of inactive waiting on the bank or of desultory casting at a venture ; then follows a burst of flies with its attendant excitement and activity, a short or long blank spell, another hatch, and so the variety and sequence may be kept up throughout the day. This intermittent species of sport, scarcity and plenty alternating, has an irresistible fascination, and we know not what we enjoy the most, the patient hopefulness, the strain on every sense, or the crowded intervals of speedy movement, quick decisions, and well-rewarded energy.

May

With the advent of May the angler attains at last to such contentment as can be his, envying no man save him whose every day is a fishing day. He is no longer seriously limited in his choice of locality, and his sole and happy predicament lies in the difficulty of making a selection that will satisfy him. That of course is impossible ; but one thing is certain—viz., that he will set forth on every possible occasion, for the merry month is the period during which fish and fishers alike are in their best humour.

In the country the freshness of spring still prevails ; early districts are still capable of yielding abundance of sport, while the later streams and lochs are quickly approaching, and within the month will reach, the summit of their excellence. Mountain lochs are an exception, but we think meantime only of places of easy access, so many in number that we can the more contentedly neglect the remote solitudes until the long days of summer, when we can take more complete advantage of every opportunity presented of these pleasurable expeditions which reward expended energy with forgetfulness of the world below.

Occupying a position intermediate to spring and summer, May exhibits their characteristic qualities in a modified degree, so that we enjoy the most attractive features of both and suffer not their extremes. Seldom is it so hot that the trout lie dormant in the deepest pools and ignore our most painstaking efforts; only very infrequently indeed does the temperature drop so low as to forbid the flies of the water-side to venture out. The river is still flowing fresh and sweet; the fish are not confined to the quiet flats or the most gentle glides; they are spread throughout the stream even to the rushing necks; we may have difficulty in reaching a favourite corner which in the height of summer seldom, if ever, fails to yield a victim, but there are many fruitful places which later will be barren.

While we await the rise or as we take a well-earned rest, we find much to look upon; Nature has fully awakened from her winter sleep; primroses deck the woodland glades; the old brown beech-leaves make room for the young; birds are busy, too busy to sing; the scent of the hawthorn hangs heavy over the loaning.

Disappointments now come less frequently, for there is a wealth of insect life which ensures sport for some time at least, if not throughout the day. Trout have ceased to crowd their feasting into an hour at high noon, and if, perchance, some cold snap should retard the insect hatch, still the fish will not persistently look upon our counterfeits with disdain, because they have awhile been welcoming the floating banquet and have learned to expect it. The day must necessarily be cold indeed if the hardy Iron Blue is not seen sailing down the pool and bringing up the trout to inspect.

If, on the contrary, the sun streams fiercely down, let it be remembered that it beats also upon the sandbeds, wherein lurk the young sandflies waiting and wearying for its coming. Over the sand they gaily sport, and a puff of wind, a mere breath, comes along, blowing them on the water, where await the trout longing for such great delicacies, and the angler must be there to reap the harvest.

Even sometimes another race of flies which love the gloaming will be born anew, and so the day may be prolonged into the night.

On the river the flies that may be expected are numerous, too numerous we might almost say, but the variations in size and coloration are so exceedingly minute that not all are worthy of imitation. Perhaps the time may yet come when the education of the trout will reach such a state of perfection that it will be necessary to attend to every detail, but the day is not yet. Greenwell Quill, Medium Olive, Iron Blue will on most waters be sufficient, but the sand-fly is indispensable on those streams which rejoice in the environment necessary to its development. It may be plentiful on some reaches of a river and altogether absent from others, the nature of the bank being the determining factor. The Grannom or Greentail is also due, and on suitable evenings a floating Red Quill will account for many trout.

The hatch of flies may on occasions be pheno-
menally large, causing the trout to rise with apparently complete unanimity, and rendering the angler
as excited as the fish themselves. As is well-
known, it is very difficult under such circumstances to deceive an experienced specimen, the
artificial representation having poor prospect of
success amid so much competition, but the probability of acceptance is considerably increased
if attention is concentrated on one individual.
If the unfortunate conclusion must be made that
it is indifferent to all attempts at deception then
another should be selected ; but hurried movements and haphazard casting will almost certainly
prove utterly useless.

The angler, however, may, and should, conduct the campaign on a totally different plan,
and he will readily do so if he will but remember that a hatch is confined to a comparatively
small area, that it is not occurring over a large
extent of water at the same moment. The temptation to remain in close proximity to rising trout
is certainly very great and admittedly difficult
to resist, but the tendency must be overcome if
sport rather than disappointment is to be his fate.

When confronted with such an occurrence we
tear ourselves away from what we now know
will fill us with irritation, and seek a favourite
or promising pool either up or down stream, wherever fancy directs, so that we shall be well placed
to take advantage of the first of the hatch there
or, alternatively, the final minutes of the rise in
progress. Such tactics have seldom in our experience failed to succeed. and we have always felt

convinced that more sport was thereby obtained than would have been ours had we remained beside the gorging trout.

The loch is, in point of attractiveness, second only to the river, and many there are who would reverse that order. No matter what loch we visit, the ghillie is nearly certain to inform us that it shows its best form in the month of May; perhaps the remark is made to enable us to bear with greater composure the burden of a light creel, but the greater probability is that in the majority of cases average results tend to prove the statement true. We are convinced at any rate, and at no period of the season do we step aboard the boat with greater expectations that a pleasant day lies before us.

The trout are thoroughly alive, and take with a freedom unknown in the height of summer; nor do we often have to complain of short-rising, but instead rejoice to see the trout coming boldly to the surface, taking the dry-fly well, infinitely superior and more interesting sport than is usually possible earlier in the year, when the flies must be sunk to the depths and the rise, or rather offer, remains unseen.

The choice of a place for the fray is bewildering, but, if we could, we would make cheerful preparations for a day on Loch Voil or Loch Katrine. We know what these delightful waters can provide in July, but report has it that they are incomparably superior in May.

June

What shall we say of June, the month of leaves and roses and long, long evenings? Can we cease

to praise it, the month of kindliest weather and
superb, but wary, trout ?   Shall anyone remain
away from the waters for one single hour that is
his own ?

Without limit are the joys of the loch and stream
in June ; in peerless condition are the lusty trout ;
everywhere is loveliness.   Where should the angler
spend his days and evenings with the rod ?

He may devote them entirely to the faster streams,
where the stone-fly abounds, and come home tired
and happy under the joyful burden of the heavy
creel ; but, though it still will lure fine trout to their
doom, that bait has lost its attractions for us.
Why that should be so we cannot explain satisfactorily even to ourselves, and good it is that
reasons are not always necessary.   We prefer to
use a delicate copy of the fragile dun, the fluttering
sedge, or the suggestion of a tiny midge, and seek
thus to tempt the discriminating trout, that roam
the pools and throng the gravelly streams in June.

The burning sun drives us to the shade of the
quivering trees, where, too, the busy spinners have
retired ; there we lie in wait on the dappled turf
or thick carpet of pine-needles, eyes gazing on
the pool, longing for the advent of the first glad rise
that makes us spring to attention.   Eagerly we
scan the water in an effort to determine the species
of fly that brings the waiting to an end.   It may
have been but an adventurous froghopper that has
hopped too far from his grassy spire ; if so, our rest
is only briefly interrupted.   It may have been
only a wandering spinner dashed down by that
wheeling martin, but it was not, for there the rise
is again repeated : the heavy sucking swirl stops

our vain conjectures and sends us out to mid-stream to make investigation.

Now we see all clearly; one or two little duns float past, Pale Olives without a doubt. We tie one to the cast of tenderest gut, and cautiously wade in behind the feeding trout. Everything is in readiness, even to the length of line required for the distance and, as again a fly disappears for ever, we send out the tiny artificial with an underhand cast. There it floats with wings acock, following up the eddying water. That is something worth seeing, but it is not all; up comes the trout with confidence, and the quickly answering rod does its duty.

Although flies are fairly numerous on the pool, only that trout now resting in the creel seems to have been interested in them. Why do the fish ignore the varied assortment of duns, olives of more than one shade, a few Iron-Blues that apparently have misread the temperature, and even a big, brown, blundering sedge that really should have delayed its aerial adventure until evening? Even a dry-fly cannot compel a trout to rise; it is not more alluring than a natural insect. It is needless to attempt the impossible, so stealthily we move up, well back from the bank, to the waving head of the long, silent pool.

It occurs to us that the trout congregated here will have sharper appetites, and may, if they have reasoning powers, as they certainly seem to have, consider that should they allow a fly to pass over them it will be lost to them for ever, and be snapped up by a rival below. Therefore we determine to test the surmise and, fixing another Olive to the cast, we lay the questing pair across and up the stream, working our way gradually to the neck. The journey upwards is slow and occasionally interrupted ; the creel opens now and then to receive a victim, and we retire to the trees again to rest ourselves, and likewise the stream.

But in June we think mostly of the twilight hour, that mysterious hour between sunfall and the night when all is peace and a hush descends over the land.

If you would see us supremely happy, set us afloat then on bonnie Loch Dochart when the great peak of lofty Ben More is tipped with the final ray of the setting sun, when the wind has gone to rest and the reeds stand straight and motionless, when the water lies calm and dark beneath the hazel-clad rocks of the northern shore, when the castle stands out clear and sharp against the western light. Grant us a boatman keen and skilled, able to steer a silent craft with one deft touch of ready oar, let us revel among the weeds and let the trout commence the evening banquet.

We face the blue heights beyond Strathfillan, watching, waiting for the signal. There by the edge of yonder reeds the water is faintly dimpled, and the circles spread and spread unto the shore ; now there is another and yet another, and the wavelets meet and rock together. Forward silently moves the boat ; as silently it stops.

High above the concentric rings the fly is cast ; daintily it lowers itself on spreading wings until it gently touches the water ; there it rocks on the tiny vortex, a living thing ; beneath it the trout rises slowly and delicately, confidently takes it down ; the rod gives to the strike, the reel protests, and the hooked fish lashes the water as it vainly strives to gain the sanctuary of the tangled weeds below. The rod, nothing yielding, for to yield is fatal, keeps command until the net embraces the plucky captive.

A trout already and the rise just beginning! The triumph is repeated, and again many times repeated. An error in direction, a want of delicacy now and then, a hold giving way, a strike too forceful, but serve to make us more careful.

At length darkness falls, and only we disturb the eerie silence of the loch. Ashore we reluctant and yet contented go, and there on the dewy grass we arrange a dozen gleaming trophies whose rare beauties we can guess but dimly see. Is that a most remarkable hour, the best hour of a season ? No, it is just Loch Dochart.

Again, we may seek Loch Leven, where a June evening is likely to prove more generous than a full day. There is not time to go far, and we perforce content ourselves with the Graveyard Bank or the Thrapple Hole, unlovely names, no doubt, but more romantic spots are beyond our reach. The long, level rays of the setting sun throw long shadows across the loch, soothing the breeze to a gentle zephyr, calming the rolling waves to a pleasant ripple. The sun drops behind the farthest peak of the Ochils, and nerves begin to tingle with anticipation. There is no visible reason for excitement, and yet the feeling pervades that something is about to happen.

Meanwhile the rod has not been idle ; all the way from the pier we have cast at a venture across the waves, not in expectation but merely to put the wrist and rod and flies into working order. Now the boat lies across the breeze, and we cast assiduously all around, simply because we cannot remain inactive. A faint but familiar sound bids the eye rest on a swirl away to right of us, a hundred yards or more, and we pull off line, as if we would reach the mark, but the action is only a sign that we are making greater effort to deserve success.

The light is waning, doubt begins to lay its grip upon us, and all at once the surface breaks. The dry-fly rod is mounted, the work of a minute or two ; the rise is beginning, and of it we must take full advantage. As soon as all is ready, there is a mark to cover ; once more the water parts, and the air is pierced. The near boatman ships his massive oar, grasps his ponderous net, and stands aloft ready to swoop upon his prey. We steer the boring, plunging fish round to the windward side in true Loch Leven style, and bring it within reach as soon as possible, and perhaps sooner than advisable. There we seem to lose much of the sport of playing a fish, but, whether it is because we are anxious to get it in the boat that we may the sooner be fast in another, or because we do not like to keep the boatman waiting, we really do not know. We act according to the custom of Loch Leven.

There are days when the angler may be doubtful of sport on the main river, and yet be unable to content himself with idling until the evening shadows fall. No happier expedition can he then make than to one of the clear, sparkling burns among the hills, now gurgling unseen into great depths in cool, dark glens, now opening out upon the moor into gliding flats with fine entering streams. These are the waters we enjoy most on hot, still days of June, waters of youth which are filled with happy memories. We must go bewadered now and keep dry, whereas formerly happiness varied directly with the amount of mud and moisture acquired. Numbers used to be the supreme necessity; now it is quality. The pools are not quite so deep as they were, nor is the burn a river, but the distances seem to have grown greater. A small pink worm on two-hook tackle used to be the killing lure, but now it is the floating fly, and if the angler will follow that example, he will be amazed at the response.

June is the angler's month. He can fish early and late, anywhere and everywhere, in burn and river, loch and mountain tarn, and find sport in all, with trout in the prime of condition, but wary enough to demand the cautious approach, every refinement in tackle and, above all, a floating fly.

July

The scent of new-mown meadow grass is heavy on the air; the tortured herd invades the favourite pools; a flickering haze vibrates across the holm; away on the open moor the shady side of a turf-dike affords the bleating Cheviots a slight protection. The angler on the river, under the merciless sun, is glad of a trout or two from the rougher streams.

It is July, a month of many disappointments, but perchance a little kindness, of much labour and still some possibilities. By day sport may be very poor, but on occasions it may be excellent, and the flies that will cause the waters to give up their trophies are the Blue Hen Spider, the Red Quill, and the Black Midge. The Badger Hackle, useful also at times during the previous month, is now indispensable, and capable of many victories, when the waters are besprinkled with tiny smuts.

Only seldom are we out at noon of the trying days. We prefer to set out at the dawning, creel on back, and rod in hand. It is then good to be out, the morning air is so sweet; there is such a wealth of life that later in the day hides itself from prying eyes. Along the road innumerable rabbits frisk about, and lordly pheasants fearless strut; on the hill we catch a glimpse of the red fox homeward bound; we hear the lark salute the morn; we flush the wary heron at the ford.

We fish the early morning July rise, when the music of the stream is hid in the melody of the woods, before the first pillar of smoke floats away from the herd's cottage on the moor, as the sun begins to pierce the moist warm air, dispelling, if luck attends, the gentle shower which delights the thirsty midges. Then we learn again some of the greatest joys in life.

The trout are awake, the big ones are out, each on its own special feeding-ground, and we may take one of them if we know the spot and hasten to get the worm or minnow over it while there is yet time; they will not linger long, but will depart as the light grows to the safe shelter beneath the bank or the stronghold of a sunken snag. If such a prize is denied, there are still trophies awaiting, the pounders, whose appetites are keen at early morn. We select, if possible, a western stream and fish up towards the sun, easily forgetting the terrors of early-rising in the enjoyment of the scene and the sport.

The trout are rising in the pool, dimpling the water daintily, taking down indiscriminately any species of fly floating over them. Our lure is an upright Greenwell, and whether it resembles any insect on the water we really have not time to discover. We wade along a high bank, stepping carefully among the grass-topped masses torn off by winter floods, sometimes on little gravel patches between and sometimes on the yielding grass. Instead of casting in the usual manner, for that happens to be nearly impossible, we use the shortest of lines and dap the fly over each rise within reach as we progress. It is an exciting and a deadly sport, striking being almost impossible of failure, and the trout taken are mainly large and in the prime of form.

Quite as interesting it is when no fish are seen rising. They are, we know, eager for food, but the supplies have been delayed. Our fly is therefore heartily taken. It certainly is a fine sequence of happy things, to spot a rise, lay the fly, an exact counterfeit of the living insect that has just been swallowed up, lightly and accurately to the mark, watch it with strained eye as it slowly follows the floating bells, see it vanish beneath, and hear the song of the reel as the fish strives to break the restraining bonds. That undoubtedly yields pleasant sensations and intense satisfaction, because care and skill and knowledge are all demanded, but we hold that there is something still better.

Across the pool, irregularly waving, broken by

stones and rocks, seen and submerged, weed-masses
and projecting banks, there is not the slightest
indication that one single trout awaits below.
Yet up the bank we quietly proceed, casting as we
go, not at random as might appear, but laying
the fly on the likely spots, places where trout are
sure to be.

We may continue for an hour or often more
without the least result, when suddenly without a
warning the water breaks in a great swirl. First
we have to realise its meaning, which takes some
time if the monotony of useless effort has dulled
the senses, and then we have to strike. We know
not which is the greater pleasure, but we would
dispense with neither. Fishing the stream demands
a knowledge of the lower waters and the ways of
a trout, and its pursuit provides many startling
awakenings from semi-consciousness to activity,
while it requires quite as much neatness and skill
as does fishing the rise where the target is clearly
indicated. Practice in one or other will come on
any July morning, and seldom indeed will the creel
fail to open.

Not all days of July are difficult. There will be
a few days of cool East wind, when even the Iron-
Blue may arrive, and then the Black Spider is extremely deadly. There may be wet, blustery days,
especially on the Uplands, when even the wet-fly
is not altogether unprofitable, and there may
occur a flood to clean out the streams. If so, good
fishing conditions may be the rule for many succes-
sive days.

After the flood begins to subside, the water
assumes a rich blackness: for a few hours the

natural minnow is without a rival as a means of
luring trout, but, that period past, the floating
fly is almost as eagerly accepted as the more substantial bait. It is difficult to know when the fly
should be tried, especially if no hatch or rise occurs
to provide a guide, but the time comes always
sooner than one would expect, and that is some sort
of indication.

While yet the water sucks at the grasses of the
bank, the dry-fly should be laid close to the edge
of the near side, and allowed to come down a yard
or two before being sent forth again. Long-casting
is quite unnecessary and even fatal; but, as the
waters continue to fall, and the gravel begins to
shine through, the fly may be sent farther and farther
towards mid-stream and beyond.

Under different conditions the angler must be
prepared to indulge in the art of trout-stalking,
and many days full of interest he should be enabled
to spend. If unwilling to put himself to so much
trouble, he may find all the sport he requires at
eventide. For the period about sunset, the Blue
Hen Spider and the Red Quill are the best flies,
but for the gloaming rise few patterns can compare
with the Corncrake and Cinnamon Sedges. A
breath of wind and a hatch of flies are the two
main requirements. If the water is calm, he
should not lose confidence, but rather acquire
it. He should place his fly at once on the rise,
and he will immediately be engaged with a fighting
fish.

But July is the time to visit the hill-loch. In
the cool of the morning we face the arduous climb
through the bracken and the heather; on the

way we may sometimes regret having left the plain, but it is wonderfully easy to forget the toils after the goal is reached. In the evening we return contented, but feeling the effects of the heavy air of the hill. We are happy after our day on the little loch, every creek and corner, every headland and islet of which we have visited, and the creel holds a goodly number of trout, small perhaps, but plucky beyond description. We have seen the nesting-isle of the seagulls, have startled the mountain hare from its form, and plucked the ruddy cloudberry from among the heather.

Possibly the dry-fly will be declared unnecessary on these distant mountain tarns ; it is pronounced a super-refinement. There is no doubt that the wet-fly will take trout from these lochs, plenty of them, but if the floating fly will capture more and better fish, it is surely sensible to employ it. As a matter of fact, the dry-fly is almost a useless lure on some hill-lochs. The behaviour of the trout in any particular loch will depend on the type of food that they are in the habit of receiving, and the angler's lure should be a representation of that form. If in any loch trout are seen rising to take flies from the surface, then at that time the angler, who desires to obtain the maximum of sport, will lay a floating artificial on the rise, even though he is convinced that a wet-fly, as carefully and accurately cast, would be probably accepted.

As long as there are burns and lochs of the hill to fish by day, and rivers to seek at eventide and early morn, July will continue to yield many a good trout to the floating fly.

August

Not many trout-fishers feel jubilant at the approach of August, generally agreed to be the least profitable month of the angling season; they look forward to it with little hope, knowing that the trout are only on exceptional days in taking humour. In all probability the sorely harassed fish have experienced a long period of low water, and of a certainty they have been called upon to withstand the attacks of innumerable holiday anglers, with the consequence that they have become very shy and suspicious.

For long, supplies have been unstinted, and the wary trout can afford to go without for a time; winter is still afar off, there is no indication of its approach, and therefore the call has not yet come to prepare against the hard times that lie ahead. There is reason for the general despair, and the angler sets forth expecting only a light creel, but now and then he may strike a lucky day.

On the river prospects may be very bad indeed, sport depending entirely on the weather conditions. If the previous month has been rainless and the drought continues, then the streams become mere trickles of water, and every stone on the bottom is covered with a green, slippery deposit, while the edges and the quiet backwaters become filled with the same vile accumulation. Fishing then ceases to be a pleasant pastime, the trout are dull and lifeless, though towards nightfall they sometimes develop some activity. The floating fly is the only possible lure, any other coming continually in contact with the foul growth, necessitating constant interruption to clean the hook, a great strain on the temper.

Fortunately a flood usually occurs in August, and, if it comes as expected, all is well. It cleans out the river-bed, making all sweet and pure again; the weed is torn from its moorings and hurled seawards. We are somewhat sorry for the worm-fisher who never goes in pursuit of the trout except when the flood is rising or is at the height of its ugly yellowness; the floating rubbish covers up his bait most effectively, so that he is forced to delay his slaughter until the next spate calls him out again. When the waters begin to subside there is sport to be had which makes us forget the weary times that have gone before. The trout, welcoming the refreshing full water, repair again to haunts long denied them, and feed boldly as one could desire.

Under the new conditions prevailing, cool water and warm atmosphere, a plentiful hatch of duns by day and of sedges in the evening is almost a certainty, and the welcome sight of free-rising trout is seen again. To take full advantage of the opportunities, the floating fly must be used, and of these the best all-round pattern is the Greenwell Quill. We have even seen in August a hatch of the autumn brood of Iron-Blues, and that is a signal for a good rise and many captures. The dark Olive Dun and the Rough Olive are also fine patterns to use, and the Black Midge is deadly among the August grayling. That fish is not yet quite ready for the angler, but its capture adds a little variety to the day's sport. It often mistakes its aim, but, unlike the trout, it will rise again and again as if determined to die. It is usually the fish inhabiting a deep, slow glide that err in this way ; those that frequent rapid shallow necks of pools seldom miss the fly, we find, but it requires a watchful eye and a ready strike to send the hook home.

There are other two flies which are sure to appear in August, and of which the angler would do well to possess copies, viz., the Black Sedge and the Needle Brown. With the former, we once, many years ago, took a basket of eighteen beautiful trout from the lone Potrail, a fact which had quite escaped our memory, until reference to an old diary brought back clearly all the details. The fish approximated very closely to half a pound in average weight, an astonishing and almost incredible average for that small but delightful tributary of Clyde, or more correctly, Daer Water. We remember also that the loss of the fly, the only pattern in our possession, brought the sport to an abrupt termination. Curiously enough, we did not replace the pattern for many years, but again, after seeing the welcome accorded the natural fly in the Cairn and elsewhere, it holds a high place in our esteem. The value of the Needle Brown has only lately been impressed upon us, but that it is a good fly we are thoroughly convinced.

The flood that freshens up the lochs and rivers ultimately reaches the sea and the silvery fish eagerly awaiting it. The salmon and sea-trout answer and come, each to its chosen river. The shoals of herling or finnock or whitling, by whatever name they may be known, crowd the streams, not always in the same enormous numbers, it is true, and we are apt to neglect our friend the yellow trout.

The dry-fly, while not so generally useful a lure for sea-trout as the wet-fly, has nevertheless great attracting power and will on occasions prove the more serviceable lure of the two. During the last seven years we have with good results devoted many days exclusively to dry-fly fishing for sea-trout in Scottish rivers; and in the lochs of Connemara and the Hebrides, on dull days when the fish showed no interest in the sunk lure, we have turned failure into comparative success by means of the floating fly.

On the loch, anglers are usually subjected to brilliant suns and gentlest breezes, when lunch in the shade of some wooded island is apt to become a protracted affair. Any day, however, may bring grey skies and a fine wave, and consequently a long, fruitful spell on the water. Loch Leven sometimes fishes very well in August, but only if there is much cloud, and then the trout are in their very best condition, which in itself is sufficient to make a visit there attractive. Frequently, the dry-fly is the correct lure, though on dour days a sunk lure will reward patient unceasing labour still better.

Some of the hill lochs will still provide sport; but the highest of these suffer from occasional night-frosts, which have the effect of driving the trout into deeper water. Consequently the angler should not fish the shallows in the morning; but as the day advances, he may approach the shore again, in case the trout have returned to their more usual haunts. For dry-fly work on these lochs, probably the best pattern is the Rough Olive, as it may pass for various species.

In spite of any attempts we may make to persuade ourselves to the contrary, the fact remains that August yields the poorest sport of the season. It is not without its redeeming features, but it arouses little enthusiasm. Still if the angler betakes himself to the water-side on every available opportunity, he will sometimes find a rise in progress, and find his floating fly well received.

September

September is the evening of the year. It is to the season what eventide is to the long summer day, and just as the angler waits, with whatever patience he may possess, throughout the breathless hours of June and July, for the coming of the gloaming, when the trout awake to cruise about in eager search for spinner and sedge, so he longs for the passing of August.

Long have the trout remained rather indifferent to his efforts, persistently they have defied his skill; but at last they come boldly forth once more. They now realise that the time is fast approaching when the supplies will be scanty, and that they must be in the height of condition if they are to withstand the exhaustion of spawning as well as the rigours of winter. They do not ignore the showers of autumn duns; they feed boldly and at every opportunity; no fly that ventures on the water can escape their keen eyes. Their appetites are insatiable, and so sport becomes reminiscent of happy spring.

Thus it is that anglers dare long for September, for, while it is the end, it is a great and glorious end. It sends them away at the close of the season with the happiest memories of final days of fine sport and magnificent scenes. These make the beginning of the period of enforced idleness the more easy to bear, and, before the waiting ends, anticipation intervenes to keep them cheerful. They may, of course, carry on into mid-October; but, before that time, the trout have earned their respite and should be left unmolested, if sport is to continue down the years.

At no time is the country more attractive than in September. Through thick grass drenched with dew, among yellowing bracken and purple heather, the angler walks in the misty air to the water's edge. He hears the song of the river, long before he reaches the banks, and at last he finds the water running full and clear, for the effects of August floods have not completely departed.

A bank of fog fills the valley as with a sea, and through it loom unexpectedly objects which should be familiar, but are distorted and magnified out of recognition. Above the gloom the tree-tops appear, and up the river rocks suddenly show and as quickly vanish from sight, weird and bewildering.

A great stillness holds the air, but soon a faint breath steals through; the light grows less dim; vertical columns drift slowly past, damp and chill; the red sun pierces, is hidden again, and finally it bursts forth victorious. The enveloping fog is mysteriously wafted away, and the whole gorgeous scene is spread before the gaze.

Every shade of green is seen, but here and there

amid the riot of leaves he detects a golden flush, the beauty of which he admires, but whose significance he chooses to forget. Along the banks, delaying progress, the long, trailing, clinging sprays of bramble are clustered with rich, dark fruit; hazel-nuts are browning; rowan-berries add a touch of brilliancy. The melody of the woods is still subdued, though the silence of August is broken. The cuckoo has sought other climes and will not mock the autumn fisher; great clouds of lapwings wheel overhead, collecting for their short adventure. There is much to distract attention on a September day.

As soon as the sun charms away the mists of morning, the flies of autumn will venture out, some of them peculiar to the season, while others resemble those of spring. The redoubtable Greenwell, the little Iron Blue, the Dark Olive, and the Rough Olive may be brought forth once more, and will do their duty.

In the strong lights and gentle breezes of September, the trout, though eager, are cautious enough, and demand all delicacy in the lure and its manipulation. They have had many escapes during the long season; some indeed have been hooked, and fought their way to freedom; all have learned many and many a time that numerous enemies thirst for their blood. Still they dare not abstain from food in view of coming events, and therefore a capture is an ever-present possibility.

The floating fly, unprofitable yet almost alone useful during the previous month, is again fit for great conquests, and many enjoyable days are to be spent on all rivers. Blanks are infrequent, victory is the rule and not the exception, so it is easy to forget that we are all actually bidding farewell to the trout.

On the loch a similar experience awaits, unless, as is not unlikely, a dead calm prevails. If, however, flies are numerous enough to bring the trout up to investigate and make them cease their pursuit of elusive shrimps and late-developing nymphs, interesting and exciting sport can be enjoyed stalking the rising trout and laying a fly neatly in the centre of the spreading rings.

Then must the angler above all things beware of the too forceful strike, which results in the loss of fly, time, and trout. It is easy to err, for the rise is expected, the line tight, and the fish heavy. If he can restrain himself, and be content with but a gentle tightening on the fish, all well-intentioned offers should be accepted, and each be followed by a long, plucky fight, culminating in merited victory.

If weeds do not prevent, it is really better to conduct the campaign from the bank than from a boat. The shy trout, which anglers have been educating throughout the entire season, are more easily and quickly approached, provided that they do not lie beyond reach ; they readily take alarm at the oncoming boat, propelled, as it probably is, by splashing oars. At any rate, we prefer to be afoot.

We can wander at will down the bank, shelter from sun or shower under the still leafy trees, with no one to consult about choice of ground and annoy with our laziness or untiring energy ;

we can work hard when there is inducement, and take things easy when invitations are few. There is as much variety as on the river ; long casts and short are in demand ; we have to study direction, and accurately lay the fly on a rise, close to a bed of weed or clump of rustling reeds, or over a submerged rock lit up by the sun.

Anglers are all happy in September, for they live only in the present, and refuse to remind themselves that they are about to lay aside for a season the faithful, deadly dry-fly rod.

CHAPTER XVIII

A DAY ON CLYDE

ACROSS the broad rough holm, terrifying the meadow-pipits, over a dry-stone dyke threatening to collapse, we hurry under the broiling sunshine to reach the river's bank. Full well we know there is no need for haste, and yet we are filled with eagerness to start the unequal fight. We consider it a day in which we shall have to be content with small events, but many a time we have expected much and received little, while not infrequently our anticipations have been far surpassed. Truly, we never can foretell what fortune intends to bestow.

Is this the brimming river that we knew in the far-off happy days of spring, when the broad, swelling pools and cheerful streams seldom failed to bring supreme contentment? The curves of the distant hills, green darkening to deepest blue, remain unchanged ; we recognise the banks, though they are draped with greater luxuriance ; the tributary burns enter where they did, yet surely they sing a sadder song, and the river is only the shadow of its former might.

A bed of dry gravel spreads gleaming white where often the rod has become a straining bow and the reel has shrieked its protest ; a pool that we imagined of mighty depth is still a pool, no doubt, but clearly to the bottom we see and find its mystery has vanished; a broad flat, which has yielded freely of its store and made us happy in our work, is now a thin shallow in which not a single trout appears to dwell.

A feeling of despair and hopelessness strives to lay its grip upon us, but we are resolved not to be overwhelmed with disappointment until we have put fortune to the test. Though the sun is brilliant and large cloud-masses intensely white float slowly across the sky, the wind is gentle from the east, endeavouring to give a little coolness, and at times, as it puts forth a greater effort, not altogether failing.

Some there are who love not the east wind, but we find it friendly on many rivers, or rather we believe that it is kindly, and that is an equivalent. It opposes the puny current, a stroke of luck to place against the many unfavourable conditions, a happy circumstance which dispels some despair and hastens on the preparations for the day. While the tails of the pools may be unaffected, the streams are appreciably longer and more ruffled, which means more water to fish, shorter distances to walk and, we hope, more sport to enjoy. If that wind were absent, we might acknowledge defeat without a trial, but its presence makes probable the impossible.

Before us lies a long, still pool, on our side a broad belt of gravel fringed and sullied with the foul green weed, the invariable accompaniment of drought, while opposite is a high, rush-tufted bank on which the long grass scarcely waves, and between them glides softly the silent water.

Detaching ourselves completely from all the sounds and scenes around—and very difficult it is to ignore the play of light and shade on the hills, and refuse to hear the sky-lark's song and the curlew's far, wild cry—we watch with unfaltering attention ·the deep black shadow beneath the bank. We have already noticed that down the pool floats an occasional tiny black smut of white glistening wing, and that all are allowed to pass on unmolested; but in expectation of the welcome being merely delayed we have attached a Badger Hackle of smallest size to the very finest cast in our possession. We watch and wait.

At last the faintest disturbance appears on the surface close to the bank; so very faint indeed is it that, had we not been watching the spot in hope of it occurring, we should probably have failed to detect it; we might even conclude that we had merely imagined it, were it not repeated again and yet again.

At one time, had we accidentally seen such a mark, we would probably have said that it was nothing but a minute air-bubble rising from the bottom, or considered it caused by a diminutive minnow rising quietly, but we have investigated and found that it is made by an exceptional trout raising itself slowly towards the surface to suck down a fly. Sometimes, but not always, a bell of air remains to mark the spot. The rise is the deadliest of all the many kinds of rises, the one that we most rejoice to see, for the fish that feeds in this quiet fashion is worthy a place in any basket, not only because of its size and quality, but also for the care that must be exercised, the delicacy that must be displayed, before its capture may be effected.

Having made certain that the Badger is absolutely dry, and that every part of the apparatus is in readiness, we switch the fly across to the bank. It alights softly close to the edge and about a foot above the floating bubble, and slowly down it comes, the line obedient to the gentle current gradually straightening out. The fly with its white glinting points suggesting the wings of the tiny smut is quite visible, as fortunately it rides clear of any foam-fleck. Will it reach the fateful spot before, in reply to the floating, pulling line, the fatal drag supervenes?

As if in answer it suddenly and silently vanishes, but we are all-prepared for this event, and almost as quickly the horizontal rod flashes downstream. The trout is hooked. It bolts below, making the reel sing and the line hiss through the rings. Not knowing yet the foe we have to deal with, we hasten, with rod held high and eyes on the line cutting through the water, to the gravel, in an endeavour to get below the captive, a manoeuvre which we always strive to carry out, as surely it is advisable to make the water assist the rod and not the trout.

The dour fighter comes to the top and lashes wildly, shoots across the pool in an attempt to reach a submerged mass dislodged from the bank, now cruises sullenly about the depths, without warning tears through the slimy shallows as if it would end the battle by throwing itself upon the gravel; but the hook holds, and the high rod-point answering every move prevents disaster to the frail cast. The end of the struggle is near, and in deep water we steer into the net as gallant a pounder as ever we hooked.

Elated with this early success, greater than we dared to expect, we repair to our former station to scan the surface for a similar invitation. That is withheld, and, our patience soon exhausted, we walk up the pool a few yards until we are opposite a narrow ditch draining the holm ; ordinarily it is quite a merry stream of bubbling water, whose music we can hear even from the tail of the pool, but now it sends only a feeble drip over the high bank.

Just above it a bubble floats, perhaps wafted there by the gentle breeze from the tiny fall, but it may be that a trout has left it there a few minutes ago in exchange for a fly, so across we flick the lure. Whatever the reason for the presence of the air-bell, a trout is there and, moreover, seems to have been expecting the fly to arrive, for it snaps it up at once. Duly it pays the penalty for its mistake, a short but merry fight enough, for, though only a half-pounder, it is not lacking in pluck.

Entering this pool is a stream, which is one of the most generous bits we know, where a floating fly is always certain of attention, sometimes, very seldom, only a little and sometimes as much as anyone could desire. On one occasion, after struggling for a time against a downstream gale, receiving nothing but half-hearted rises, we changed our tactics, and took from it half a dozen fine trout on a Red Spider, fished wet.

At summer level it is only about a foot in average depth and of fairly steep gradient. Often it is crowded with rising trout, especially at the gloaming, and what a glorious, exciting sound trout make when rising greedily in a steep stream! The bottom consists of the finest gravel, with not a single large stone to provide cover, so that it may safely be concluded that any trout in it are there for the sole purpose of feeding. Even though the flowing surface was quite undisturbed, we would not omit to search it thoroughly, for we cannot recall a blank day on it.

At that point where the ripple of the stream fades away in the pool, there is a fish quietly feeding on small duns sailing down the current, a small company truly, but evidently quite sufficient to attract attention. Of these our Pale Olives are a fair representation. The substitution called for is soon made, and the new fly laid above the last eddy of the stream ; gaily it bobs for a moment, and then sails placidly along. The trout splashes wildly over it, a good fish not destined to be ours. We think that it rose with the best intentions, determined to accept, but at the last moment took alarm and changed its course.

Taking the hint, we replace the fly with one of the same pattern but smaller in size, and greedily look over the waving water. The small hatch seems to have passed, and we are too impatient to wait for the arrival of another detachment. Our fly may pass as a belated individual or as a fore-runner, we really care not which.

Gradually we work up the short stream, casting the fly ahead, laying it over the favourite lines of the fish, remembered from past days, and, though offers are fairly frequent, only three times is progress interrupted in the way we most welcome. Two of the fish are fine average specimens, which display remarkable resistance, being assisted, vainly however, by the strength of the current ; the third is an immature fish, an interloper in this fine piece of water.

As a rule, having fished the pool and its stream, we would return to where we commenced operations and there wait until the disturbance had died away sufficiently for the trout to recover their equanimity, but to-day we have a desire to revisit old familiar haunts on a full mile of water. Our next halt is made at a great pool with a very sharp bend in it, where we have never had great success, and only once have we seen trout rising in it, and that was on a sultry, thundery day, when the water was covered with ants and the rod was being given a rest. The neck of the pool is a strong rush with a high wave, whither we would not expect trout to repair in search of surface food.

We do not care to pass the place without giving it a trial, and happening to remember that we possess a large Red Quill adorned with a stiff detached body, we decide for amusement to float it down the rapids. As it sails along from trough to crest at great speed, a trout throws itself clear of the water upon it, and making no mistake in aim firmly hooks itself. Without ceremony we hurry it into slack water and run it ashore, a bright little fellow of six ounces. In spite of this immediate success we have not experimented further with detached bodies, as, though they are very natural in appearance, we imagine that only by a lucky chance will an offering fish be hooked, as the stiff body will usually interfere with the strike.

The wind meantime freshens to a strong breeze, but still, fortunately, from the same direction. The air is decidedly cooler and more pleasant, so that we give up quite cheerfully the next two pools, the fishing of which would demand greater exertion than we deem worth while, as they are unfavourably placed as regards the wind.

A short walk across country and through the stream brings us to a pool which, though exceedingly well stocked with trout, continues to defy us. To-day, as usually is the case, we secure two good fish at the tail, where it is simple fishing ; but it is at the head that we receive innumerable chances and score as a rule an equal number of failures.

An island of gravel splits up the river into two channels, that on the right bank being too steep and shallow to hold trout, while the opposite branch is a narrow, deep, curving, twisting stream which at the end strikes against a rude wall of stone built for the purpose of keeping the river from altering its course. The two branches meet to form an easy cast, which seldom, however, holds a willing trout, and to-day is no exception.

Again we stand on the gravel within sight of these trout that for years have baffled us ; as usual they are rising freely and quietly in the far-off stream. Deep water containing many currents lies between us and our wary foes, hence we have to suffer the first great handicap of a long line which, moreover, must be thrown loosely, or the drag that follows is horrible to behold. The cast produces a rise almost as a matter of course, and an ineffectual strike completes the unhappy sequence. Line must be lengthened as we search farther and farther up the stream, for of course we continue the agony to the bitter end.

As we take what we mean to be our last cast in the inhospitable place, we receive the almost inevitable rise, and, according to custom, we strike fiercely in reply. There is little danger in that, as so much line has to be pulled straight before any movement can be communicated to the fly. In amazement we discover that we have hit something more substantial than water, and we have a wild fight with a plunging, spinning fish. Gradually we overcome it and bring it down, but still it twists and writhes in disconcerting style. The explanation of its contortions and exceptional power becomes apparent when we discover that the fly is lodged at the root of the pectoral fin, a sure hold. That half-pounder will not tantalise us on our next visit, but there are dozens more in that tricky corner to carry on the work.

The opposite bank, high, bare, and vertical, we find no better as a base from which to conduct the campaign. We have attempted the downfall of these trout in almost every conceivable way, but a solution seems as far off as ever. A sixteen-foot rod would assuredly make several captures probable, but we are not burdening ourselves with such a heroic weapon on a trout-fishing expedition.

We leave the place more contented than we generally are, for we feel that at last we have accomplished something: luck undoubtedly has contributed to the success, if it is not alone responsible for it, and yet the satisfaction is in no measure diminished. In good humour—we are doing well on this inauspicious day—we pass on to the next resting-place, a long broad flat, such as we would expect to find twenty miles lower down the river, very deep at the sides and everywhere too deep to wade, an unpopular stretch with most anglers, but a great favourite of ours when a strong upstream breeze blows.

The current is slow, gentle, and uniform, nowhere is there any serious likelihood of drag, and therefore we attach two flies to the cast, both of the same pattern, viz., the small Pale Olive, which is still on the water. A break here and there, an eddy slowly fading away downstream, shows that they are as readily welcomed as ever.

We choose the right bank, high and grassy, because it is more favoured by the best trout than the other. At one time we used to pass by without a cast, but we discovered that it is possible to work slowly along the base of the bank, an occasional grasp of the overhanging grass being required to help us to pass a difficult part. The basket is an encumbrance that must be left at the tail of the pool, the landing net is another, but as it would be impossible to land a trout without it, it has to accompany us on the journey. Only underhand casting can be indulged in ; accuracy in direction is thus rather difficult to obtain, but quite frequently the dropper-fly rectifies a mistake.

Dry-fly fishing is at times not without its discomforts, but these are readily forgotten in the excitement of the sport. In the circumstances it is impossible to confine ourselves to rising trout ;

we might see a rise forty yards ahead, but we would certainly not hurry to put ourselves within casting distance. Too much labour all at once would be thereby entailed, besides which only a short period of time will elapse before we see a trout rising much nearer at hand; in the intervals of waiting for a mark we " fish the stream."

Imagine us crawling along the face of the bank, sometimes pulling ourselves round a projection, while all the time the rod switches the flies ahead or, by way of variety, stretches them across the current. If they do not fall exactly where we desire them, there is no harm done, for, when a number of trout are rising in a pool, it simply means that the other inhabitants are refraining from doing so from necessity, not choice, that they will rise when there is a fly to rise to, and that fly may be ours.

For a time there is no response, and we are busy considering whether a change to another pattern would be effective—a change would involve much trouble—when suddenly, as the cast falls parallel to the bank, two trout rise almost simultaneously and both are hooked. Now we have something to keep us really busy, and we shuffle into a firm foothold, with back pressed against the bank. We must play the fish from where we stand, hold them with an easy pressure, and allow them to exhaust one another.

It is a lengthy struggle and uncertain; the victim of the dropper is the first to turn over, and after what seems an hour, though in reality it is but a few minutes, the other follows. Gently we bring them within reach, luckily they drift close together, and a sweep with the net lifts the pair of beauties to the bank overhead. We throw the rod up after them, and scramble downstream to the first place where we find it possible to leave the water. We bring the creel along as well.

We sit down to rest awhile after these strenuous labours, pleased with all the world. Often have we landed two trout at once; never before have we been forced to stand motionless during the process, and not until now have we so clearly realised the assistance that running water can be made to give in such a case. In a loch, too, there are difficulties which can all be overcome if the angler who would reap the full benefit of his good fortune will exercise great patience and ignore the net altogether, until the lower fish is ready for it.

We find we cannot rest, as the trout below continue to rise; they may cease at any moment, so we toil to our post again. Almost immediately we raise a trout to the dropper, but owing to a short, tight line or an excess of force, or a combination of both, we leave the fly in its mouth. Rather than take the trouble to replace it we continue with the single fly. A fish rises in mid-stream, a fine boil indicative of a heavy trout; we pull off line sufficient to reach it, make a tremendous effort with an overhead cast, and succeed in hooking a thistle-top behind us on the bank.

This lapse necessitates a slow walk to the tail again, and involves a loss of time in repairing the damage, but it is time well spent. It serves to quell our excitement, and we determine to avoid further errors. By slow degrees we work up the edge, getting a little encouragement now and then

in the shape of a rise, but the trout, probably now
well satisfied, are not rising in the same deadly
style, and the great majority of the offers end dis-
appointingly.   Nevertheless by the time the stretch
is completed two fine trout are reposing somewhere
on the bank waiting to be picked up, and as the
landing of each required caution and restraint, the
sport obtained on this long and difficult reach was
much greater than may appear.

The day is drawing to a close, but there yet
remains one pool to fish, one of the choicest bits of
the whole river, one that we cannot think of omitting,
so many and so great are the victories we have won
there.   In some respects it is like the first pool,
slow and stately, where only the most delicate work
will yield a trophy ; in one particular it is different,
the gravel bed being steep and crumbling, very
trying to walk upon.   We are tempted to put on
the Badger again, or by way of change a Blue Hen
Spider, so eminently suitable a place it is for a
dainty hackled fly, but we resolve to retain the
Olive which has already done so well.   No trout
are visible, but yet we cannot pass it by ; so many
fish of the finest quality are here that it will be
surpassing strange if we do not come across one
willing to accept one fly more.

Over to the far side we cast the flies, and though
we lay them softly time after time there is no result.
Still we persevere.   Off a projecting cape near the
head the water is faintly ruffled, both by wind and
current, and, deeming it a sure place for a trout to
be lying expectant, we throw the tail-fly lightly over
it.   The rise of the fish and the fall of the fly seem
simultaneous, and, the line being tight and the rod

in position, the strike succeeds. At once the trout throws itself high above the water, a good three-quarter, and then dashes in headlong flight down the pool, every yard of its course being completed with a wild leap, very trying and exciting tactics ; but this excessively agile trout accomplishes its own defeat, for by the time we have come up with it, it is lying exhausted on its side and requires only to be steered ashore.

Such is the day that we thought would prove a lamentable failure, and instead yielded as bonnie a basket of trout as one could hope to get. We are tempted to declare that only the dry-fly could have given it, but we refrain, as every now and then we are convinced afresh that predictions regarding trout are wholly vain.

CHAPTER XIX

THE DAER WATER

AMID the silent solitudes around Queensberry is born a tiny stream—Daer Water—destined to become a great and noble river. As it trickles along it gathers to itself innumerable hill burns, until it becomes a brawling torrent, tearing over a boulder-strewn bed. In time it checks its impetuous haste and sleeps now and then in a long, still pool, opening gradually out until, when it welcomes Potrail Water, it is fully entitled to be called a river. On it flows at leisurely pace, sweet and pure, clear and gentle, winding through a broad, grassy holm, and at last it receives the insignificant waters of Little Clyde. Here it ends in a fine, deep pool ; the name of Daer goes no farther.

With the reason that allows a negligible streamlet to give its name to the glorious River Clyde and ignores the full-flowing river which receives it with little more concern than it would a raindrop, we are not meantime interested : we are out to fish the Daer, and that is sufficient to occupy completely our attention.

Right at the start we should be busy, for the pool that is the last on Daer has at its head a long glide, one of the grandest stretches for the dry-fly on the whole water. A favourable wind on it would lead us there from many miles away, for it contains numerous trout of fine size and quality which are generally in taking humour. The left bank is high and much crumbled away, so that care must be taken when wading along it, but that is the side from which the angler must fish if he desires to lure the wary, keen-eyed trout.

It will take him nearly an hour to search thoroughly, provided that he moves slowly forward and lays his flies at many angles across the stream from each halting-place. He must beware of advancing and delivering the cast at the same time : that bad habit, easily acquired because very natural, is one reason why many offers are unaccepted. In estimating the time required for fishing this stream, we assume that a rise is not taking place ; but should such additional incentive to careful work be granted, progress will be still slower, for the trout are not situated far apart, but spread all over the glide in great numbers, a fact that can be verified by anyone who cares to walk down the high bank. Then he will see many dozens of the finest trout hurrying for the shelter of the deep pot at the mouth of Clyde's Burn.

At the next bend the river runs in a narrower, deeper channel, a sure place for a kill when trout are keen and eager, but it is not one of our favourite bits, and we can pass it by without regrets. It is not so with the next pool, which rejoices in the possession of a smooth-flowing backwater, where we feel grievously disappointed if we fail to hook a half-pounder or weightier specimen. Here we can be content to wait for quite a long time until we see a rise, and then without hesitation we strive to place a floating fly with all possible delicacy right into the centre of the ring ; if it is done neatly and at once, then a fine fight is certain to ensue.

Now follows Crookedstane Ford with the long shallow flat immediately above it. This must be a grand flat for the night fly and, when the water is black after a flood and the wind is right, the angler need not leave it until the day is done. It is an impossible place, if the water is low and clear, and when, in addition, the breeze is absent or down-stream. A stiff wind blowing against the slight current means that, when the deep waving run at the neck, where the grayling lie, is reached, the creel will be very much heavier, unless fortune has arranged a succession of untoward accidents.

Crookedstane Pool is a fine bit of water, broken up by cairns of stones, built for the purpose of per-suading floods to keep to the river channel, into several deep holes connected together by gravelly shallows. It contains very big trout that know as much about lures as the angler does, but we once tempted one of them, a comparative youngster of $1\frac{3}{4}$ lb., with a floating Greenwell, and it kept us in good humour throughout a cold, wet, blustery July day. From the topmost shallow, quite a short stretch, we once basketed during an evening rise six magnificent trout, and that denotes sport of the highest order, when the captures are in the finest condition, and few casts are unrewarded.

With a careless cast or two we pass over the next flat, because it has always yielded only small fish, and the following pool, because the bottom is so soft and muddy that wading is somewhat uncom-fortable. We never have failed to take one good trout at least from the pebbly stream at the top, and there we once got a fine grayling of $1\frac{1}{4}$ lb. which afforded satisfactory sport.

This spot is well worthy of more attention, but we have little time to spare it, as we are always so eager to reach the pool beyond it, which for some reason contains trout of finer average size, we should say, than any other, one alone excepted, on Daer. In fact, if the angler hooks a small fish here he should at once conclude that the favourable time has not yet arrived, and should lie down on the gravel to wait, until the big ones begin to feed. If that does not suit his temperament, he may proceed upstream searching the pools, five in number, clearly defined but differing in no essential from those mentioned, until he arrives at the mouth of Potrail.

Here he is at the parting of the ways, and must decide which of the two waters he will fish. We can never resist the temptation of turning off up Potrail and following it as far at least as the White Bridge ; if sport is good we continue farther, but if there is little doing, owing to want of water, adverse wind, anglers ahead, or other cause, we return to the Daer. We are always amazed at the little Potrail ; it produces so very beautiful, bright-coloured trout, and of a size remarkable, but we must not neglect the Daer.

Glenochar Pool, where three waters meet, is a very long stretch, which, we notice, most anglers pass by. We cannot understand their objections to it, for we have had excellent sport on it by casting a long line from the banks when the wind was strong upstream. In other conditions we also would move on to the rocky corner beyond, which is exceptionally good; here more than once we have had the pleasure of hooking and holding two trout at one and the same cast, and quite an exciting event that is.

From this point onwards the pools are fewer in number and farther apart, so that we find it easy to remember their names—Watermeetings, Nunnerie, Allershaw, The Bend, Watergate, and Wintercleuch, great names and great pools. all easily negotiated and all well stocked.

These pools that we have mentioned are all ideal parts for dry-fly fishing; on them that is the most efficient lure at most times, and specially when waters are low; a wind fairly strong from the right direction is all that is necessary to make it extremely deadly. Above them all we prefer The Bend, a long narrow pool that slips along with barely perceptible current. The right bank is a steep gravel bed, while the left is low and grassy, but—and this is the reason of the pool's excellence—it is also much undermined. On any given day we probably take more trout from each of the other pools, but we always approach The Bend with caution and expectation, for great events are always possible there. All the trout in it are grand fish, and there is always one at least, the capture of which would make a season memorable.

To see these trout on a summer evening rising along the grassy bank in that quiet manner which scarcely betrays, and which many might fail to observe, makes us halt to test the cast and examine the fly. The water is absolutely calm and still; no kindly breeze assists, there is not even the eddy of a rise on which to lay the fly. Often we have failed to raise a trout, but sometimes we have succeeded, and we remember clearly the frantic rushing to and fro in the confined space, the repeated efforts to reach the recesses below the bank and, lastly, the culminating triumph. Seldom, if ever, have we scored more than one success, as the commotion caused by the captive effectually brings the rise to an end.

Beyond Wintercleuch the character of the stream completely changes, becoming rough and rapid, and more adapted to fishing with the creeper and worm, the dry-fly, though exceedingly deadly, being rather difficult to manipulate among the moss-covered stones that in all directions pierce the surface. Great takes of trout are sometimes taken in these high reaches with the worm when the floods are out, but we infinitely prefer the slowly moving pools and the gentle streams of the lower parts, where the fish are wary and well-fed, and where we can place the floating fly over the dimpling rise or into some difficult corner.

CHAPTER XX

ON DUNEATON WATER

OF all the tributaries of the Clyde none appeals to us quite so much as does the Duneaton, which, rising in Cairntable, on the borders of Ayrshire and Lanarkshire, falls after a long and varied course into the main river about a mile below the village of Abington. We find it difficult to give a satisfactory reason for our preference, which is none the less decided on that account. It is true that we have always had and can depend on having better sport on Daer Water, but we look upon that delightful stream not as a tributary but as the Clyde itself.

The Duneaton is a typical moorland stream, winding through a broad strath bounded by smooth rolling heights, slipping along between high grassy banks, chattering over gravelly shallows, gliding through long flats. No sound breaks the silence of the holms save the song of the sky-larks above, the bleating of the sheep, the lone far cry of the restless curlew, the music of the water, or the sudden shriek of triumphant reel.

It is a place where we may spend pleasantly and contentedly a long summer day with rod in hand and bag on back casting a questing fly as fancy directs, and every minute is one of enjoyment,

there is so much to do and see. The fresh breeze
of the moor cools us as, after the labour of an hour's
patient fishing, we lie deep in the grass gazing
skywards, watching for the mysterious birth of a
cloud, its growth and flight across the heavens;
we revel in the great distances. Here we do not
feel confined; here is freedom, here is space, and
it is only when a stronger breath of wind wafts to
us the gentle living voice of the water that we take
up the rod again.

There is no monotony; there can be none beside
flowing water, and least of all by a moorland stream.
Where shall we find more variety? Yet we may
easily destroy it all and thus miss the joys that
await.

We may crouch upon or even wriggle along a
high bank that we may lay, ourselves unseen, a
dainty fly over a glassy pool; we may have to
wade deep that our presence remain unsuspected
and cast a straight line to an intricate corner; we
may have to switch a fly round a projecting point
where the eye may not follow, and listen for the
sound that calls forth the strike; we may place
the fly on the grass, and with gentle touch of the
line bring it softly to the water where a fine trout
lies expectant; we must take every precaution,
if we would hope to lure the best of these lively
fish that have learned to fear the dangers that
surround them. And we may do none of these
things, but simply draw off a fair length of line
and blunder along the banks, scaring many trout
and raising few, and these few only innocent young
things. Not a tree shades the stream; here and
there a bush may dip a twig into the water, yet

difficulties thickly throng the angler's path, and the greatest of all is the wariness of the trout themselves.

An upstream breeze foretells that the creel will not be empty when the day is done, but, should the water be flowing full and slightly tinted from the brown peat of the moor, then sport should be fine ; and these are the conditions that we hope to meet on Duneaton. Such a happy combination has not yet been granted us, but we always keep a watchful eye on the weather and cloud-carry that we may hurry off whenever they send the signal. It has been sent and we have not answered, but that is unavoidable. We will not hesitate when it is possible to accept.

It may be difficult to retain confidence in a stream that always denies us its best, but a few trout here mean more than many taken in other waters, because the quest is made in such alluring environment. We never seem to learn the water thoroughly ; we cast diligently up a long pool, wind favouring and assisting the work of the rod, and suddenly we find the breeze strong against us. We feel our luck is out, that the wind has changed its direction, but the trouble is due only to a great bend in the stream ; and as likely as not in the rough water where the two winds meet we take the best trout of the day.

When we are out for a day on a small water we are accustomed to decide beforehand that we shall fish for a certain distance, and then return to try once more those streams and pools which have attracted most or given the greatest encouragement. That arrangement we find impossible to carry through on Duneaton, for the simple reason that, when we arrive at our destination, we look ahead and find such an enticing bit of water that we proceed at once to test its worth. When that has been thoroughly searched, we are in sight of another reach which seems superior to all that we have tried; it simply must be fished. And so on we go, up and ever farther up the stream, until we have covered so many miles that we have no time to search out our carefully marked places.

In such a miniature stream the angler might expect to find the trout correspondingly diminutive, but in that he will be agreeably surprised. Of course, there are many which must be carefully unhooked and returned to the water; but the average weight should be quite good except on very unsuitable days, half-pounders being fairly numerous, while there are a few grand specimens which will defy the most expert. The fortunate man may succeed when the efficient angler may fail, and may be lucky enough to encounter and land a trout that will make him proud of his skill. A schoolboy, fishing probably with worm in a flood, once made himself famous throughout the entire valley by the capture of a grand five-pounder.

In parts the stream is perfectly adapted for dry-fly fishing, long steep glides, gently moving flats, streamy water at the heads of pools occurring frequently and at regular intervals, so that the rod is seldom idle. From that it is not to be inferred that there are no barren parts; on the contrary they are fairly numerous, though not of great extent.

We cannot at the moment recall any stream

where, at comparatively small cost, very substantial improvement could more easily be effected. By a judicious disposition of small concrete blocks, or by the removal and redistribution of the larger stones, many places at present useless could easily be converted into excellent haunts of trout. An enthusiastic angler resident in the district could in a few hours accomplish much, but it never seems to occur to some people that such things are possible.

The last visit we paid to Duneaton Water was on the closing day of April, a day of gentle east wind, unclouded sky, and remarkably high temperature. Scarcely a single fly hatched out—the *Ephemeridæ* of spring like sterner conditions—and not one natural rise was seen throughout ; the water was at lowest summer level, the long green trailing weed was already conspicuous, and therefore results were meagre. We found it extremely difficult to fish, everything but the wind being against us, and yet we wandered contentedly enough for miles above the sequestered village of Crawfordjohn.

The trout were in their most aggravating humour, rising with great freedom but refraining from taking a firm hold, presumably bold enough at the outset but spluttering over the fly at the last moment. We must have raised more than fifty fish, from which we conclude that the stream is well stocked, but we succeeded in capturing only four trout, from a quarter to half a pound in weight, and a grayling somewhat heavier. The best trout put up a capital fight, struggling valiantly as we sought for a gravelly bank whereon to land it, but the grayling, not being in condition, allowed itself to be pulled about in any sort of fashion. Of course, there were in addition many immature trout that fastened securely, and bad luck was in constant attendance as we raised, ran, and lost a few trout better than any we secured.

In spite of all misfortunes, though our good day, the day of east wind and a black water, is still to come, we shall continue to have confidence in Duneaton Water. We have never gone expecting a great basket, for the conditions have never raised hopefulness of that within us, but a pleasant day, with a few beautifully marked trout, well fed, pink-fleshed, and full of sport, has always been ours, and what more can angler desire?

CHAPTER XXI

A DAY ON TWEED

THE long, long series of rainless weeks is ended. A night of heavy rain brings us to a morning calm and fresh, with just the slightest drizzle that sways not ,from the vertical. The air is warm, and we set out with greater hopes than we have had for many days. Surely to-day the flies will hatch and the trout rise as we would have them.

The sun-browned grass already is touched with green, the crab-apple trees by the road-side have shed a part of their too abundant crop, the trim hedgerows have lost their powdering ; but we are eager to be on the river, and much escapes our notice.

We strike the water beside a broad stream flowing with gently ruffled surface over a bed of small stones into a great still pool. It is little more than knee-deep throughout, a splendid bit for a floating fly, and we feel certain that many trout will have come up from the depths to welcome the flies that must arrive. With these we shall compete, and sometimes not in vain.

The shallowness of the stretch is itself a difficulty ; a wildly waving rod will be seen by these trout of extraordinary shyness, and at the first glimpse they will seek safety in flight. A long line would overcome the trouble only to introduce another, the impossibility of effective striking; an under-hand cast will make great events probable.

We note with satisfaction a belt of clear water between the gravelly edge and the befouled stones farther out; the river has risen an inch or two in answer to the rain, and that at least can do no harm, while it may enliven the trout. In the absence of any guide from the waters—possibly we are too impatient to look carefully for a sign—we attach a Black Midge to the tail of the cast, and a yard farther up we affix a dropper, a Blue Hen Spider, a tolerable imitation of several delicate yellow-bodied duns, or, rather, their spinners, and a deadly pattern it is on Tweed. Out we wade carefully and quietly through the calm, casting and lengthening line until we come within reach of the rippling water.

As we search the far edge, more to ensure that all parts of the apparatus are working smoothly together than with hopes of response, we happen to detect a break in the surface upstream. Without hesitation we lay the cast across the spot; the trout rolls over the dropper; the hook sinks home, and the captive, with a lightning dart, shoots straight past us to the pool, where we dare not follow, as lower down the gravel is loose and treacher-ous, sure to run away if we set foot upon it. More-over, there are ledges of rock, whose exact location we do not yet know; there on one side we have two or three inches of water over rock, and on the other the awful blackness of great depth.

We give the fish all the line it asks, freely at first,

but later with a grudge. We put on a little pressure and recover; the trout would fain remain in the current, when it is denied the still depths, but we insist as strongly as we may on it coming between us and the shore. It essays little rushes, finishing each with a high leap; then it begins an unpleasant tugging action which threatens the gossamer cast, but, bringing it round with the straining rod, we slowly let it fall back to the sunken net. Proudly we bear it to the bank, and transfer it to the bag, a bonnie trout well over half a pound, a modest but very suitable beginning to a grand day.

Feeling full of guile, we remove the Black Midge, and for it substitute a duplicate of the death-dealing fly. Out again more confident than ever we go, casting as fancy directs over the stream, waiting and watching for a promising mark over which to place the flies. In a minute or two it is granted. From where we stand it is a long cast and the water is here already lipping the waders, so that we dare not venture farther. Pulling off line we make the attempt and overshoot the mark with the tail-fly, but the dropper comes to the rescue, rectifying the mistake and falling softly and precisely on the spot. The trout rises again and is hooked. It seeks safety upstream in the fast-flowing water, but that part is still to fish and must not be disturbed. Who knows what it may yield? We turn the fish by a sidelong pull and force it to come down. It is even livelier than the first, though a trifle smaller, but in time it is our own. Taking no risks, we wade ashore and lay it beside the other, a bonnie brace indeed. We feel quite cheery; this is to be our great day on Tweed.

No sooner do we return to the fray than we are met with a terrific shower of rain, which drives us to the shelter of a leafy tree. With it comes the wind, a hurricane ; the rain ceases, but the blast continues. For long we fight against it, striving to fish ; it plays tricks with the cast, tossing it high in the air, slapping it on the water ; it bellies out the line, making the flies come down at speed, furrowing the water. No self-respecting trout would touch them ; one glance is sufficient to make them flee in alarm. We also are driven away to look for a " bieldy bit," as they say on Tweedside, and find none. Why were we not on the water an hour sooner ? We are filled with vain regrets ; our promising day is finished.

The gale soon absorbs the moisture from the gravel, and we lie down at the edge of a narrow pool, slightly less exposed than the rest, partly in hope that conditions will improve and partly to watch for a rising fish. If either event occurs we are ready to seize the rod and begin to live again.

Our eyes wander from the pool to the stones at our feet. Here is a nymph, a dark brown, squat, venomous-looking creature, mounting a semi-submerged stone ; it lies motionless for a time, and then something begins to take place. A head emerges ; the brown mass heaves a little and a yellow banded body is slowly dragged forth ; one after the other the crinkled wings are spread, and before us stands uncertain in the wind an Olive Dun, complete to its short antennæ and long flowing setæ. A handsome big fellow he is, as he stands clinging to the stone, quivering to the gale, drying his wings preparatory to a flight on this inauspicious day.

It is the same fly as we have frequently seen hatching out at all times of the day, even just before nightfall in July, when especially it forces the trout to take notice. It is likewise our old, esteemed friend the dark Blae and Yellow, with which we have done considerable execution on the loch and in the gloaming on the river.

In the interval of watching this specimen, several more have come to land. We are specially interested in one of them ; something goes amiss, for in spite of great effort it fails to extricate itself from its confining envelope, and presently all is still.

We are induced to look more closely into the water, and we perceive dozens of the nymphs crowding the upper surfaces of completely immersed stones. Apparently to them the call to the air has not yet come. We raise a hand to lift out a stone generously dotted with them, but at the first movement everyone of these curious creatures within two yards disappears as if by magic.

In a few minutes they are out again, as numerous as ever ; we flick a cigarette end into the water. As it floats along it seems to sweep the nymphs before it ; with amazing speed they bolt beneath the stones. Occasionally one will swim from the shelter of one stone to another ; the eye can easily follow it on such a journey, but fails completely to do so when the nymph darts from above to beneath a stone. We do not think that trout can capture many nymphs of the Olive Dun, except at that time when they are about to assume the winged state.

We pick a stone out of the water, and by rare good luck discover a nymph on the under side.

Being concealed it must have considered itself safe, but on being exposed to the air it becomes quite inert, allowing itself to be touched. We see, or imagine we see, the breathing processes vainly striving to extract the necessary element from the film of water. Gently to the stream we lower the stone, and the nymph, as soon as it feels the first touch of the water, vanishes.

On another stone is a small mass of white jelly; it shrinks and swells, lengthens and shortens, stands on one end and waves the other, and makes astonishing progress. We can distinguish no organs. This is something beyond our ken, but it has no appealing beauty to make us desire its closer acquaintance.

More interesting are the caddis-tubes, scores of them, all nicely decorated with minute pieces of gravel. We are inclined to think that there is some attempt at a colour design, the red, the white, the black and the rest being so well intermingled. They are absolutely still, for they have shut themselves behind a gravel grating to rest until the time comes for them to take wing. Now we see a tiny twig from a miniature tree, or so it appears at first, but a closer view shows it to consist of six short, smooth tubes, lightly attached together, and each of them contains a life which we do not allow our curiosity to destroy. What a wealth of life there is in Tweed!

Here beside us on the dry gravel, neglected until now, are two duns of exceeding minuteness and frailty, smaller than the autumn Iron-Blue, and that is small indeed. Yet they stand up to the wind, but refuse to venture a flight. Near them is another delicate creature, a pale Olive Dun, and here is another, a mammoth by comparison, of no remarkable feature except its size. Trout may have been rising in great style for the last hour, but we have been too busy to think of fish or fishing, and now it is time we were home.

CHAPTER XXII

EVENING ON TWEED

ALL day we have been inconsolable, tired of the stifling heat, stung by the glare of the dusty road, whiling away hours under the shade of drooping trees beside Tweed's fair river, now no more than a prattling stream. We might have summoned up sufficient energy to repair to Yarrow or Ettrick or the pleasant waters of the Cheviots, but these have well-nigh disappeared, and their trout, the few that have eluded the vigilant poacher, have resolved to remain in close hiding, until rain comes to restore their confidence and allay their fears.

The sun is slowly sinking to rest behind the triple crown of Eildon as we walk quietly down towards Mertoun Bridge, where begins a fine series of grand streams. On the way there is much to interrupt anticipation. A weasel lopes across the sun-browned grassy track, making an easy burden of a baby rabbit ; a cock pheasant rises heavily at our feet, and with a rattle of wings hastes to the shelter of the trees ; the grey heron, standing motionless in the dancing shallow, allows us to approach within a hundred yards and with a harsh protesting croak flaps away to roost. The gulls are screeching merrily—what a crowd of white wings !—wheeling left and right, now stooping, now standing on the air, dipping, soaring, hovering, climbing ; and every sudden change in direction means one fly the less for the trout.

We halt beside a glorious stream, deep and strong, foaming and heaving, but fading away to a flowing glide, and though we do not yet fully know its capabilities we feel sure that it will suffice for an hour at eventide. The water seems to flow more lazily than by day, with a slight suspicion of a misty haze across its foam patches, but nothing as yet disturbs the surface. The gulls have gone upstream, our presence no doubt the cause, and the flies are descending to the water.

As the last ray of sunlight fades away, and the red gold spreads even to the zenith touching the fleecy clouds to radiance, as at a given signal the first glad sound comes from the waving stream, and soon the calm water below is overspread with the daintiest rings. The old Tweedside angler beside us, one of a long line of famous fishers, remarks, " The stream is dimpled as with rain from the heavens."

The first and all-important problem is the determination of the species of fly that is occasioning this welcome and promising activity, and fortunately it is fairly easy of solution. All the way down we have been watching, and already have reached certain conclusions. No doubt the trout in the calm waters of the tail are sucking down spent spinners and tiny *diptera*, but there is something more substantial for the fish that throng the broken water, and these, to begin with at least, will have our attention.

A few dark duns have accommodatingly alighted upon us and our belongings, and to represent them a large-sized Greenwell Quill will suffice, but they are far outnumbered by myriads of fluttering sedges which crowd the air and water, almost obscuring the view. Not one of our stock of sedges corresponds closely enough to the natural insect to deceive the extremely wary trout of Tweed. Despair and disappointment are about to fall upon us, when luckily we chance to remember our cherished collection of Rough Olives, which are a correct representation, save in one particular, viz. shape. By dint of some coaxing and gentle pulling the upright wings of this deadly counterfeit are induced to droop from their erect position and lie low over the hook ; and now we possess in lieu of a member of the *Ephemeridæ* a most amazingly faithful likeness of the sedge-fly, which is proving so acceptable to the trout. In great glee we affix it to the tail of the cast, leaving the Greenwell for the dropper, the place of secondary importance, the duns being most decidedly in the minority. Carefully we anoint the line and the cast, oil the flies, and cheerfully and confidently we wade out to search the fast-flowing broken stream, prepared to cover a rise whenever the opportunity is given, but determined to lay the flies on the water as often as possible.

At the union of a twin ripple behind a submerged rock a trout breaks water, just our distance, and lightly above it falls the converted Olive ; the fish refuses. We pull off a yard of line, and present the Greenwell to its notice. The rise, the strike, and the rush through the stream to the opposite

bank seem simultaneous; in fact, we can scarcely
believe that the trout leaping high in air above
the calm water beyond the rush is ours. Neither
it is; it was, but the leap and the consequent
easing of the strain have given it a chance to eject
the hook, probably merely resting on and not
penetrating some hard part of the mouth—a chance
that a hooked fish never omits to accept. Sadly
we recover line and cast, and prepare the flies
once more for their work. The quick answer,
though it comes to naught, is promising enough.

There seems to be a lull in the rise, and we almost
fear that it is about to end just after it began;
but we proceed quietly upwards, gently casting
at a venture to no place in particular, for one spot
seems as likely as another, when, without the
slightest warning, the Greenwell vanishes from
sight. We are given the same tactics as before
to answer; but the hook this time has secured
a firm hold and, keeping our eyes on the plunging, pulling trout, we manœuvre cautiously into
a position offering good footing, as well as deep
water in which to use the net. That instrument
is not required yet awhile, for it is a trout of Tweed
we have to deal with, an active plucky fighter
that knows as much of the art of escaping as it
does of the angler's wiles. Out from the rush
it must come at all costs, and we refuse to be persuaded to follow it downstream, therefore we put
on all the strain the 4x gut will permit, and steer
it into the calm water beside us. The creel duly
receives the first trophy of the evening.

A heavy trout rises ahead, and over it we place
without loss of a moment the sedge-fly; up it

comes again with resounding splash, but the answering strike meets no resistance. How narrowly
have we missed triumph!

Out across the stream we throw again; a gleam
of silver pierces the failing light, and we hook a
dancing fish which feels light on the rod, yet struggles
gamely. Impatiently we pull it to the net, as
we see it is but a lively smolt, about eight inches
in length, an exact facsimile in miniature of a
salmon; tenderly we unhook it and carefully
lay it in the water; it lies on its side exhausted
for a while, but by and by it recovers and disappears. How different, we think, is its behaviour
from that of a trout of similar size, which would
have been away with a lightning dart the moment
it touched the water! We believe that we
could, without breaking the law, have retained it,
but who would be guilty of slaughtering such
innocents?

The Rough Olive now comes into its own, raising, hooking, and holding in rapid succession three
magnificent trout, which provide splendid sport,
offering a vigorous resistance before they acknowledge defeat. Two of them reach nearly three-
quarters of a pound each, and Tweed trout of
that size, taken in a strong stream on fine tackle,
would greatly surprise any angler who has not
had any experience of the river. We marvel
principally at the fact that these fish were rising
in the roughest water at the neck, where we might
not have thought of placing a floating fly, after
sunset especially, had rises to the natural fly not
invited us to do so.

To hook such trout requires the greatest rapidity

of casting and the use of an absolutely dry fly, and demands that the rod be in the striking position from the instant the lure alights upon the water ; a short, tight line likewise contributes materially to success, but there is not the slightest doubt that the fish must be rising with deadly intent, and not merely amusing themselves, if any success at all is to be obtained.

Now the small sedges pass away, and in their place arrives a much larger variety whose presence we are soon made aware of by a tickling sensation on hands, face and neck. Obeying the sign we replace the cast with one of stouter build —larger flies demand heavier gut—and to it we attach two specimens of the Cinnamon Sedge. These are not very satisfactory imitations of the particular fly on the water, but it is the best we can do until we become possessed of patterns of the Auld Hen, a famous Tweed night fly. That represents a large caddis- or sedge-fly which appears in June and July just as darkness falls ; it is usually fished wet and downstream, but we prefer that it should float on the surface as the living creature does.

It is rather early yet for the trout to take this pat· tern freely, but, not knowing the moment the late rise may begin, we start once more at the bottom of the stream and fish up. Without the least encouragement we almost complete the stretch, and are on the point of deciding that no sport remains for us when a trout rises some distance downstream. Carefully gauging the length of line required, we lay the flies on the track, reaching out and lowering the rod as the line straightens out. The trout comes up and makes no mistake in aim, but it proves a fatal mistake nevertheless. The Cinnamon Sedge has shown itself worthy of a trial.

The light has gone, and no longer can we see our flies on the water. We reel up and set out for home, supremely contented with our basket of five excellent trout, the product of less than an hour's fishing. Moreover, we have clearly seen them rising to accept our fly, and been able to enjoy to the full their fighting power; we have taken no mean advantage of them by fishing for them under cover of night or with coarse tackle. Certainly the take compares very badly with what is sometimes obtainable even in the same time, but it is infinitely better than we have had.

CHAPTER XXIII

AMONG THE HILLS

AGAIN we are beside the old familiar river. We know every stone and corner, every pool and stream, the haunts of the best trout, the barren parts and the fruitful stretches. There are places that we hurry past, fishing carelessly or missing altogether, but there are others which we linger over, expecting something to happen at every cast.

We enjoy a first visit either to loch or river. There is so much to discover, so much experimenting to find the killing fly; the water is all to learn, for it certainly has peculiarities of its own which distinguish it from all others; the trout, too, may be large or small, bold or wary, quick or slow in the rise, sullen or lively in the fight, and a first day is never so successful as it might be.

We like none the less the well-known stream. We know what to expect, though we may expect what never comes. Should we fish up a stretch without response we know that ahead lies a pool that never fails; it always is farther and farther up, and if by the end of the day we have not reached it, still hope has carried us ever onward, and the pleasures of anticipation are probably the sweetest.

Memories of the past crowd upon us; great events may take place where they have before occurred; where a fine trout fell to the lure, a worthy successor may lie in wait; the monarch of the pool, which once we raised and lost, may rise again, and we tremble with excitement as we approach the well-remembered spot.

We recall conversations with other anglers, and hear again their accounts of wonderful days of the long ago, when trout were not expert entomologists, and rivers ran full and undefiled throughout the year, when pollution was unheard of and the dry-fly unnecessary. Despair may readily overtake the angler on an unfamiliar river; but on a favourite stream hopefulness cannot altogether leave him.

Still we have disquieting thoughts to-day. While the river is in grand order, very clear but of fine volume, with every stone washed bright by the flood of a week ago, yet that is the only favourable condition. It is a day of late August, dull, sultry, and heavy; thundery clouds hang low over the hills; across the valley stretches a thick rain-curtain, and down towards us it comes on the wings of the light South-west wind. We shall have to cast against the breeze, a prospect none too attractive.

Almost before it reaches us the rain vanishes, the sun pours through a cleft in the clouds, and we begin to feel somewhat cheery as we stand fitting up the rod on the gravel beside the first stream. Not a fly sails the wave or flutters past in the breeze; not a rise disturbs the quiet pool or the sparkling stream. We have only two hours at our disposal, and therefore can wait for neither

hatch nor rise ; difficulty attends the selection
of a fly, but memory of past successes decides in
favour of the Rough Olive for the tail, and the
dropper we elect to reserve for experimental purposes.   The first choice for that position is the Greenwell Quill. These are two of the finest patterns
ever made, and the presence of either on the cast
gives the confidence necessary.

Like all anglers, we have our notions and fads,
and one of these is now in evidence. We confess
that only when a good healthy rise is in progress
do we select a new fly, that, when there is little or
no activity amongst the trout, we submit for their
inspection a fly that has already seen much service
and accounted for several fish. After much experience day after day on the same river we have been
forced to the conclusion that a well-used fly, provided that it is complete in every detail, is infinitely
more effective than a brand new specimen that has
never been laid upon the water.   There is a great
temptation to use one, so bright in all its glory of
freshness, so attractive to angler's eye, but the trout
require something more than beauty.

After a fly has been dragged under water a few
times, whisked backwards and forwards through
the air, removed from the mouths of two or three
trout, the wings divide out more or less into their
separate fibres, and thus acquire a transparency
which is more natural than a heavy opacity. We
are convinced that the trout are less suspicious of
such a lure, though when well on the rise they will
readily accept a fly out on its maiden voyage.
Therein, too, we believe, lies the deadliness of the
hackled pattern, in which the wing is only suggested.

Some anglers use this type exclusively, but we obtain, or imagine we obtain, the best sport by using hackled flies on calm or gently-flowing water and the winged varieties on the rougher streams.

Preparations completed, we fish carefully up the long stream right in the teeth of the freshening wind. At times the cast flies out beautifully straight, and lightly enough, it seems to us, to bring up a trout ; now and then an error in timing causes it to be blown back, but the result is always the same. Not a fish honours us with the slightest attention, so far as we can see, and we begin to wonder if the river has been completely cleaned out.

This is a really fine stream, which used to yield good sport ; in fact, we do not remember drawing it blank, and we persevere. Almost at the top the Olive raises and hooks a trout, but it is undersized and is returned. As soon as the line is lengthened out again the same fly brings up another, a bright little fellow rather less than a quarter, but good enough for a start on this inauspicious day.

Now we have a stroke of luck. The wind suddenly fades away altogether, and almost immediately comes again, but out of the North-west. It blows with just the right strength directly against the stream, and we hail the change with delight. Such good fortune does not often follow us, and we hurry on to a favourite flat, a beautiful stretch with a fine glide deep and slow down the far side. An eddy here and there breaks its smooth expanse, betraying the existence of a current ; the bank is built up with stones and branches, so that there is provided adequate shelter for many trout, while the glide affords them a happy hunting-ground.

In answer to the invitation of the quiet water we
substitute a Black Spider for the Greenwell, but
we allow the lucky Olive to remain. Success is
immediate ; a good trout, dark in colour but lively
enough, makes the fatal mistake, and the Olive
scores another victory. Almost as soon as we
could desire a fine golden trout of slightly larger
size falls a victim to the same pattern.

Then follows a succession of rises missed ; the
small fish, of course, take a firm hold, but their
larger brethren annoy us. We shorten line, we
hasten the strike, we cast straight up in front ; but,
in spite of all, the irritation continues, and we move
onwards to the next pool, pleased to learn that so
many trout have escaped the snares of poachers.

This has never been a favourite of ours, but hence-
forth it will be, and we shall hereafter fish it with
the greatest care and attention. Similar in appearance to the last, it is rather faster and more shallow,
and one would not expect it to be the home of any
but the smaller trout. Gradually upwards we go,
searching only the centre of the waving current.
Beneath the Olive we see the gleam of a golden
flank. We lift gently to the strike, the hook sinks
home, the rod curves to a strong resistance, and
the trout makes one long, fierce, thrilling rush right
into the foaming neck.

Already we know we have something beyond
the usual to deal with, and we seek the dry gravel.
The fish comes down with a glorious, stirring, yet
dangerous dart through the shallows, across to the
depths and secret difficulties of the high bank,
downstream with heavy pull on the line, then it
rests at the surface as if to recover breath, and we

rejoice to see a great trout. Wading out, recovering line as we go, we advance the net, but at sight of it the captive awakes and dives below, the reel screaming merrily the while. It makes a bold endeavour to plunge into an island of weed, but is prevented; then into another farther down, but we keep on all the strain the 5x gut permits, and succeed in steering it past these danger zones. Full fifty yards from where we hooked it we take command and lead it unprotesting to the net.

A more rousing fight we have seldom had. We lay the superb trout, exactly $1\frac{1}{2}$ lb. in weight, upon the grass, and stand over it in admiration. It is the finest specimen we have ever taken from the river. Throughout the season it has seen many hundreds of flies and has ignored them all; it has baffled dozens of anglers; it has eluded the poacher's net, and at last it has succumbed before the deadly Rough Olive.

Filled with a great contentment we carry on, caring little whether we fish or not, but now another Olive takes the place of the Black Spider. The time passes quickly and pleasantly among the hills, and now and then the net reaches out to embrace another victim. Soon we halt and arrange on the grass beside the favoured pool eleven beautiful trout, headed by the great trophy, followed by two or three half-pounders, and so through a tapering series to the first fish of the day.

CHAPTER XXIV

UP THE RIVER

GONE are the brimming pools and the broad swelling streams of the merry springtime, the cool fresh breeze, the fleet of duns, the rise of deadly intent, and the contented creel. Here a few weeks ago we almost feared to wade, so deep and strong was the full-flowing current, and now it is but a stone-strewn stretch of thin, lifeless water. Pools there are still, no doubt, but they are far apart and few, and when after painful toil under the heat we reach one, we find it dull, stagnant, hopeless.

For many days the sun has ridden unchallenged across the heavens ; by day not the tiniest wisp of cloud relieves the monotonous expanse of everlasting blue ; at eventide a few filmy streaks collect in the West awaiting in their vanity to be adorned with golden brilliancy, but before the dawning they melt away, and we are left with but a memory of their glory. The promise given of most necessary help is withdrawn, and we awake to another day of sun and calm.

The terrified trout have fled their accustomed haunts to search out refreshing deeps under the rushing white force of a steep, stony stream, sadly attenuated though it be, among the rocks of a still, dead pool, beneath a hollowed bank, within the mazy recesses of tangled roots, and from none of these retreats will they be tempted by any lure save that of the foaming flood which will (but it is yet afar off) bring with it life and liveliness. We look across the broad flat and see as through a sheet of glass clearly to the farthest corner, but not a single fish can we detect, if we except a shoal or two of happy minnows, basking, questing, darting, splashing, now without an enemy. Our most careful efforts are vain, our daintiest flies are useless, ignored absolutely, as are the few living insects that ride the stream.

At sundown and for perhaps an hour or more thereafter, a few trout dare to leave their hiding-places in the depths of the pool and venture into the smooth thin water at the tail or the edges of the entering stream. Even in the late hours only a slight reward is given to patient and careful effort ; it was not always so, but then never was there such a drought, rocks, whose existence was suspected by a faint rippling wave on the surface, now standing clearly exposed. Those adventurous trout rejoice to annoy us by rising to, taking, and rejecting all in the same second our choicest spinner. The water here is unfriendly, unkind by day ; in the late evening the reward is poor return for the sacrifice involved and the irritation experienced. We must fish. Let us away up the river.

Off we go thirty miles up the river, where it is a cheery streamlet, flowing along merrily in a narrower channel between higher banks, so fast that only here and there is a stone befouled by yellow and green unloveliness. We are on the open moor, and though the sun burns here quite as brightly as it does away down beside the cities of the plain, the breeze is sweeter, stronger, and there is a finer, cooler draught sweeping down the glens.

The trout are wary enough, but food is not too plentiful; they do not like this unceasing sunshine any more than we, and yet they dare not allow many flies or nymphs or beetles to pass unheeded. They have to reach some day the same form as their brethren of the lower reaches, and they have less time for the purpose as well as smaller stores to draw upon. Therefore there are no lazy days, no wasted opportunities in the life of the trout in a swift moorland stream; there are many hard days of hunger in the winter that must come, no matter how cloudless skies may be now.

Sunshine assists us to combat their craftiness, for it plays upon the glinting gravel and the ripple, giving the lure many points of light, obscuring its deficiencies, and helping to make our approach more difficult of detection. We welcome all the assistance we can get when waters are at their lowest recorded level.

The river here in these green uplands would usually be designated a typical Scottish wet-fly water, fast and free, fretting among boulders, sliding down a steep glide, gurgling in a little pot, slipping along a broad pool, tumbling over a rocky ledge, singing over a gravelly shallow. We say it is an ideal dry-fly water, for so we find it, and the simple reason is that in summer at least, when we know it, the floating-fly utterly vanquishes the sunken variety.

There are places, the swiftest streams, for example, where a little pink worm will easily prove itself superior to either, while in some of the deep necks a natural minnow neatly spun by a carefully concealed angler will bring to close inspection trout that would seldom if ever condescend to take anything less substantial. We have tried all lures many a time, and in summer the longest continued spells of fishing, the least amount of walking, and the maximum of sport are undoubtedly the results of using the floating fly.

To produce conviction on the point no trial is necessary. It will be sufficient to watch the manipulators of other lures at work. They would all without exception pass over as impossible the long still stretches of the pools—and such form a large proportion of the water available—confining their attentions solely to the streams and necks. The dry-fly man finds trout in places which others ignore, as well as in what they regard as their most fruitful hunting grounds. A high upstream wind would help all, but it would certainly not bring all to the same level.

The angler who objects to fishing with the dry-fly unless he can find a rise to cover will not be happy here, for he might wander by the banks for a week or more without receiving one solitary direct invitation to test his skill in the accurate, delicate placing of a fly. Even if he did observe a trout rising, it is extremely improbable that he could rigidly adhere to his principles which lay down that he must present for the acceptance of the fish an artificial representation of the fly that has just met its fate.

The unfortunate insect may have been the sole survivor of its race, or a member of a species not classified or even before observed : the trout may have made a mistake, rising to a grass seed or a piece of straw, and it is quite prepared to attempt the next thing that comes along. We have had many an offer to the knot which attaches cast to line, but it is the fly we next put over the rise, not always unsuccessfully. We have heard of such anglers, though we have never seen one. If there should really be such a one, he should overcome his objections and learn the joys of a day on the burn amongst the hills.

It may be true, as has often been stated, that trout will not feed freely on any species of fly until they have become accustomed to its presence, but it certainly does not apply to the smaller mountain streams, for if it did then the unhappy trout would never know the flavour of any fly. Trout that inhabit rapid water, where food is not too abundant, sample first and reflect afterwards ; anything moving down the stream may be good to eat. Their brethren of the placid river may inspect from safe range and then either reject or accept according to their conclusions ; they can afford to be saucy, one fly more or less is of little moment.

We open the campaign on a long, narrow pool, overhung on one side by a high grassy bank, very deep and still at the tail, with a fine twisting stream at the neck. We entrust our fortunes to a single fly, for in such a stream it is usually necessary to aim at a very minute target, a little run among moss-covered stones, an eddy behind a rock, and whatever accuracy is attained may often be immediately converted into miserable failure by the presence of a second fly exerting its evil influence on the well-delivered cast. For the same reason we use the shortest of lines and instead reach the desired goal by cautious approach, crouching behind a boulder or tuft of grass or even by wading if no cover is available. A long line floating on the surface, as it is almost certain to be moving at a rate different from that of the fly, makes effective striking impossible, while it likewise makes a rise extremely improbable by reason of its retarding or accelerating effect on the lure.

The lightest of summer zephyrs fails to disturb the calm surface, but still we think it not unlikely that a willing trout awaits under the shadow of the bank. For the occasion we select a little Greenwell Quill, though we would be equally contented to test the seductive powers of a Black Spider. With an underhand cast we flick the fly lightly to the very edge, but there is not an answering dimple throughout the entire journey up the pool.

Now we arrive at the entering stream; a stone projecting above the surface breaks it into two portions just where it comes sweeping round its final bend. We search both branches in turn, but without result, and then stop to study how we shall lay the fly beyond the stone.

It is a difficult cast; not an inch of line must touch the water, the fly has only a second in which to float free and naturally, but if a trout is at home, that length of time will suffice. Risking everything, even the loss of the whole stream, we place the fly on the grassy bank; the cast hangs clear above the water; by hand we give a gentle twitch to the line; good luck attends and the fly falls softly to its goal. At the same moment, all unsuspecting, a trout rises to meet it and takes it down. The captive strives to rush up the stream, but that we cannot allow, for we have still use for that curving, wavy water, and we force it to come down to the deeps where we lead it on to the gravel—a plump little trout of the moorland. Back we go to fish out the stream and secure another but smaller victim.

Soon we reach a little pool, a basin hewn from the rock it seems to be, but it is floored with fine gravel, while here and there dimly show larger stones, which we are sure will shelter some fair trout. Into the white foam of the rush we place the fly; it floats, but the hissing water pulling on the cast would, if it had time, drag it beneath. Before that happens, however, a golden trout, the monarch of the pool, has launched itself upon it. There ensues a hurry to and fro, a sharp conflict all over the pool; so quick and unexpected are the movements of the trout that the eye is unable to keep pace with it; but the hook does, and in time we find a creek whither we lead the plucky fighter.

And so gradually we work our way upstream among the rocks, over the grassy hummocks, picking up a fish now and then, until the time comes for the return. It has been a strenuous day of incessant casting, fine practice in the art of accurate delivery, and we have taken trout or tried to take them from almost every conceivable variety of water; we have been alone in the solitudes and, while the trout reposing in the creel are smaller than the broad river could give if it would, they afford us infinite satisfaction and help us to forget the poor days under the merciless sun.

CHAPTER XXV

THE DRY-FLY FAILS

I T had been a day of intense heat, unclouded sky, and but an occasional feeble breath of wind; merely to move about was laborious, to fish the loch with expectation demanded such faith as is not possessed by even an angler. Absolutely hopeless was the outlook; not a trout would rise in such a day, but the more generous evening was still to come, and we waited patiently, contriving even at times to become cheerful.

The loch, on which we were privileged to fish, is a small sheet, but as good as it is small. We had been told that it held trout of excellent size and quality and, in addition, an overwhelming supply of weeds. The first glimpse of it, as we reached the shores on a June evening, was sufficient to convince us that in the latter respect report was very accurate, while the conditions pointed to the impossibility of being able to arrive at conclusions regarding the trout. Still it was pleasant to be in such a place, the little loch with its protecting belts of trees, its little wooded islet, its bays studded with water-lilies, its marshy headlands a mass of flowering bog-bean, forming a beautiful picture on which the eye rejoiced to rest.

The water lay calm and still save where a swan

glided lonely about—his ancient mate was on the island seriously occupied imagining a vain thing— and playful coots indulged in their merry antics. Even the topmost twigs of the trees remained motionless, and long clean-cut shadows were thrown across the loch. The absence of wind helped to make more clear the unfortunate state of the water ; great patches of weed were dotted all over the surface, and to them clung foul, decaying green accumulations, of which smaller clumps, not yet having found an anchorage, floated all around.

We had therefore little cause to become filled with enthusiasm. Still in the fading light trout sometimes, generally in fact, prove not altogether indifferent to our offerings. We always hope for the best, and we had come to fish. Consequently it was useless to remain idle on the bank. We mounted the rods, boarded the boat, and the keeper pushed off. Now and then a slight zephyr came out of the East, raising a tiny ripple, but no sooner it came than it died away. Drifting being impracticable, the boat was worked backwards and forwards, gradually approaching ever nearer to what from a distance appeared to be an impenetrable maze of weeds.

Occasionally a fish would rise in half-hearted fashion, though never within casting distance ; the sun still blazed, and we wearied for its setting ; the floating fly seemed to be the lure that would produce a rise, but it entirely failed. It was evident that there had been a strong hatch of the pale watery dun earlier in the day, as now the surface was most liberally besprinkled with the spent spinners lying motionless with outspread wings. Here was a feast

prepared, and yet, save for a few negligible instances,
it was being ignored ; we hoped that acceptance of
the minute dainties would come later, or, better
still, that a swarm of sedges would arrive and be
received with greater favour by the trout.

The bow-rod diligently searches the waters with
a quartette of tiny doubles, while we from the stern
strive to lay a floater neatly on a likely spot, or
with great effort struggle to reach some far-off
promising mark. An hour passes, uneventful if
we except a few offers made without serious intent,
and yet the feeling persists that reward may come
at any moment. It is somewhat dreary fishing
blindly in a calm, almost as monotonous as doing
nothing, and several times we are on the point of
deciding to suspend operations, when a trout comes
up to inspect. So the attention never wanders
far.

Surely that is a boil in the vicinity of the sunken
lures. We are not mistaken. The strike is administered in time and with judicious strength, and
the shriek of the reel announces that at last a fly
has found a victim. Before the long line can be
recovered, the trout dives for the nearest weed bed
and succeeds in reaching it, but obedient to the
steady, unceasing strain it is forced to come out
into more open water. As the fish tears off across
the bows, the cast shows above the surface ; three
of the flies are decorated with green sliminess ; but
the fourth is fast in a noble trout. The fight is long
and for a time uncertain, but at length the net is
called for. The spell of patient toil is rewarded at
last ; a trout of $1\frac{1}{4}$ lb. is able to produce forgetfulness.

This success may be the signal for the commencement of a glorious time, but instead not a single rise is forthcoming, and all the while the sun sinks slowly down. At last it falls beneath the horizon, but still the afterglow is too brilliant to gaze upon. The breeze, never more than a breath, falls likewise, and a silence betokening great events fills the air. A wary old mallard leads her brood from their downy nest to the shore and out among the weeds. Will the trout also gather for the feast awaiting them ?

From a little bay the answer comes. A great trout breaks the surface in a mighty swirl and, excited, we hasten to cover it. But what is this ? The trout does not trouble to go down again ; it ploughs through the water scooping up the spinners, gulping them down by the dozen, lashing its corner of the loch to a wave. We endeavour to put the flies not over it but in front of its tortuous path, but it is all in vain. Close at hand others follow the example, and our fly, taken from one mark to another, laid on the route indicated as delicately as possible, is absolutely unheeded, as if it were not there.

Which is the greater trial : to cast at random nowhere in particular and receive no response, or to reach with accuracy and neatness a clearly defined target and be ignored ? The results are identical ; we are defeated. The trout continue to rise, but never by any chance do they select our artificial.

We actually see two trout starting out from different points and arriving at the same destination ; for a time there are signs of a weighty conflict, and then the waters fall calm again. We move onwards to other creeks and bays amongst the weeds, where we undergo the same tortures and achieve the same results.

By and by the light fades, a less impotent breeze springs up, caddis-flies of more substantial frame appear, not in countless thousands but a few from time to time, and divert the attention of the trout from the irritating spinners. Off the stern one of these sedges disappears from view, and we, having now discarded the futile floater in favour of the wet-fly, bring the cast across the wavelets over the mark. There is a lunge at the Woodcock and Yellow; we strike, and at last, after nearly three hours of complete failure, we feel that we have hit something. The thought of the first capture bids us be careful, but caution is needless, the fish being only a little fellow of six ounces, plucky and lively enough and extremely welcome, even though we were but a short time ago laying our flies in the track of cruising three-pounders.

The line and flies must be cleared from the omnipresent weed, a slight tangle caused by the contortions of the trout must be straightened out —occupations not too easy in the semi-darkness— before we may tempt fortune again. Almost at the first cast the reel screams out its message ; the resistance informs that we have encountered a worthier foe, but the cast is sound, and we refuse to grant much liberty, as the many obstructions in the way might readily bring disaster. We hold the fish on a tight, short line as much as we dare, or perhaps rather more than we should, but all ends well. The trout is a finely proportioned specimen, just failing to reach a pound, but well worthy of the long-sustained effort under conditions so difficult.

This late rise is of the shortest duration, only a few minutes altogether, and the bow-rod unfortunately does not get a single opportunity of aiming at a mark within his allotted area. So luck swings round in fishing as in other things.

Now it is as dark as a June night of unclouded sky can be ; the air is quite chilly, seeming to promise a touch of frost on the uplands, but no mist is wafted over the waters, which remain silent and undisturbed. The keeper, even more anxious than we are ourselves, spares himself no pains, rowing us up to the very choicest corners where good fish are wont to feed, and encourages us by every means in his power to keep the flies on the water. His efforts and ours are of no further avail, and we reluctantly conclude that our basket of three trout must suffice.

We set a course for the boathouse not too contentedly, we confess, for the diminutive water can, when conditions permit, afford magnificent sport. During the evening we have seen several huge trout dining riotously on flies and, if we remain, we may yet lure one of them. Still we must leave, but we shall return in another season, when the trees are budding, and before the weeds have had time to reach the surface and curtail the fishing area so much.

Often indeed is the angler disappointed, and yet, no matter how frequently he is subjected to adverse weather conditions, or received with complete indifference by the trout, or harassed with misfortune, he remains optimistic through it all, persuading himself that next time all will be as favourable as he could desire, and that he will have his great day.

CHAPTER XXVI

A FAVOURITE LOCH

WHILE it undoubtedly gives us great pleasure to be afloat on the waters of some unknown loch, a pleasure born of a love for experimenting with different types and sizes of flies, for studying the configuration of the shores and deducing therefrom the nature of what lies hidden beneath the surface, we are equally keen to revisit familiar haunts, scenes of past triumphs.

Of course speculation and experiment can never be entirely absent from a day's fishing, for the trout in a loch vary their moods from day to day and seldom exhibit the same behaviour, although conditions may be to all appearance precisely similar, but it is a considerable advantage to be able to commence operations armed with some previous knowledge ; without hesitation we select a bay and drift across it full of hope, well knowing that, if the fish are in the humour which most strongly appeals to us, we shall be amply rewarded. We know the flies most in favour; and, moreover, we can with confidence predict the species which will ride the wave if wind and weather are such as are likely to tempt them forth.

Continually we are reminded of the past ; off that low-lying ledge of rock we hooked and after a fight of long-doubtful issue landed our best fish for many a year ; on that drift we took on one great day the record basket of the season ; down yonder bed of swaying reeds once we on a calm windless evening had one memorable hour after sundown, when the trout found the seductive floating fly completely irresistible.

With such thoughts crowding upon us we stand impatiently by the shore of Loch Dochart, waiting for the completion of the preparations necessary before we may embark. We seem to be fortunate in the weather, for the sun, long absent, promises to shine through at intervals, and a fair breeze from the West raises a good fishing ripple, and yet we dare not allow ourselves to become too sanguine of success. Autumn is fast approaching, while still snow gleams white on Ben More, conclusive evidence of the untoward conditions which have prevailed during the season. The long-continued rains confer one benefit in that the too abundant weeds are well covered, and consequently the extent of fishing area is greatly increased.

It is not until we row out that we realise to what degree the loch has lately been flooded ; the reeds show that they have been entirely submerged, and now the points, projecting a foot or more, display an incrustation of fine dry mud, from which we deduce that the rise in the water had been very sudden and its subsidence equally rapid.

We decide to try first the lagoon at the mouth of the river Fillan, a usually fruitful part characterised by deep water bordered by sandy shallows, on which fish love to rest. It was formerly, and most probably still is, tenanted by trout of grand average weight, but only one condescends to accept our lures, and we change to that belt which lies between the Castle Island and the south shore.

We arrive there in time to welcome the fore-runners of a hatch of Medium Olives, for which Loch Dochart is justly famed, and which it seldom fails to produce. A resounding splash here and there shows that the trout are as pleased to see them as we are, and we lay whenever possible our floating representation where a worthy trout is found to be waiting. For a time the sport is sufficiently fast and furious, and the quality of the fish coming aboard quite good enough to satisfy the most exacting of anglers, but there is one require-ment above all that must be possessed if a rise is to terminate in a kill; and that is ability to strike quickly.

We have never in all our wanderings encountered trout which are so quick in their movements as are those of Loch Dochart; the speed with which they can accept and then reject a fly is astonishing, so that the answering strike must be very quick indeed. After they are hooked they show an equal agility in enveloping themselves in weeds, unless they are held firmly and worked smartly into the net.

To be successful with these nimble trout a vigilant, ever-watchful eye is necessary, especially when the lure employed is the floating fly, for they, the larger fish in particular, can and do frequently suck it down almost without betraying the fact. The sudden disappearance of the fly is all that indicates the event, and should the attention waver for an instant the longed-for opportunity of dealing with a fish may be gone for ever.

Up to the present we have been doing so well that we complain bitterly when we are compelled to change our methods and resort to the wet-fly. The reason is that the wind has risen to a gale, which drives the boat at great pace before it, so that we cannot keep our line and flies floating to our satisfaction. The hatch, however, continues as merrily as ever, a matter for surprise in this cold windy weather, and swallows and trout alike are feasting to their hearts' content. It is therefore no wonder that we are annoyed at being forced to diminish our chances of sport, however unavoidable the change of lure may be.

Now we are on the long drift between the island and the out-flowing river, sheltered slightly from the gale, and by keeping the rod point low and dragging the flies across the path of the boat we manage to circumvent the gusts. Sport is being fairly well maintained, the credit of which belongs partly to the willingness of the trout themselves, perhaps also partly to the tactics employed, but chiefly to the efficiency of the boatman, whose services we are decidedly fortunate to secure.

His knowledge of the loch is complete; he lets slip no opportunity of putting us within reach of a rising trout, which is accomplished neatly and quickly by a deft touch of an oar; he shows his satisfaction when his and our united efforts result in a capture, but the gale prevents him showing the finer points of his skill. In a gentle breeze he would as of yore work the boat in and out the edge of the reeds, the floating Olive would vanish from sight, and the air would be filled with the music of the reel. Still in the adverse conditions he works

wonders, and the creel begins to bear witness to
the fact.

Now with every sense alert we approach expect-
antly the most critical point, the entrance to the
river.   There the wise, old, wary trout are gathered
together waiting for what the wind and the wave
and the current will bring, and there many of them
have in past days fallen to our fly.   To-day there is
no exception to the rule, for the instant the tail-fly
alights it is seized, and a fine fish wildly leaps in a
vain endeavour to shake free the piercing hook.
We have some anxious moments before it is safely
in the boat, but then we see that it is the finest
trout of the day, a beauty in every respect.

All too soon the day passes, and we seek the shore
again, there to arrange but first admire our thoroughly satisfactory basket of twenty-five lovely
trout.   What more could anyone desire, a day in
the fresh, keen air amid the picturesque surroundings of Loch Dochart, a fair measure of sport, and a
dish of really handsome trout to distribute among
one's friends ?   Surely that is enough to please and
satisfy anyone, and yet the results are mediocre and
serve only to indicate what great sport could be
obtained on a favourable day.

Loch Dochart stands pre-eminently our first
favourite among lochs, and our reasons for putting
it in this high position are many and varied. · It is
easily reached ; a blank day on it is unthinkable,
except when a terrific storm makes it impossible to
launch or manage a boat ; the trout are of excellent
quality, full of sport, numerous and of good average
size ; boats and capable men are usually if not always
available ; the loch itself is generally acknowledged

to be of surpassing beauty. We have frequently heard anglers complain that the loch is scarcely worth visiting, and the reason they give is that the trout are diminutive specimens, but they would in all likelihood be readily persuaded to alter their opinions if they would take pains to develop an increased readiness in responding to a rise, for we confidently assert that it will be only on an extremely bad fishing day that the fish basketed will average less than one-third of a pound.

Of course it must be carefully pointed out that the most effective lure there is without doubt the floating fly, the truth of which statement will be rendered apparent to anyone who cares to use his powers of observation. On no loch known to us is there such a superabundance of insect life, consisting, too, principally of *Ephemeridæ*; almost every day in the season they are in evidence, and never have we seen a hatch unaccompanied by a corresponding activity on the part of the trout. This fact alone is sufficient inducement to us to visit it and to hold it in the highest esteem.

The fish are accustomed from almost daily experience to see flies sailing on the surface, and they rise, we venture to affirm, invariably with serious intent. Even when we have repeatedly failed to hook rising fish, we have never felt inclined to comfort ourselves with the inference that they are indulging in that irritation known as short-rising, but rather have we blamed ourselves for being guilty of tardiness in our actions. The only point against the loch that we can admit is the prevalence of weeds, which, especially in a dry season, may become a positive nuisance to the boatman who has to propel his craft through them, no light task against a strong wind, but to the angler they should cause little annoyance except in so far as they curtail the amount of fishing water.

CHAPTER XXVII

ACROSS THE MOOR

A LITTLE, irregular patch of blue on the map, four miles across the moor, over ground that promises considerable exertion, is all our invitation. We might go by road all but the last half-mile, but there is one good reason why we should select a more varied route.

Early in the morning we set out along the stony, winding, island track, by the side of a prattling burn ; the sound of the tinkling waterfall bids us halt as it does every day, and as usual we peer cautiously through the clusters of pink roses adorning the bank into the deep little pot, black in the shadows, golden in the sunshine. Two or three plump trout, quarter pounders they seem to be, cruise about, sucking down occasionally some unfortunate midge or rising to examine some object floating in the foam ; one a little better than its fellows poises itself in the bubbling water of the fall ; the monarch of the pool occupies the best position. Some day, perhaps we may stop to offer them a fly, but it is not likely ; we would rather have them where they are than in the creel.

In any case we cannot linger to-day, for ahead lies an adventure. The expedition is one of uncertainty ; there are many possibilities, but what they are we cannot foretell. Perhaps disappointment awaits; perhaps great fortune will be ours. The loch may be full of weeds; but again it may be filled with trout; fish of some sort must roam these distant waters.

A walk of over a mile brings us to a loch which has already furnished us with the grandest sport, baskets of bright, lively trout, between two and three to the pound, beautifully marked, magnificently proportioned, short and deep, keen fighters all. Many a time we have enjoyed drifting the fine curving bays, the long indented shore, the calm belt under the trees, and, more than all, the peculiar lines of tall reeds, which never fail to call forth the music of the reel. Here we have fished the rise of the July gloaming, often with conspicuous success, sometimes almost in vain; once or twice, when the chilling mist was wafted along in weird columns, we have been sent empty away; but even that experience has not been invariable even under these depressing conditions.

In spite of these memories, we refrain from putting up the rod, the better to withstand the temptation of these bays, for nothing must be allowed to prevent or even hinder the projected expedition. If that fails altogether, then we have the kindly loch to cheer us on our return in the evening, and therein lies the reason for the route selected. Boarding the boat, we row at speed straight to the opposite shore. We feel like pioneers as we draw the craft far up the beach and, shouldering the pack, set off across the moor. With no guide save our memory of the map and its easy contours, it is possible that, owing to frequent detours necessary to avoid the inevitable peat-hags, we may miss for a time the object of our search. Still, confidently enough, we move forward.

The way is interesting ; but the pack is heavy. A long day lies before us and we are well, probably too well, prepared. In addition to a complete equipment for both dry-fly and wet-fly fishing and a generous lunch basket, we carry along wading stockings and a pair of canvas rope-soled boots. The latter are almost useless for wading a river, where weight and plentiful nails are required to enable one to withstand a strong current ; but for use in a loch they are highly satisfactory, and they do not, moreover, add seriously to the burden on the back. It is well to take them to an unknown loch, for it may possess shallow bays, where wading must be undertaken if the trout are to be reached.

Contentedly we plod along under the sun over the open moor. The fine, fresh breeze is welcome, not only because it is pleasantly cool, but also because it promises good fishing conditions. We reach a loch, long, narrow, and completely filled with weeds and reeds. It is one of our guides and, being expected and impossible of confusion with the object of the expedition, the sight of it occasions only a little alarm. We had noted it on the map as lying on and directing our route, and we had also entertained hopes of casting a fly over it on the return journey. It may be well stocked with fish, but it is unfishable, and it arouses fears that the farther loch may be similarly impossible. We carry on less confident than before.

At length on rounding the shoulder of a hill, we see lying before us a beautiful sheet of water, surrounded on all sides by an irregular ridge which delays dis-

covery from any direction almost until the loch is
reached. No weeds line the shores, though a few
patches are seen beyond the longest cast from the
bank ; the bottom is of large gravel ; it looks a
troutful water, as it sparkles under the brisk
westerly breeze. There is no boat visible, and we
are thankful that the waders have not proved a
superfluous burden.

Although a rest after the arduous walk across the
moor would be advisable, we cannot halt until we
have searched the rather excessive wave. Waders
are donned, and the two rods mounted in a few
minutes. No fish are showing, therefore we make
a start with a cast of four Loch Leven wet-flies,
standard size. Just before us lies a long, narrow
neck of water, more like a river than a bay in a
loch, towards which the wind is blowing and raising
a great jabble. Nothing arrests the progress of the
flies, though they are subjected to very varied
treatment. Are there no trout in the loch ?

More for the sake of variety than with any expectation, we take up the dry-fly rod, put on a brace
of flies, the Rough Olive and a dark Greenwell,
lengthen line, and send the cast across a calm
frothy belt. At once a trout comes wriggling up, a
good fish obviously, and we wait for it patiently,
striking as it turns to go downwards. The hook
takes hold and the reel sings merrily ; a sharp fight
ensues, but in time the rod claims command, and
we step out into deeper water to use the net.

Back to the shore we come to unhook and examine
the victim of the Olive. Fully a pound it weighs, a
handsome fish, the first from a new water ; it inspires
with hope to continue.

Out again the flies go, and immediately another trout accepts the same fly. It duly pays the penalty. In the first four casts we capture four trout, all very fine fish ; but the first is slightly the best of the lot. This is sport of a truly remarkable kind. We fish a certain piece of water with the wet-fly, and receive no response ; without any invitation from the water in the shape of a rise to the natural fly, we try the dry-fly over the same stretch, and with it take four fish in as many casts, trout that would look well in any company.

We do not know the reason for such a pleasing reception, but we venture to suggest an explanation. Even on the stormiest day, there may be seen on the loch lines of foam and long, oily lanes waving slightly but not ruffled ; these persist and retain their position for quite a long time. The angler on Loch Leven must know them well and, if he will watch how the boat edges its way across them, he will realise fully that a boat seldom drifts straight down wind, but at an angle to it, and so favours one occupant of the craft more than the other. That, however, is not the matter at present under discussion.

Flies driving before the wind sooner or later arrive at one of these foam-flecked patches, and there their journey ends ; for a circle of froth surrounds each of them, and prevents further movement. Results seem to show that trout are well aware of this, and that they lie under such bits of water sucking down the flies congregated there. So often have we caught trout in these places, at times, too, when there was nothing doing in other parts, that we have come to regard a cast into a calm, frothy patch as very likely to succeed in bringing up a trout. Even a wet-fly will in such a case often score a victory ; but a floating-fly of almost any pattern is decidedly more deadly.

On the river, also, a foam-covered backwater is almost certain to conceal trout. One would think that flies floating on foam would be invisible to the fish below ; but that they are not is quite easily proved. In our earliest days we discovered how easy it was to get a trout on the fly, when there was such an aid to concealment, and even yet we do not allow such an opportunity to slip. It always gives us delight to see the black circle appear in the surrounding whiteness, when a fish takes down the fly.

Our marvellous run of luck in the far-off moorland loch seems to be due not so much to any superior virtue in a floating fly, but to the fact that the lure was placed where the trout expected to see it.

Further trial shows that the merry period has come to an abrupt end, repeated casting over the generous stretch producing no result, and reluctantly we wander up the bank, encumbered with two rods and net, but leaving the remainder of the apparatus behind. Our theory seems to have broken down, or the other trout have become alarmed by the struggles of the victims ; but the change probably has some connection with the fact that the weather conditions are undergoing modification.

The wind, under the influence of the strong sunshine or other cause, is perceptibly fading away, and in time it becomes only a gentle breeze, a state of affairs very much to our liking, even though it seems to have had some bad effect, only temporary we hope, upon the trout. Provided that it does not fall to a flat calm, we shall remain hopeful that a hatch of flies will arrive, and that the surface of the loch will be plentifully disturbed by the rings of leaping fish. The previous conditions were calculated to supply moths and the like from the surrounding heather, but such accidents are not to be relied upon ; we infinitely prefer a less violent gale, a moderate breeze, enough to make casting easy.

Slowly we proceed up wind, watching, when possible, the water for a rise, but more frequently choosing our steps ; for at very short intervals marshy places, dangerous with black ooze, covered here and there with an oily film, occur, and then it is wise to decide that the long road is the shorter. All along the shore, the water is extremely shallow, only a foot deep twenty yards or more from the bank, and not a trout is seen rising or moving away in alarm at our approach.

A great, broad bay curving round an island of weeds arrests our steps, for here, if anywhere, we are convinced that sport will be forthcoming, if and when the rise begins. Feeling the effects of the strong air of the moor, and having already obtained a few beauties from the loch, we are able to remain inactive for a time, listening to the green plover calling ; but our eyes never wander far from the water.

Without warning, first one trout, and then another, rises close to the edge of the weed-bed ; their position is easily fixed, but, before we can wade out far enough to lay the deadly Olive on the

mark, the longed-for sign is seen all around.   Meantime we heed none but the original marks, and
succeed with both casts.   Slowly we work round
the weeds, covering a rise now and then to right or
left.   The sport is good, very good, interrupted
chiefly by visits to the shore for the purpose of
relieving the net of its burden.   One trout keeps it
nicely weighted for slipping it below a second victim,
but two occupants make it awkward and unwieldy
to carry.   Before long, the rise ceases altogether,
as suddenly as it began, and not a fish will move to
either lure.   Though short it has been productive,
for the total catch is the goodly one of seventeen
trout, all very fine specimens.

We spend a long time over lunch and rest, follow
it by a spell of fruitless fishing, and finally, deciding
further effort vain and the creel sufficient in all
respects, we say farewell to the kindly loch of the
lonely moorland.

CHAPTER XXVIII

A FINAL CAST

FOR a whole month, almost the last and one of the best of the whole trouting season, we have been guilty of neglecting the trout. Instead we have attempted to induce dour, irresponsive salmon to leave attenuated waters, but at length, realising the folly of the one and the futility of the other, we set out to the Clyde at Elvanfoot for a final cast with the little ten-footer.

After an absence of five years from what was wont to be our favourite stretch, we are keen to renew acquaintance, and we hurry through the rushes and twisted grass of the broad holm, putting together the rod as we go, though the haze of early October plainly indicates that of haste there is no need, that hopefulness must be awhile delayed. We reach the banks of Clyde and halt in amazement.

Never have we seen its pure waters so intensely clear ; right to the bottom of the deep pots with their almost vertical sides of crumbling gravel we see plainly ; here and there we notice patches of bright white sand, with now and then a clump of weed ; not a single trout do we detect, and we begin to wonder if one has managed to survive the season's fishing.

That is not the end of our troubles. The wind

is from the south-west, strong and downstream, which means that we have failed to follow our own advice, and deliberately selected a stretch which is not suited to a breeze from that direction ; but that is only an apparent lapse, for ahead lies a pool, our main objective, which is favourably placed, and which in itself used to be sufficient to make such a choice thoroughly sound. Presently the mist is wafted away, and the sun pours forth from a sky of unclouded blue. Thus the prospect of sport is of the poorest, but still it is a pleasure to be alone in these broad solitudes. The glorious freedom delights ; the smooth, swelling heights are distant.

As far as we can see, and from a grassy mound we can examine nearly three miles of water, not another angler plies his craft ; but that is the one favourable feature of the day The wind and the sky, the water and the scarcity of trout will render the day a comparatively poor one as far as sport is concerned. We shall have to work hard for any reward. A less inauspicious day might have been granted for our final offensive against the wary trout of Clyde.

And where are the birds of the holm and the water side ? Even the little meadow pipit fails to welcome us ; the curlew's eerie whistle, the music that takes us to the moorland stream and gives forgetfulness of the city, is not heard ; the peewits do not swing and wheel, nor fill the air with clamorous plaint. From the rushes, it is true, we flush first one blackcock, then another, and also a solitary old grouse, but even the skylark's song is silent. Faithful as of old, however, the white-breasted dipper nods from his water-worn stone, but says nothing, and, sure sign that no one has disturbed the pools this morning, a heron rises beyond the bend.

What a change of scene is this! On our last four expeditions we have been poking among trees, doing all sorts of intricate swings, both elegant and the reverse, with a hefty salmon rod, shooting the line and recovering it in coils on the bank, where of course it would often succeed in securely attaching itself to brambles and thistles; wading in a boiling stream where every stone is a thing of life and full of guile; dodging behind and casting over bushes mercifully trimmed to make the work less impossible, and the reward was ever the same—tired limbs and extreme weariness of heart, and glorious rises from mighty salmon immediately we had passed them by.

Here all is entirely different. Not a tree, not even a bush, interferes with the long, free sweep of the cast; wading in the stream is more comfortable than walking on the bank, though an incautious step on loose gravel beside a pool might result in total immersion; the trout when he rises, means to feed: when the line passes over him he retires to the depths, flees in alarm from the dangerous place; he does not rise to taunt us. As for the recompense of labour, that is still to be discovered.

The little rod feels a mere toy in the hand. We wonder at first if it is all there, so light and useless it seems, but after an hour of incessant casting the wrist is left in no doubt that work has been performed. Its action is awhile unfamiliar, and yet the same handy little weapon has brought to the net or bank many hundreds of trout from this very

stretch.   Here it took fifty pounds of trout in one
week, but then the water was in perfect order, the
wind right, and the fish feeding all day long.

Once here we were ordered out to obtain a dish
for some friends ; for the first four hours we covered
two miles of water without receiving as much as a
rise, but in the next hour, probably the most crowded
hour we ever enjoyed, we took nineteen trout of the
very best quality.   It is difficult to be entirely
hopeless when such memories come, but to-day,
we are sure, will not witness great events.

Though the river sings a merry tune as it dances
over the pebbly shallows, the water betrays no sign
of life.   Not a spreading ring marks the breezy
surface of the pools or the broad calm belts along
the bank ; not a fly flutters through the sunny air
or sails the sparkling stream ;   the thought comes
strong upon us, and it persists all day long, that
very few trout remain where once a magnificent
stock was maintained.   The great problem presented
for solution concerns the flies which should be
placed upon the cast.   Possibly one pattern will be
as good as another, and until some indication arrives
from the water we decide to entrust our fortunes
to a Black Spider as being sufficiently suggestive of
the late Iron Blues, a very probable arrival, and a
Rough Olive, a generally useful pattern and one
not unlike the Autumn Reds and Browns.

The wind is as bad as it can possibly be, but at
Bodsbury Flat the river makes a great swinging
bend, so that the water actually heads to the South.
That part will offer easy casting, and its immediate
surroundings will be comparatively simple to
negotiate.   Thither we go, reminding ourselves that

ONE OF THE OLD CLYDE SCHOOL.

on each of two similar occasions the little stretch
yielded six pounds, but the flat itself grants but
a single fish, a lively quarter-pounder which falls
victim to the Black Spider, a modest but withal
satisfactory beginning.

If Bodsbury can do no better than this, prospects
are bad indeed, and we may as well retire now
as endure further disappointment, but round the
bend there is a deep hole into which a brisk stream
enters, one of the readiest bits we know, a cast
that is almost certain to grant a trout. It is not
an easy place to fish at any time, being narrow
and very steep, demanding a short line and a cast
straight up the middle of the run if the fatal drag
is to be circumvented, but to-day the adverse breeze,
half a gale rather, adds enormously to the difficulties. The fly takes only a second or two to
complete its journey, a rise has to be observed and
answered without a moment's hesitation, but if
fortune favours and enables the cast to be neatly
and correctly executed and the dangers to be overcome, then a rise from a trout beyond the average
is almost a certainty.

With an effort we succeed in cheating the wind
and laying the Black Spider exactly as and where
required. At once a trout gleams through the wave
and we strike quickly and firmly ; the reel sings out
that the hook is fast and screams in protest as the
fish bolts through the current towards us down to
the depths of the pool below. We follow, and in
the brilliant sunlight see it flashing, gleaming, and
boring ten feet below ; it searches the irregular
sides apparently striving to reach some hidden
recess ; we observe, too, that the hook is fast in the

tail, and now understand the reason for the unusual tactics. Exercising a little care and applying a minimum of pressure, we gradually lead it farther down to shallower water, where we may follow. In time we bring it to the surface and the net, but not without a grand fight worthy of a pounder hooked in the mouth. This stroke of luck puts us in good humour ; fortune has not quite deserted us, but instead has given us a good trout, rather more than half a pound in weight, and a few minutes of sport which might easily have been less exciting than it was.

The flat seems worthy of another trial, and we return across country to our starting-point. Round the base of a cairn of stones the water is slightly broken, and the wind driving against the current raises a fair wave, a place likely to hold a good fish. The tail fly is laid beyond the first of the miniature billows ; it bobs along a foot or two, and then in a trough a trout arrests it. The strike fails to send the hook home. Not until we arrive at the generous rush at the neck do the flies receive further response ; but the Rough Olive this time is the winner. The captive behaves exactly as the previous victim, and for precisely the same reason. As soon as the trout drops into the net, the hook comes away, and, on proceeding to touch it up for future conquests, we perceive that it transfixes a tiny scale. Three trout already are in the bag on what we consider a hopeless day. Surely it is worth while continuing, even although two of them are the victims of their own bad luck.

The next stretch is a great, long, broad flat, the top part especially of which, and the glorious glide at the neck as well, used to be very good.   In the glide a pound grayling was almost certain to suck down the fly, and along the high bank fine trout were often to be enticed to rise.   Now all is changed. A bold bluff that used to send the water round in a swirl has been sliced off by some flood, the entering stream has altered its character and course, and, though the bright green weed-beds still flourish, we cannot help thinking that the old was better than the new.   Still it gives us a beautiful half-pounder, which shows no hint of the approaching spawning season either in condition or power of resistance.

We go over the stretch once more and yet again, raising a trout occasionally and at long intervals landing one, until, when it is time to bid the river farewell for another season, the basket contains no fewer than ten trout, a take we consider very good and much better than we dared to expect at the beginning of the day.

INDEX

DARK OLIVE DUN

IRON BLUE DUN

MARCH BROWN

OLIVE SPINNER

PALE WATERY SPINNER

CINNAMON SEDGE

BLACK SEDGE

GRANNOM

NEEDLE BROWN

NATURAL FLIES

1   2   3   4

5   6   7

8   9   10

11   12   13

14   15   16   17

18

ARTIFICIAL FLIES

Featured Titles from
Westphalia Press

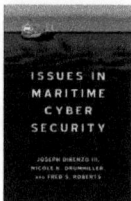

Issues in Maritime Cyber Security Edited by Nicole K. Drumhiller, Fred S. Roberts, Joseph DiRenzo III and Fred S. Roberts

While there is literature about the maritime transportation system, and about cyber security, to date there is very little literature on this converging area. This pioneering book is beneficial to a variety of audiences looking at risk analysis, national security, cyber threats, or maritime policy.

The Rise of the Book Plate: An Exemplative of the Art by W. G. Bowdoin, Introduction by Henry Blackwel

Bookplates were made to denote ownership and hopefully steer the volume back to the rightful shelf if borrowed. They often contained highly stylized writing, drawings, coat of arms, badges or other images of interest to the owner.

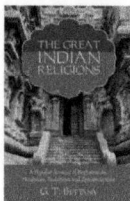

The Great Indian Religions by G. T. Bettany

G. T. (George Thomas) Bettany (1850-1891) was born and educated in England, attending Gonville and Caius College in Cambridge University, studying medicine and the natural sciences. This book is his account of Brahmanism, Hinduism, Buddhism, and Zoroastrianism

Unworkable Conservatism: Small Government, Freemarkets, and Impracticality by Max J. Skidmore

Unworkable Conservatism looks at what passes these days for "conservative" principles—small government, low taxes, minimal regulation—and demonstrates that they are not feasible under modern conditions.

A Place in the Lodge: Dr. Rob Morris, Freemasonry and the Order of the Eastern Star by Nancy Stearns Theiss PhD

Ridiculed as "petticoat masonry," critics of the Order of the Eastern Star did not deter Rob Morris' goal to establish a Masonic organization that included women as members. As Rob Morris (1818-1888) came "into the light," he donned his Masonic apron and carried the ideals of Freemasonry through a despairing time of American history.

Demand the Impossible: Essays in History as Activism
Edited by Nathan Wuertenberg and William Horne

Demand the Impossible asks scholars what they can do to help solve present-day crises. The twelve essays in this volume draw inspiration from present-day activists. They examine the role of history in shaping ongoing debates over monuments, racism, clean energy, health care, poverty, and the Democratic Party.

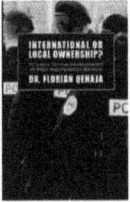

International or Local Ownership?: Security Sector Development in Post-Independent Kosovo
by Dr. Florian Qehaja

International or Local Ownership? contributes to the debate on the concept of local ownership in post-conflict settings, and discussions on international relations, peacebuilding, security and development studies.

The Bahai Movement: A Series of Nineteen Papers
by Charles Mason Remey

Charles Mason Remey (1874-1974) was the son of Admiral George Collier Remey and grew up in Washington DC. He studied to be an architect at Cornell (1893-1896) and the Ecole des Beaux Arts in Paris (1896-1903), where he learned about the Baha'i faith, and quickly adopted it.

Ongoing Issues in Georgian Policy and Public Administration
Edited by Bonnie Stabile and Nino Ghonghadze

Thriving democracy and representative government depend upon a well functioning civil service, rich civic life and economic success. Georgia has been considered a top performer among countries in South Eastern Europe seeking to establish themselves in the post-Soviet era.

Poverty in America: Urban and Rural Inequality and Deprivation in the 21st Century
Edited by Max J. Skidmore

Poverty in America too often goes unnoticed, and disregarded. This perhaps results from America's general level of prosperity along with a fairly widespread notion that conditions inevitably are better in the USA than elsewhere. Political rhetoric frequently enforces such an erroneous notion.

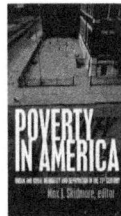

westphaliapress.org

www.ingramcontent.com/pod-product-compliance
Lightning Source LLC
LaVergne TN
LVHW041151080426
835511LV00006B/556